A Trail of Money and Death

Matteson and the Morris Murders

William G. Kohler

D1127153

ISBN: 978-1-7373816-0-0

DEDICATION

To Nancy A. McCaslin, educator, attorney, and editor
for all the encouragement received for over fifty years, and without whom
this narrative would never have come to fruition.

And to Markus Schmitt, for not only indulging me in every new interest,
but so often, for finishing the projects I start.

Acknowledgements

Cover: *Michigan Farm*, painted by Deloris Hays Kohler (1925-2013)
Clark Historical Library, Central Michigan University for the Elias Morris papers
Gunnison Chamber of Commerce for the photo of the M.D. Matteson house
Markus Kohz for technical support

CONTENTS

1

FOREWORD

There in the newspaper, set in bold capitals, separately spaced and centered, the words practically sprang off the page at me.

"M. D. MATTESON IS THE MURDERER"

The words carried weight with them. Obviously, the editor had not wanted them to be overlooked.

Once, before the Internet and powerful search engines came to their rescue, genealogists had no choice but to sift through dusty library shelves in the hopes that they might run onto the occasional index. Or they sat for hours at microfilm machines, without an index, and scanned old newspaper archives in search of an occasional nugget of family history. On some days, there was no treasure to be found.

Genealogy was the reason for my visit to the Decatur library that day. The regional history room there was my ground zero, as my family's ancestors had been among the early settlers in Van Buren County, Michigan. But perusing the collection this particular day, I stumbled onto a scrapbook labeled "Morris Murder Mystery." It was a familiar story, always referred to as an unsolved "mystery". The story began when answering a knock at the door on a moon-lit September evening in 1879, a young prominent farmer named Morris was shot through the chest and neck. His wife was then chased through the house and shot repeatedly at such close range that her night dress caught fire. The killer had then stolen Morris's best horse and ridden through the night to South Bend, Indiana, where his trail vanished. The details of the case were familiar to me but the name Matteson was completely new.

The newspaper article I found in the scrapbook, however, read differently in context:

It is openly asserted by some that they believed

M. D. MATTESON IS THE MURDERER

3

or that his money hired it (the murders) *done, because, they say, he is the only person who could have any reason for wanting them* (the Morrises) *out of the way.*[1]

The editor's peculiar print setting, however, aroused my curiosity. Who was this M. D. Matteson and why had the editor seen the need to present Matteson's name in such an accusatory manner? Furthermore, if this was indeed justified, why had I never seen the name mentioned in all the recurring newspaper accounts I had read?

That single bold-set phrase led me to unbelievable tales of forgers and counterfeiters, of a school teacher who pistol-whipped a pupil's father and who was so cruel, parents would keep their children out of school. Also, money loaners who foreclosed mortgages on widows, a private investigator who had guarded Lincoln, and any number of untimely deaths, not to mention a further murder shrouded in mystery. The trail of money and death that unfolded weaves its way from New York to the Michigan Territory to post-fire Chicago, to an assassination in Rockford, Illinois, and a pistol-whipping in Iowa, and all the way to a "skyscraper" in the mountains of frontier Colorado and ultimately back to the affluent Lakeview district of northern Chicago. This was the Gilded Age in American history, a time of particularly rapid economic growth, and the Matteson family proved to be eager participants.

The most familiar version of the Morris murders typically begins at the scene of the crime and ends the following morning with Morris´s best horse being abandoned in South Bend, Indiana. But the trail of money and death is much longer. This book is designed to give greater insights into the Morris and Matteson families, to provide potentially new evidence in a case long considered to be cold, and to encourage future generations to question and investigate the findings anew.

Decatur

1

LITTLE PRAIRIE RONDE

The western frontier and its lawlessness are rarely associated with areas east of the Mississippi River. Early film images depicting lawlessness are likely to bring to mind images of outlaws blowing open safes at town banks, schoolmarms cowering with their pupils in the corners of one-room schoolhouses, tensions rising as gunslingers enter saloons, hostile Native Americans attacking wagon trains, and the lone sheriff with his hand poised next to his holster while the images we personally are likely to associate with the frontier include the golden hue of prairie sunsets, clouds of dust, and the occasional wind-blown tumbleweed.

But at one time, the lush forest areas and vast prairies east of the Mississippi River presented as many challenges as life on the western frontier, if not more. While some of the virgin forests became the basis for lumbering industries, the early subsistence farmers needed, first, to find arable land and find it fast. Their quickest solution was the grassy clearings which, for centuries, the native tribes had burned off to facilitate hunting, and it was here that the settlers found the opportunity to cultivate the soil more easily and harvest corn and wheat necessary to see them through the year.

Such was the lay of the land when, in 1828, Dolphin Morris travelled by ox and lumber wagon from Ohio to the Michigan Territory. During that winter he explored what French traders had dubbed Little Prairie Ronde, and by early April he was able to bring his family to the simple log cabin he had built there. For two years the Morris family were the sole white settlers in what became Van Buren County, Michigan, and the conditions under which they first lived were challenging.

There were no roads in this wilderness except the St. Joseph and Sauk Trails, routes left to the native population by the mastodons. Throughout the 1830s the only road planning was done by the settlers and the only direct paths were from one settler´s home to the

next. Transportation was slow and tedious. Oxen were more common than horses, and if a family were fortunate enough to own a horse, members of the family often shared the animal, a practice referred to as "riding and tieing" because as one person walked, the other rode ahead to a point where he would dismount, tie up the horse, and continue on foot. When the second person reached the point where the first had dismounted, he would then dismount, tie up, and have the horse waiting to be ridden again.

While confrontations with native tribes were more dramatic elsewhere, the Morrises enjoyed relative peace. The exception to relative peace in this region was due to the actions of a Potawatomi chief named Shavehead who once boasted of owning a string of 99 white men's tongues.[1] Apparently an enterpriser, Shavehead charged tolls for ferry boats plying the St. Joseph River and was generally hostile, even to other native tribes.[2]

Other than Shavehead, the Potawatomi around Little Prairie Ronde, particularly the women, were friendly to the Morris family. Dolphin Morris's eldest son Samuel recounted how his first playmates were Indian children; and according to Samuel, the contact was so frequent that he could speak their language and learned from them how to hunt by bow and arrow. Morris's son Elias reminisced how Indian women actually helped his mother with household chores.[3]

While the Indians would bring venison, maple sugar, and berries to exchange for salt pork and flour, it was white bread that lured the Potawatomi, and after Grandma Hathaway, a neighbor who lived south of the Morrises, confronted an Indian chief with "White bread costs money", no bread was ever requested by the Potawatomi without offering game in return.

Pioneer life could be grueling in the Midwest. In 1831 seed corn crops failed, so Dolphin Morris sent a man working for him and another settler's fifteen-year-old son 100 miles to Fort Defiance, Ohio, for two bushels of seed corn that would save the settlement that year.[4] The following year, Morris traveled the 25-mile trip to the nearest mill in Niles, Michigan, and was caught in a snowstorm, keeping him away from home for fourteen days. His wife Nancy and the children were dangerously low on supplies and they feared for Dolphin's safety.

Eventually, Dolphin managed to return home with only his team, his two front wagon wheels, and a single bag of flour.[5]

In June, 1835, the land experienced a frost so severe that it wiped out most of the vegetables, wheat, and corn, and the settlers were put to the test again. While game was plentiful, the woods were also full of wolves, bears and wild cats, all eager to prey on livestock. Samuel Morris recounted how he once had to defend the sheep from a pack of seven wolves.[6] Nearby, the swampland was full of poisonous water snakes, and until the Swamp Road was built in 1849, enabling the settlers of Little Prairie Ronde to reach Decatur, they had to wade the mire and risk contracting malaria.[7]

Morris had come to Little Prairie Ronde with his wife and three small children. He settled on some of the most fertile land in the entire region, and began farming. Crops and livestock allowed for the farm's expansion, and although only six of his eleven children would live past their twentieth birthday, four of the children grew into strong boys who helped the farm prosper.

From *History of Berrien and Van Buren Counties, Michigan,* 1880

Morris and his family lived in a small cabin on the farm, and this humble cabin housed the first school in the county. Although he had no formal education himself, Morris, along with his own children, learned to read and write. The rustic cabin gave way to a stately frame farmhouse and by 1865, Dolphin Morris was a stockholder in the newly organized First National Bank of Paw Paw.[8] His tireless efforts had resulted in his amassing eleven hundred acres on Little Prairie Ronde before he divided it up into parcels for his sons Samuel, Amos, Elias, and his daughter Susannah Morris Anderson. Dolphin´s youngest son Charles Henry was only 22 when his father died in January 1870. He had just married Esther Jones a few weeks before his father's death. Charles Henry inherited the family homestead from his father and so the newlyweds stayed on with Mother Nancy until she, too, passed away in 1877.[9]

The Morris name would have enjoyed prominence merely by having been the first pioneering family in the county. Not only was Dolphin Morris's cabin the site of the first school and sermon, the first birth

and death occurred here as well. Through industry, fertile soil, and good yields, the Morris family was well-known throughout the entire area. Even more so after Dolphin´s death, when the Matteson-Morris forgery case was meticulously followed in local newspapers due to suspicions that Milo Matteson may have been involved in the murder. Each week witnesses' testimony was front page news, fueling questions as to why an affluent family was in need of such high financing and whether an unscrupulous money loaner, assisted by a local attorney, had committed fraud by forgery. The case gripped the community for much of 1873 and was not finally decided until 1879 until the Michigan Supreme Court rendered a decision on appeal and the mortgage was finally surrendered at no cost.

The Morris family had made a name for itself by being the first settlers in the county, and four decades of expansion and affluence only added to the family's prominence in the community. Then, every week for seven years, the Morrises were the subject of weekly newspapers reporting every detail of the mortgage forgery cases in which they were named. But no scandal or tragedy could grip the community as intensely as the cold-blooded murder that occurred on a moon-lit September evening in 1879.

The Morris Farm   *History of Berrien and Van Buren Counties,*1880

2

THE MORRIS MURDERS

On the morning of September 29, 1879, Jennie Bull, the Morris family hired girl, stumbled onto the body of 32-year-old Charles Henry Morris on a side porch of his home. He was wearing only his nightshirt and had been shot dead, with bullets penetrating his chest and neck.

Initially, neighbors summoned to the crime site could not locate Mrs. Morris, but a trail of blood led them through the dining room, parlor, and bedroom to the body of 29-year-old Esther Morris, slumped in a closet, shot three times at close range. Robbery was not the motive, as the murderer left cash and gold watches untouched. The hired man, returning to the farm that morning, was the person who discovered a missing horse from the barn—Morris´s best—although no saddle or bridle had been taken. As he left the barn, he noticed Charles Henry Morris's trousers discarded on the manure pile.

Although widely reported throughout the region and beyond, the testimonies of the hired girl, Jennie Bull, and the hired man, John Klinger, seem most complete in Cassopolis's *National Democrat* on October 2:

MURDERS MOST FOUL

Henry Morris and Wife of Little Prairie Ronde, Murdered in their Own House

Plunder Not the Object of the Assassin, as Money and Valuables Were Untouched

No Clue to the Perpetrators Yet Discovered

Monday morning last the fearful statement was made on our streets that Henry Morris and wife, of Little Prairie Ronde had been found murdered in their own house. The statement was barren of incidents attending; the manner in which the horrid deed was committed or the cause. A reporter for the Democrat was immediately started for the locality to ascertain for our readers all that could be learned of the terrible event.

The farm of 320 acres belonging to Henry Morris, is in Van Buren County, coming to the Cass County line. The residence, a large frame house in good repair, and well furnished, is situated back from the road which forms the dividing line between Van Buren and Cass counties, 60 rods, and is connected by a lane with the highway.

Below we present a diagram of the house which may assist to be a better understanding of the case. (Author's note: a more explicit description and diagram of the bloody pursuit through the house was offered by *The Decatur Republican*):[1]

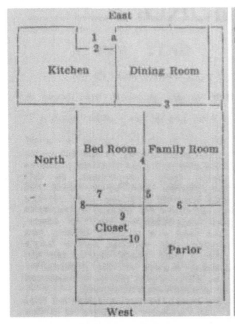

East

1 a
2

Kitchen   Dining Room

3

North   Bed Room | Family Room
4

7   5
8
9   6
Closet
10
Parlor

West

The open space at the east is the open stoop, where Mr. Morris was shot.
1 is the place where he fell.
2 is where the ball lodged.
a is the door opening onto the stoop from the dining room.
3 is the door opening into the family or sitting room.
4 is the door leading into Morris' bed room.
5 is where the third ball lodged after passing through Mrs. Morris' body.
6 is the folding doors opening into the parlor.
7 is the location of the bureau hit by the fourth shot.
8 is the door leading into the closet from bed room.
9 is the place where Mrs. Morris fell and where the fifth and sixth shots were delivered, which passed through her body, lodging in the floor beneath.
10 is a door leading out of the closet into an unoccupied bed room in rear of parlor.

The first person to discover the horrid work that had been going on during the night, was Jennie Bull, a young woman who had been at work there for some time, and whose statement will be found in full now.

Probably the next person to visit the home was the hired man, Johnny Klinger, whose experience is also related in detail now.

When Elias Morris and wife Rosewarne and perhaps fifteen or twenty neighbors had arrived at the house, not far from 8 o'clock, a horrid scene was presented; the murdered man lay on the east porch, naked all but his shirt, with a little pool of blood discoloring the floor under the wound in his side. An examination of the body showed that a ball had entered his right side and passed clear through him, striking and passing through the side of the house, then through the wood and plastering and striking against a cupboard in the pantry, fell to the floor. The other ball had entered the neck just below the ear and passed in a diagonal direction downward, coming nearly to just below the left point of the shoulder blade, from where it was cut by the surgeons in attendance. The first shot must have caused death almost instantly, from the relative position which the body occupied with the bullet hole in the siding, shows that he never moved, except to fall after being shot.

The general supposition is that the assassin called Morris to the door, either by rapping or halloing, and then crouched back behind the corner of the house till his victim unsuspectingly came out on the porch, when he shot him down in cold blood. The second [shot] must have been fired after he fell to the floor, the murderer bending over him and holding the muzzle of his pistol close to his victim's throat, as his chin was filled with powder grains, and discolored. Morris probably hearing an (illegible), and it being early in the evening, supposed it to be some of his neighbors or his hired man, and grasping his pantaloons in case he needed them, went to the door, and not seeing anyone stepped out on the porch, when he was cruelly shot down.

The next bullet mark that was found is in the north-west corner of the sitting room, on the door leading into the bed room; the bullet did not pierce the latch, but rebounded and was picked up from the floor. It is supposed that Henry's wife, hearing the shooting, had started to the assistance of her husband, and was met by the villain who fired at her the above shot; still followed by the fiend, for the next mark of his work found is where a bullet tore its way through the upper, right hand short drawer of the bureau, and buried itself in a corner of the drawer, where it was subsequently dug out. The marble top of the bureau was sprinkled with blood. So far nothing had been found of Mrs. Morris, and Mrs. Charlotte Morris, accompanied by a man, thoroughly searched the upper part of the house, while her husband, Elias, pursued the search on the first floor. Neither found the object of their search, until Mrs. M. opened the door of the closet off the bedroom, where the spectacle of Esther Morris lying cold in death, her body pierced by three bullet holes met her gaze.

Two shots had evidently been fired after she had entered the closet and fell to the floor, one probably from the door, as the ball entered the left side in a diagonal

15

direction, and ploughing a furrow of an inch or two in the hard oak floor, stuck fast. The other wound was in the left breast, not more than four inches from the other, but was evidently fired with the villain standing directly over her, with the weapon close to her body, as the bullet was directly downward in its course, and passed clear through the floor, while the flash of the explosion had set fire to her night dress and burned out a hole 8 or 10 inches in diameter. She also had a flesh wound on her left arm, between the wrist and elbow. The generally accepted theory is that the same bullet which inflicted this wound, passed on through her body and into the bureau drawer. In that case six shots were fired, and that many slugs and places where they lodged have been found. There are others who think that seven shots were fired, believing that the bullet which entered the bureau, did not touch Mrs. Morris.

When found, she had lying by her side, as if dropped from her hand, a revolver belonging to her husband, with all the chambers loaded, and not cocked. It is supposed that she started in the aid of her husband, carrying the revolver, but then was met by the ruffian, was shot down before she could use it. The balls were very conical and had two creases at the base; they have been examined by parties in Decatur, who think they were discharged from a Remington, instead of from a Colt's Navy, as was the general impression.

THE ESCAPE

Appearances indicate that the bloody villain after his devilish work was done, immediately fled, taking along with him a pair of pants belonging to Morris, and leaving them at the stable. He probably seized them mechanically, as no attempt was made to secure money or valuables in the house. In the bureau drawer through which the ball passed, was a pocket book containing $110, two gold watches, bracelets, and other valuable jewelry all untouched. He then took the fleetest horse in the stable, a favorite driving horse of known powers of endurance, and it is supposed put upon him a saddle and bridle which he had brought with him, and made good his escape. It is probable that the horse had been saddled and bridled and the large gate opened previous to the execution of the horrid deed. He was seen twice while making his escape, as related below by young Rosewarne and Hathaway. A person riding fast was also met in Jefferson Township, a little after midnight, and again this side of South Bend (Indiana) five or six miles by a man giving his name as Stickney, between one and two in the morning. He claims to recognize the horse as one that he saw during the night, and the rider he described as a man

16

muffled up, and wearing a black slouch hat pulled down so that he could not recognize his features.

THE CORONER'S INQUEST

Word was immediately sent to J. G. Haynes, of Decatur, to come and hold an inquest over the bodies of the deceased victims of this terrible tragedy.

As the news of the horrible murder spread, hundreds of people came to the scene, and upon the arrival of the justice, a jury was impaneled consisting of the following persons, all of whom were from Decatur:

Dr. H. M. Broderick, foreman; Dr. G. L. Rose, Dr. J. T. Keables, Ransom Nutting, W. H. Clark, L. D. Roberts.

After viewing the bodies of the deceased, the testimony of Jennie Bull, the hired girl of the deceased, and John Klinger, the hired man, was heard, and the verdict rendered that the deceased came to their death from wounds by a pistol, fired by someone to them unknown.

MISS JENNIE BULL'S STORY

This witness is an intelligent, sprightly appearing unmarried woman, about 25 years of age; her parents live in the vicinity, and has always borne a good reputation. Her story as related to the Democrat reporter, and to the coroner's jury is as follows:

"Had been at work for Henry Morris and wife for about five years, and had always got along pleasantly with them, never knew them to have any trouble with each other. Last Sunday we all went away visiting, leaving the house alone. I left about eleven o'clock in the morning, and went to Charleston. Henry and wife were still at home when I left, but were expecting to start for a visit to Johnny Gould in Porter township, Van Buren county, soon after. I returned, reaching home about four o'clock in the afternoon, but found the family had not got back. The house was locked, and after waiting a short time, I went over to my father's, which is near by, and staid until nearly six o'clock. It might have been a little after six when I got to the house, and found they had not yet returned. I sat down on the bench on the east porch, near where Henry was found, but having no paper, nor anything to read, I thought of a short ladder standing near by which I carried around to the west side of the kitchen, climbed up to the window which is only six or seven feet from the ground, and crawled in. I unbolted the kitchen door which opens on the east porch,

and getting a paper, sat down on the bench again, and commenced reading. Henry and his wife drove up soon after, and he put up the horses. His wife and myself helped do the chores, feeding some corn to the hogs, while Henry went for the cows. The chores being done, we all returned to the house, and I spread a cold lunch, of which we all ate. Did not get any warm supper. While we were eating Mrs. Morris inquired if anyone brought me home, as she had noticed a fresh buggy track turning into the lane as if it came from the east, on the highway. I told her no, I came home alone, and on foot. There was general talk about going to bed; Henry saying that he wanted to get up early. I went up, staid (illegible) soon after going to bed; felt tired. I sleep in a chamber over the dining room. The blinds were open on my window, and the window up, that night. The window opens to the north over the porch under which Henry was found dead. My room door was closed and held with my trunk, which I usually shoved against it. I heard nothing during the night, although I have a vague, indistinct recollection of having been partially awakened and going to sleep again, as if in a dream. I felt stiff and numb in the morning, and cannot account for my sleeping so soundly, as I usually sleep very light and arouse readily. When I awoke in the morning, the sun was shining into my windows; should think it was half past six o'clock. Was surprised that it was so late, and that I had not been called as Mr. Morris was in the habit of doing. I went down stairs, and as I stepped into the dining room saw that the north door leading onto the porch, was open; the wire screen door was closed, it shuts to with a wire spring. Saw Mr. Morris through the screen door, lying on the porch with nothing but his shirt on; supposed him to be sick; passed through the dining room and pantry into the kitchen, and unbolted the kitchen door, which opens onto the north end of the porch; then saw the wound in his neck, and blood on his shirt. I screamed, and ran to Mr. Gillett's, the nearest neighbor, alarmed them, and then went to my father's. When I returned, a number of people had collected, among them, John Klinger, the hired man, my father, Mr. Rosewarne and son Charles, Elias Morris and wife, and others. Charlotte Morris said to me: "Oh Jennie, this is bad for you!" I could not reply for I was almost exhausted. The revolver that was found lying by the side of Mrs. Morris in the closet, I have often found when making the bed, under the pillow on the side of the bed where Henry slept. Do not think Mr. Morris had much money about him; he had been selling some wheat but got no money for it; he had sold some hogs and got $122 on them. He discharged a hired man named Riley Huntley a few weeks ago, because he drank so much. They did not part in anger. Have no suspicion as to who committed the murders."

JOHN KLINGER

Who was employed by Morris after the discharge of Riley Huntley, about eight weeks ago, to do chores and work on the farm, is a beardless youth, who has scarcely attained his majority, but is married. His wife lives about a mile and a half away, near Nicholsville, and since working for Morris, he has lived with him most of the time, going home to stay nights occasionally. His account of the transactions of the fateful Sunday and the day preceding and after, as related to the Democrat, is substantially as follows:

"Began work for Morris about eight weeks ago; my home is at Nicholsville where my wife lives; staid at home nights part of the time; staid here every night last week, because Morris asked me to. Saturday last I drew a load of wheat to Decatur, Morris driving over in a buggy. We both got back about six o'clock in the evening. Do not know whether he had any money; had not been around with him in the village any. The following day, Sunday, I went home; did not leave until about noon; when I did leave Henry and his wife were both down to the barn. Upon reaching home I found my wife was sick, and I sent back word by Mr. Rosewarne that my wife was sick, and I would not be back to do the chores that night; Mr. Morris got the word, as he stopped at Rosewarne's on his way home that evening from Gould's. Monday morning I went over to Morris's, reaching there I should think, about six o'clock. I went to the barn first; noticed that the large gate was open leading to the lane, and also the stable door; went into the barn and gave the horses hay, when I noticed that one of the horses was gone. I then started to go up to the house, and as I went out of the door saw a pair of pants on the manure pile; left them where they were and went up to the house, when I saw Henry lying on the porch, and thinking he was sick took hold of him to help him up, when I discovered he was dead. I fainted, I think; when I came to, I ran to Rosewarne's and told them, and they notified Elias Morris. Then returned to the house; I looked for horse's tracks and found fresh tracks looking as if made by a horse while running. There was no saddle or bridle taken, not even a halter or strap." *The reporter suggested that Jennie Bull thought she was a light sleeper,* a look of incredulity spread over his face, and he said: "Why, Henry often has to call her two or three times in the morning, and I have had to do so myself, when they told me to call her."

Besides the testimony of Jennie Bull and John Klinger, *The National Democrat* included testimony of the person who most likely first sighted the murderer:

THE MASKED ASSASSIN SEEN – CHARLEY ROSEWARNE'S STORY

Charley Rosewarne, a young man, son of Wm. Rosewarne, one of the nearest neighbors to the deceased, was out Sunday evening; attending a Sunday school concert at the Valley school house, commonly known as the "Sogger Hill school house," about two miles and a half west. The concert concluded (and) the young man started home with a horse and buggy, not far from 9 o'clock. When about a mile west of Henry Morris's he saw a man riding horseback coming towards him at break neck speed. As they neared each other the horse neither slacked its speed nor turned from the road. When within a few rods young Rosewarne recognized the horse, by its white feet, white face and general appearance, the rider he did not recognize; he had a tall soft hat on pulled well down on his head, and something covering his face so that it could not be seen. The horse had a bridle on and either a saddle or an oil cloth, something for the rider to sit on. Rosewarne came on home put his horse out, and went to bed without saying anything to anybody of what he had seen. The clock did not strike ten until he had been in bed some minutes.

The National Democrat included one other first-hand account of the strange rider by the grandson of Grandma Hathaway ("White bread costs money!"):

THE MYSTERIOUS HORSEMAN AGAIN

About two miles and a half from the scene of the tragedy, between 9 and 10 o'clock Sunday evening, Abner Hathaway met a horseman going south-west, riding an animal corresponding in description to the one taken from the barn. When Hathaway first heard and saw the horse it was going rapidly, but was slackened down into a walk as it passed him. The moon was shining brightly and he had a fair look at the man, who appeared to be of medium size, wearing a tall slouched hat and a false face, the apertures for eyes being large and looking hideous; his beard escaped below the mask, and was dark grizzled gray. The horseman rode slowly by with averted face, but after passing turned and looked at the occupant of the buggy for a moment, and after a distance of a few rods struck the spurs to his horse and dashed away at a keen lope. Hathaway said nothing about this until the following morning.

THE HORSE FOUND

Information was received from South Bend, (Indiana) by telegraph, about 11 o'clock Monday morning, that the horse belonging to Mr. Morris was found loose in the streets of that city, which is about forty miles distant from the tragedy. The horse had nothing on him when found, but had marks of a saddle, and gave evidences of recent hard riding. Flakes of white foam were dried on his hair clear to his eyes, but he was cool when found, indicating that he must have been turned loose two or three hours before.

THE MOTIVE

It being apparent that plunder was not the object, the mind naturally seeks for some adequate motive for the fearful deed. Inquiry develops the fact beyond dispute that Henry was universally liked, he was one of those easy, social good-natured men, who make friends of all with whom they come in contact.

His wife was a prepossessing, beautiful woman, of intelligence and culture, with rare graces that made her valued in all the relations of life, and probably had not an enemy in the world. During this period of excitement, the most trivial affairs were brought to mind and considered, to see if they could possibly furnish a sufficient motive to even the most devilish mind for the execution of this horrid murder.

THE DISCHARGED HIRED MAN

The fact that Henry a few weeks before had discharged a hired man for drunkenness, was spoken of, but an investigation of the circumstances, soon relieved him from all suspicion. The facts in relation to that matter are as follows: Riley Huntley, a man 35 or 40 years of age, has worked for Morris two or three years, and has always been considered a good hand except when in liquor. Lately the habit of getting drunk has increased in frequency. About 8 weeks ago, Morris went away one Sunday, leaving Huntley at home, and he too soon left for Decatur, where he got in a drunken condition and returned home. When Morris returned in the evening, he inquired if the chores were done, to which Huntley responded no; he had got done doing chores; that he had never got any thanks for doing them. Morris undertook to reason with him, but finally told him he was too full to talk with, but to come around in the morning, and they would settle, which was accordingly done.

Morris not having the money in hand to settle the balance, Huntley staid with him a few days until the money was procured, and then left with apparent good feeling, and in conversation with the help of some neighboring farmers admitted that he was largely to blame, that he drank too much &c. Huntley lives in Hamilton township and passed through this village Tuesday on his way to the scene of the murder, and to attend the funeral. He stands clear of suspicion in the minds of the people in the vicinity.

A PENDING LEGAL CONTEST

There is now pending in the U.S. courts a suit to foreclose a mortgage purporting to have been given by Henry, but not signed by his wife, on his farm of 320 acres, to secure the payment of $11,000. There has been no interest paid, and the sum total now claimed to be due would not be far from $20,000. This mortgage [has] been contested by Henry on the ground that it was a forgery. Henry was also an important witness a few years since in a similar suit, wherein his brother Amos was a defendant, and the public are discussing the question, as to whether, out of these difficulties, any person could have acquired sufficient malice, or sufficient prospect of pecuniary benefit by getting the testimony of Henry out of the way, to prompt the fearful murder.

THE VICTIMS

Henry Morris was the youngest child of Dolphin Morris, an early settler on Little Prairie Ronde, on the farm where the tragedy was committed. His parents are both dead, as are also two sisters. He leaves three brothers, Amos, Samuel and Elias, all well known and successful farmers, in the immediate vicinity.

Esther Jones Morris, was a daughter of Asa Jones, of Edwardsburg, and was married to Henry Morris in December 1869. She was universally beloved and respected for her many excellences of intellect and heart. She leaves two sorrowing parents, and a bereaved brother and sister.

THE FUNERAL SERVICES

Were held under the trees at the old family residence where the tragedy occurred, Tuesday afternoon, and were attended by over 1,000 people. The sermon was preached by Rev. J. W. H. Carlisle, of Decatur. The husband and wife in separate coffins, were both interred in one grave.

So far as known there is no direct clue to the perpetrator, but the case has been put in the hands of competent and skilled detectives, and nothing will be left undone that has a promise of success in bringing the perpetrator of this most dastardly and cold blooded murder to justice.[2]

MRS. CHAS. H. MORRIS   CHAS H MORRIS

By the time The National Democrat had printed this overview of the sensational double murder, "competent and skilled detectives" were indeed already on the case. The Pinkertons arrived in Decatur on September 30, and despite "no direct clue to the perpetrator", the detectives had barely disembarked the train when citizens eagerly pointed them in the direction of the chief suspects.

3

ALLEGED FORGERIES AND A JURY VERDICT

Van Buren County no longer qualified as the "frontier" in 1879. It had a sheriff and a jail, both located in Paw Paw. Smaller towns had "day constables" or "night watches" who were usually part-time officials but the position of sheriff was full-time. Horse theft being the predominant crime of the time, it was the Anti-Horsetheft Association that traveled to South Bend to bring Morris's horse home after his murder.

So it was that the Morris family turned to the Pinkerton National Detective Agency for help. Allan Pinkerton was a renowned Scottish immigrant who had accompanied newly elected Abraham Lincoln to Washington, thwarting an assassination attempt in Baltimore. Pinkerton had been an active abolitionist with ties to John Brown and during the war had operated as a Union spy throughout the Confederacy. After the war Pinkerton's agency concentrated on train robbers, and in 1874 was hired to track Jesse James. With several agents being gunned down by the James-Younger gang, the pursuit became a personal vendetta for Pinkerton but in 1876, after one of his agents working undercover next to the James farm was killed, he chose to withdraw the agency from the case.

Pinkerton wasted no time in investigating the Morris murder. After he was contacted, he immediately dispatched his son William, who arrived in Decatur on September 30, the day after the bodies had been found. His first contact in the village was a livery stable keeper who named the Matteson brothers, Milo DeHart (Hart) and James, as prime suspects in the murder.

In his report, Pinkerton wrote, "Hart Matteson follows the business of a usurer, loaning money at exorbitant rates of interest to farmers then taking mortgages on everything they had; in other words he was a dealer in cut-throat mortgages, and of course was universally despised throughout the whole country." He added, "Matteson was known as a bad character, a man who would do anything to make money, he had a brother James, who was a worse character than himself, who formerly lived in Texas, and was known as a horse trainer, had also been a school teacher."[1]

Pinkerton's report presented a picture different from earlier neutral descriptions of the family. The Matteson family had not always suffered such a damning reputation. Alamanson and Eunice Bentley Matteson had brought their two sons, Milo and James, to Decatur from Cherry Creek, New York, in the late 1860s. The 1863 draft registration indicated that Alamanson was active in the Civil War effort. In the New York State Census of 1865, Alamanson is listed as a farmer, and son James is listed as a "seaman on lake"[2], possibly on a steamboat providing passage on the 17-mile-long Chautauqua Lake nearby.

By 1868, the Matteson family had established itself in Decatur. The *Republican* named Milo as a "day constable" and one of four "best men in town" who had shackled the town terror Joe Pearson and taken him to the Paw Paw jail after one of his drunken attacks.[3] Milo DeHart Matteson was also listed as one of the founding directors of Citizen's National Bank of Niles (Michigan) in 1871, but he was foremost a private money lender, and Pinkerton wrote in his report, "dealing in cut-throat mortgages."[4]

The same year a list of mortgage sales began to appear in the weekly Paw Paw *True Northerner*. Initially, father Alamanson assigned the mortgages to his son James.[5] From 1872, however, it was Milo D. Matteson who was named in nearly every issue of *The True Northerner* as the person who foreclosed defaulted mortgages. The following notice of default and sale involving a purchase of land by Ruth O. White is an early example.

MORTGAGE SALE.—Default having been made in the payment of an Indenture of Mortgage executed by Ruth O. White to Palmer Earl bearing date the eighteenth day of April, A.D. 1870, and recorded in the office of the Register of Deeds for Van Buren county, June twentieth, A.D. 1870, in Liber 1 of Mortgages, on page 184, which said mortgage was duly assigned by Palmer Earl to M. DeHart Matteson, upon which said mortgage there is now due two hundred and eighty dollars and eighty-eight cents and an attorney fee of forty dollars and no suit at law or in equity having been instituted for the recovery of the same: Therefore notice is hereby given that by virtue of a power of sale in said mortgage and the statute in such case made and provided, that piece of land described as the north half of the north west quarter of section ten in township four south of range fifteen west, County of Van Buren and State of Michigan, excepting twenty-two and a half acres sold by Ruth O. White to George Nesbitt off the north west corner of the above described land, will be sold at public auction to the highest bidder at the front door of the Court House in the village of Paw Paw, Van Buren County, Michigan, by the sheriff of said County, on the 22nd day of April, at one o'clock p.m., to satisfy the amount due on said mortgage. Dated January 22, 1872. M. DeHART MATTESON, Assignee. Foster & Coleman, Attorneys.[6]

In multiple issues of *The True Northerner*, Ruth O. White was named as having three different mortgages that were foreclosed with M. DeHart Matteson as assignee of the mortgagor. Despite the circumstances causing the default of her mortgages, what the public likely saw was a 45-year-old woman with three children, ages 15, 9, and 7, and a 68-year-old husband losing their home.

Further notoriety came to M. DeHart Matteson in 1872, when he foreclosed on Bryant and Laura Herrick's property. Herrick had left his wife and three small children in 1871 to run off to Illinois to wed a neighbor woman, she herself being already married.[7] Whether the circumstances of his death two months later were known, or whether the public was aware of the scandal, is unclear, but Matteson's foreclosure on yet another widow and her children was repeatedly published in *The True Northerner*.[6]

Regardless of the actual details surrounding the mortgages and their defaults and subsequent foreclosures, such examples painted a picture of Matteson, for many, as the heartless villain evicting mothers and children from their homes. During the 1870s Matteson had 28 such foreclosures docketed in the Van Buren County circuit court, and he seems to have been attracted to weakened families, such as the Whites and the Herricks. However, after Dolphin Morris died in 1870, the Morris family, which at that time was known as the First Family of Van Buren County, became Matteson's obsession.

Morris had left a 67-year-old widow and children as his survivors, but they were hardly without resources. In fact, in 1871 *The True Northerner* published a list of "solid men in Van Buren County who own[ed] real estate and personal property exceeding in value twenty-five thousand dollars."[8] Only three Decatur people qualified, one being Milo Matteson's father Alamanson, and his name was directly followed by the name of Mrs. Nancy Morris:

The following is a list of some of the solid men in Van Buren County who own real estate and personal property exceeding in value twenty-five thousand dollars. The figures set opposite each name represent thousands—the first column real estate and the second personal:

F. W. Fisk Almena	30	5
J. T. Clapp Paw Paw	22	4
T. R. Harrison Paw Paw	17	10
J. M. Longwell Paw Paw	28	5
T. W. Willard Paw Paw	50	10
E. Smith Paw Paw	30	20
T. L. Ross Paw Paw	25	16
A. Sherman Paw Paw	33	40
E. O. Briggs Paw Paw	20	30
J. Lyle jr. Paw Paw	17	17
L. T. Rawson Decatur	17	10
A. M. Matteson Decatur	3	30
Mrs. Nancy Morris Decatur	25	5
J. J. Woodman Antwerp	26	35
M. L. Fitch Antwerp	35	15
A. W. Haydon Hamilton	54	10
Robert Nesbitt Hamilton	52	18

[8]

It is noteworthy that the Matteson and Morris fortunes complement each other. Whereas the Matteson wealth was amassed as personal property, the Morris fortune was in real estate holdings. These figures most certainly did not go unnoticed by Milo Matteson. If Pinkerton's assessment of Matteson was true—that he was a man who would do anything to make money—did this list influence the grim course the 1870s would take for the Morris family?

Beginning in late 1873, Amos Morris and Matteson were involved in three alleged forgery cases which held such a high degree of public interest that the detailed testimonies—direct and cross examinations and redirect examinations—were front-page news for four weeks.

One of the forgery cases was a criminal case. The charging information filed in the case of *People v. Matteson* alleged that *"on the 21st day of June, A.D., 1873, Milo D. Matteson, at the township of Decatur, in the county of Van Buren, falsely and feloniously did make, counterfeit and forge a certain false, forged and counterfeit deed, purporting to be an indenture of mortgage; which said false, forged and counterfeit deed purports to have been made, signed, sealed, executed, acknowledged and delivered by Amos Morris to the said Milo D. Matteson, and bears date the 21st day of June in the year one thousand eight hundred and seventy-three, and purports and pretends to have been given, signed, sealed, executed, acknowledged and delivered for the purpose of securing the payment of a large sum of money, to-with: the sum of five thousand and eighteen dollars"* with intent to injure and defraud.[9]

Morris admitted he had borrowed money from Matteson but argued that the signatures on the mortgages dated February 14 and 28 and June 21, 1873, were forgeries. Penmanship experts, in the form of bank tellers, artists, merchants, bookkeepers, and registers of deeds, were called to compare the signatures with other samples of writing, and their testimonies dwelled on such specifics as the downward stroke of the M and the capital letters situated above or below the line. On the subject of penmanship, Samuel Morris testified that he had overheard Milo Matteson boast, "I have no particular hand, but write as many hands as there are people. If you or any one else would write your name, I could write [it] again so you could not tell one from the other."[10]

Perhaps more significant, two Decatur lawyers, Newton Foster and Jerome Coleman, testified to witnessing acknowledgments of the mortgages.[11] Matteson ran his office, separated by a partition, out of the back of Foster and Coleman's practice, so it is was convenient to call them when he needed a witness for a signature. However, both Foster and Coleman also testified that they had neither read the documents they witnessed nor had they actually seen Morris sign them. From their testimony it appears that Coleman had considerably more contact with Matteson than Foster as they were seen driving together in a buggy, notably on June 21 to the Masonic picnic. Also, Matteson was known to have dined at Coleman's house.[11]

Although witnesses attested to having seen Amos Morris in Decatur on February 14 and 28, the date of the third mortgage, the date of June 21, was solidly called into question by others. A considerable number of people who had attended the funeral of a Mrs. Langdon on June 21 when she was buried south of Lawton attested to having seen Amos Morris driving east to Lawton—not west to Decatur—with a hayrack in the morning of the funeral and returning home in the afternoon, refuting any claims that Morris was in Decatur that day to sign the third mortgage note.[12]

At the close of the criminal trial involving Matteson, Circuit Judge Charles R. Brown charged the jury and addressed the nature of witnessing acknowledgments:

Now if as matter of fact the signature of Morris was forged it follows that though the names of Coleman and Foster appear as witnesses, they are not, in fact such. The witnessing of a paper consistes not merely in the act of writing the witness' name but in taking cognizance of the fact that the maker signs, seals and delivers the instrument in the presence and view of the witness. If this be not done, if the maker do(es) not sign, and deliver the instrument in the presence of the witness, that which purports to be a witnessing is not such, but is a falsehood—is not genuine. And so with the certificate of acknowledgment. If the maker named in the instrument do(es) not in fact acknowledge it, then that which purports to be an acknowledgment, is not such, and in that sense is not genuine.

In closing his remarks to the jury, Judge Brown intoned, "It is one of the most glorious features of American law that it is no respecter of person. The rules that it applies to the poor and despised, it also applies to the rich and powerful. When crime is committed, it requires the office of Justice to bring the person suspected of the offence, whatever his situation or standing in life into the temple of Justice to answer the accusation. The People does not wish, the law does not demand the conviction of the innocent. Justice requires the conviction and punishment only of the guilty. It is for you to say whether you are satisfied beyond a reasonable doubt that Milo D. Matteson is guilty. If you are not, acquit him. Render such a verdict as shall accord with your judgments and satisfy your consciences now and hereafter.

The True Northerner reported the jury's verdict in the same issue: "The Jury then retired and after a short absence returned into Court and say on their oath that they find the respondent GUILTY, as the People have charged in their information.[13]

The shift had begun from Matteson's being declared as "one of the best men in town" as a day constable in 1868, to his gaining notoriety as one who foreclosed mortgages on widows and children, and subsequently being identified as an alleged forger. It is of little wonder that by 1879, Pinkerton agents would describe Milo DeHart Matteson as "universally despised throughout the whole country."[14]

4

A DECADE OF LITIGATION

The guilty verdict of January 1874, branding him as a forger might have spelled an end to Milo Matteson's cut-throat mortgage business in Michigan, but the problems for him were that he had invested too much in the area with his money-loaning activities and that he was still involved in numerous court cases. The February 14 and 28, 1873 mortgages he had taken on the properties of Amos Morris had not been addressed, and in July 1873, Matteson claimed that a whopping $11,000 mortgage on the land of Charles H. Morris existed.

After the jury entered a guilty verdict against Matteson in the case involving Amos Morris and the forged documents, Matteson filed a bond for security and requested the case be transferred to the U.S. court at Grand Rapids. Kalamazoo attorney Arthur Brown filed affidavits claiming that Matteson was a non-resident of the State of Michigan, and that due to local prejudice, Matteson could not get a fair and unbiased trial.[1] A reporter for *The True Northerner* vented,

This is a dodge resorted to for the purpose of delay and to annoy and worry Morris. It is resorted to for the further purpose of adding to the expense and rendering it difficult to procure the attendance of witnesses, all going to the advantage of the defendant. The removal of Matteson to South Bend, Ind., is a sham. We do not believe that Matteson has or ever had any intention of locating at South Bend, permanently. His destination is Texas.[1]

Approximately six weeks later, the attempt to transfer the trial had failed. *The True Northerner* reported, "*We learn that the cases pending in Cass County to set aside the forged mortgages, out of which the Matteson forgery case grew, and which were sent to the U.S. District Court on motion of Matteson, have been sent back to Cass County for trial. Matteson's sham removal to South Bend appears to have been labor lost.*"[2]

The whereabouts of the Mattesons indeed became foggy. In April 1873, the papers had announced, "*The Matteson family, of Decatur, intend soon to remove to Kalamazoo for a permanent residence.*"[3] Approximately eleven months later, it was announced that Newton Foster, the lawyer who failed to examine the mortgage document he was witnessing, had "*bought the Matteson place on the corner of Phelps and St. Mary's streets, giving his former residence on Wheeler Avenue in part payment.*"[4]

Activities surrounding the cases accelerated in the latter part of 1874. In June, on the day that Kalamazoo Judge Charles R. Brown denied the motion to grant a new trial, his resignation took effect. *The True Northerner* reported,

As he is now off the Bench a new trial will follow as a matter of course, because the law, we believe requires the Judge before whom the trial was had to sign the Bill of Exceptions to remove the case to the Supreme Court. The Respondent not having been sentenced, the People are compelled to submit to the expense of a new trial or abandon the case, thus letting a dangerous man loose on the community to practice his fleecing without restraint.[5]

Later, *The True Northerner* reported, "*On Saturday last a new trial was granted to M.D. Matteson. The people have Judge Brown to thank for the entailment of expense that these new trials subject the people to.*"[6] The case was moved to Centreville in St. Joseph County for retrial in March 1875. The near circus-like atmosphere surrounding the case lasted four weeks, at which time Matteson obtained his acquittal.

The punches and counter-punches had continued throughout 1874. On July 9, 1874, Amos Morris was arrested and escorted to Grand Rapids to answer an indictment for perjury that had been procured on the claim of Milo Matteson, who was "still at large" according to *The True Northerner.*[7] The indictment, however, was dismissed by the court for lack of jurisdiction. And in August, Jerome Coleman, the second lawyer to witness the Morris mortgage documents, was also placed under arrest for committing perjury during the forgery trial.[8] In September, his bail was fixed at a noteworthy $1200.[9]

Once Matteson was acquitted in the spring of 1875, he wasted no time commencing a lawsuit to foreclose the Amos Morris mortgages. The case was first dismissed by the U.S. court for lack of jurisdiction and then heard in the Cass County court where Judge Coolidge granted a decree for foreclosure. Morris, however, appealed the case to the Michigan Supreme Court. Nearly four years later, in January 1879, the state's highest court ruled that the mortgages that had been assigned to Milo's uncle James Matteson of New York, had been "fabricated" papers, thereby finally putting the forgery cases between Milo Matteson and Amos Morris to rest.[10]

The Supreme Court verdict might have dealt a crushing blow to Matteson's activities in Michigan, but the very opposite was true. As for the Morris family, a culmination of events ended the decade in tragedy for them. Dolphin Morris's widow Nancy had died in October 1877, leaving the homestead to 30-year-old Charles Henry and his wife Esther Jones Morris who had married on Christmas Eve 1869, only two weeks before Dolphin's death; and as far as can be ascertained, the couple had no children until March 3, 1878 when their son Frank was born. Sadly, however, he only lived 6 months, and according to death records, died in September of that year due to a liver complaint.[11]

Although the local newspapers had once speculated that the Matteson family might head for Kalamazoo, the Matteson parents had settled in Chicago by 1876, and Milo, not being "at large" any longer, was in Chicago often enough to meet and marry the 21-year-old Laura Ann Shilling, daughter of Isaac W. Shilling and Mary Randolph Shilling. When they married on February 3, 1879, Milo still owned lawyer Newton Foster's former house on the northern edge of Decatur, and the newlyweds were in residence enough that on the day of Charles and Esther Morris's murders, Decatur citizens remarked how unusual it was to see the couple attending church and socializing in the local hotel afterwards.[12]

In 1880, The True Northerner continued to focus on Matteson and described an example of his earlier methods:

About 1870 Caleb M. Gardner borrowed $105 of Matteson, and gave a chattel mortgage on about all he had to secure the payment of the same – Gardner made payments from time to time amounting to $90, but continually renewing his notes and mortgages until in 1876 Matteson had his notes for $449, and mortgages on all he had. Gardner then paid $200 more, after which Matteson took the balance *of the mortgaged property. Gardner brought replevin, and after two trials in the Circuit and one in the Supreme Court recovered his property.*[13]

After the Amos Morris mortgages were deemed as frauds, Matteson turned to his claim against Charles Morris's land. In the same article in 1880, *The True Northerner* printed a full summary of the history of the *Matteson vs. Morris* litigation:

The recent trial in the United States Court at Grand Rapids, of the case of Solomon W. Steele against Milo D. Matteson, brings afresh before the public gaze the Matteson family, who have figured so extensively in the courts of this vicinity for the last eight years. Prior to 1873 the Matteson's (sic) were not strangers to the courts; but the suit commenced in July of that year, by Charles H. Morris, against Milo D. Matteson, to set aside, as a forgery, a mortgage of $11,000 dated in April 1872, was the first thing that excited the public attention. It was claimed by Charles H. Morris, in his bill in chancery, that he never knew of the existence of this mortgage until he heard of it being put on record.

Immediately after this, the report spread that Matteson had on record three other mortgages against Amos Morris, in Cass County: Amos Morris claiming too, that he never knew of their existence until told of their record. Directly on the heels of this discovery, Milo D. Matteson was arrested on the charge of forging the Amos Morris mortgages, and in January 1874 a long trial was had in the Van Buren County Circuit Court, resulting in the conviction of Matteson. A stay of proceedings was obtained ostensibly to give Matteson time to get a Bill of Exceptions settled for the Supreme Court. Pending this stay of proceedings, Judge Brown resigned without settling the Bill of Exceptions. This, under the practice of the Courts, gave Matteson a new trial. He then got the case removed to St. Joseph County, and after another four weeks [of] trial [Matteson] obtained a verdict of acquittal.

Meanwhile Matteson commenced in the U.S. court, a foreclosure of the Amos Morris mortgages, and got Amos indicted in the U.S. court for perjury in his answer to the foreclosure bill; but the indictment and the foreclosure cases were dismissed by that court for want of jurisdiction. Matteson also commenced foreclosure of the Charles H. Morris mortgage in the U.S. court, and this was also dismissed for the same reason. Matteson then commenced [an action] in the Cass County court, to foreclose the Amos Morris mortgage. Voluminous testimony was taken and Judge

Coolidge granted a decree for foreclosure. Morris appealed to the [Michigan] Supreme Court and that Court pronounced the mortgages "fabricated" papers.

Matteson also commenced again to foreclose his $11,000 mortgage in the Van Buren Circuit Court. This was fought inch by inch for about two years, until Matteson voluntarily withdrew his bill and commenced over again. By virtue of a recent act of [C]ongress he transferred this suit into the U.S. Court of the State. Before Charles H. Morris had been sworn in the U.S. Court, in his own behalf, the community were horror-stricken with the announcemment [sic] that he and his estimable wife had been murdered in cold blood in his own home.

Efforts had been made before Morris' murder towards a compromise, and his counsel were authorized to offer $5,000 to settle the $11,000 mortgage, which had at that time increased to $16,000 and upwards; but nothing came of this. In the summer of 1880, Matteson commenced taking testimony on his side, before a commissioner appointed by Judge Withey; at the close of the second day of the taking of this testimony, the cross-examination of Mr. Matteson as to his movements and whereabouts for a week or two preceding the murder, made him decidedly uncomfortable. Night came to his relief, and an adjournment of several days was obtained, during which, a previous offer of the administrator of the murdered man for a settlement was accepted, and Matteson took about fourteen per cent of his claim and paid his own costs. Of course the cross-examination was never resumed and the mortgage on the old Morris homestead was discharged. It is estimated that this whole litigation has cost all parties, public and private, not less than $40,000.[13]

STRING HIM UP

When the Pinkerton agents arrived in Decatur, only one day after the Morris bodies had been found, they were immediately directed toward Milo Matteson as a person of interest by residents who strongly suspected him of being involved in the murders. But because he and his wife had made a seldom appearance in church that morning and driven around town several times before spending most of the day socializing in the lobby of the Duncombe House, consensus quickly formed that an accomplice must exist.

Any sign of evidence at the scene of the crime, namely tracks, had been obliterated by the scores of buggies that had been driven up the lane after the alarm had spread. The strange buggy tracks Esther Morris had mentioned seeing on returning home that Sunday were hopelessly gone.

One clue, however, remained fresh. Early in the evening before the murder, four witnesses passed Anderson Cemetery, which lay just east of the Morris homestead. The road they traveled makes a small jog around the cemetery and had been carved out of land owned by Dolphin Morris and LeGrand Anderson. Just one year before the murders, the cemetery had become the final resting place for Charles Henry and Esther's 6-month-old son Frankie.[1]

A small wooded area across from the cemetery provided the perfect vantage point to observe the Morris farm where Charles Henry and Esther had lived. One could have watched the young couple drive off in the direction of Lawton, and with both the hired man and girl gone as well, the lack of activity or disturbance on the farm would have provided the intruder a perfect opportunity to sneak onto the premises and familiarize himself with the logistics vital to his plan.

On the spot where the parked buggy and team had been sighted, tracks were discovered that had left a particular mark, possibly a lead to identifying the vehicle and its driver. While a buggy was found on Floyd Smith's premises that might have produced such a mark, public suspicion most probably aided in a trail to Smith, the only person to be accused in aiding and abetting the Morris murderer. Floyd Smith had once worked for Charles H. Morris and was viewed by the Pinkertons as a prime source of information. He had worked for Milo D. Matteson as well, and by 1879 had taken a mortgage on the Matteson farm west of Decatur. Pinkerton agents worked undercover for weeks to gain Smith's confidence in an attempt to draw information from him, often employing a bottle of whiskey; but Smith remained guarded. Allan Pinkerton summed up the agency's surveillance of Smith with, "The assertion that Matteson *might* have been concerned in the murder, Smith repeated twice, but added each time that he did not believe Matteson to be that kind of a man. K. questioned him closely for over an hour, but he did not contradict himself, or seem in the least embarrassed."[2]

The Pinkerton investigation of the Morris murders lasted throughout October 1879 and was only discontinued due to the additional expense of $1000 necessary to "solve the case."[3] Smith, however, in his conversations with undercover agent K. had admitted that he was a bit afraid that Matteson might foreclose on his mortgage, and further accounts show that he was more involved with Matteson than he was willing to divulge.[4] Smith's arrest came on December 17, 1879, and *The True Northerner* reported:

The Morris murder and the Morris-Matteson forgery and fraud mortgage cases continue to occupy the public mind. The people for months have been in a state of feverish excitement. On Wednesday evening of last week a warrant was issued against Floyd Smith on a charge of complicity in the Morris tragedy, and placed in the hands of Constable Botsford, who went out to the township of Hamilton and took him into custody. On the way to Decatur they were met by a party of masked men who took Smith out of the cutter and sent Botsford and his assistant home. Just what was done with Smith is not known though all manner of rumors are afloat.

The True Northerner account continued:

It seems to be well settled in the minds of the people in that vicinity that after the Morris tragedy, Smith was the medium through which Matteson sent and received considerable correspondence. This of course, if true, has a strange look, and people wonder why a purely business or friendly correspondence should require an intermediate medium.

The reporter wrapped up the article with,

Constable Botsford was called to the stand and testified substantially as follows, as reported to us by one who was present: When he arrested Floyd Smith the first time, he was met by a party of unknown men who halted them on the road and forcibly ejected himself and his assistant from the cutter, and after securing Floyd Smith, put him back and told him to 'git', which he did. He had no knowledge of what occurred after that and to the time he made his second arrest on Friday last, except what Floyd Smith told him. He also testified that Smith further said that Matteson came to him (Smith) the day after the murder of Morris, and said that they would detain and examine his mail at the Post Office and to avoid that he (Matteson) had caused his mail matter to be addressed to him (Smith); that Matteson's mail came thus addressed with a private mark on one corner of the envelope to distinguish it from any that might be designed for Smith; that he thereafter received Matteson's mail—some through the Decatur office, some through the Lawrence, Breedsville and other surrounding offices; that Matteson's outgoing letters were delivered to him to be mailed through different offices and were so mailed. This went on until Smith's wife became alarmed when Matteson's correspondence was turned over to some one else. At this point the case was adjourned until Tuesday, the 30th inst. at nine o'clock in the forenoon. We learned that an immense crowd was present and the excitement was intense.[5]

But according to Dana P. Smith's *"The Tragic Story of Floyd Smith"*, "*On the morning of the hearing, Prosecutor Benj. F. Heckert announced that there was no evidence that would warrant holding the defendant (Smith) and that he was released from arrest.*"

Dana Smith added, "*In my acquaintance with Floyd Smith, while he never brought up the subject he never seemed to shrink from answering questions about his experience. He maintained that he was innocent, and suspicion to the contrary, never ripened into proof.*"[6]

In the 1870s the local newspapers were full of foreclosures, forgeries, accusations, and revelations concerning Milo D. Matteson. After no evidence could prove that Floyd Smith had aided and abetted the

Morris murderer, and after the sudden C.H. Morris mortgage settlement in April 1880, the name Matteson rarely appeared in the papers, except for the mortgage cases Milo had transferred to his father Alamanson. According to an 1891 article in the Chicago *Herald*, Milo Matteson claimed, "*At the time of the murder I was in Decatur, Mich. on business, but [because of] rumors connecting me with the affair I gave up my residence in Chicago and moved to Decatur. I lived there two years for the express purpose of clearing myself of any suspicion, and to afford every chance for legal investigation. I was never summoned to appear at the coroner's inquest, and there was no trial.*"[7]

But in fact, prior to the settlement, in the spring of 1880 *The True Northerner* reported:

The Matteson-Morris case, before U.S. Commissioner Judson, is postponed. Only two witnesses have as yet been examined, Jerome Coleman and M.D. Matteson, and the evidence of the latter is to be continued. It is thought it will require months to get through the testimony. Before it is through with it will involve all that has taken place in the Matteson-Morris case relative to the mortgaged premises.[8]

But only a month later, a sudden end to the decade of litigation was reported,

On Tuesday last, the 13th inst., the Matteson mortgage foreclosure case was settled by the payment to Matteson of $2,500. The entire claim of Matteson aggregated about $30,000 to the time of settlement. The proposition came from Matteson through his attorney, Boudeman, who had evidently become alarmed for his client, and the amount paid was the approximate sum that it would cost the Morris estate to carry the case through to a termination, and is somewhat less than ten percent of the pretended claim. What is the inference to be drawn as regards Matteson?"[9]

Finally, two brief *True Northerner* news items signal an end to Milo Matteson's residence in Decatur, Michigan:

In December 1880, the paper noted, "M.D. Matteson is the father of an eight pound son."[10]

And in April 1881, it was reported, "M.D. Matteson is disposing of his property in this county with a view of seeking a home elsewhere."[11]

"Elsewhere" was undefined, and it is unclear whether the locals had an inkling how far away "elsewhere" might be. They were most likely just relieved to see the family leave the area. Although the area residents must have known that, wherever he went, Milo Matteson would have his eye out for any and every chance of entrepreneurship, could anyone have foreseen how far the family would go to regain the respectability they had lost?

6

COUNTERFEITING AND DRY GOODS

Before setting out for "elsewhere" in 1881, it is uncertain how much of 1880 Milo and Laura Matteson spent in Decatur. They could hardly have felt very welcome in the community after Floyd Smith had been strung up and his link to Matteson publicized. Still, Laura Matteson was pregnant, and according to census and draft records, son DeForrest Arthur Matteson was born in Decatur on November 29, 1880.[1] By April 1881, however, the family most likely headed for the Lake View district of northern Chicago, where both sets of parents lived.

Laura had been a Shilling before her marriage to Milo. The Shilling family had been no less enterprising than the Mattesons. They had followed American expansion, migrating from Pennsylvania and Ohio to Indiana, where Laura's father Isaac W. Shilling married Mary Randolph in 1852. By the time Laura was born in 1855, the family had moved on to Paxton, Illinois, and her father was listed in the 1860 Census as a hotel keeper.[2]

One cannot say what kind of mark the following decade left on Laura. Her mother and maternal grandmother both died in Paxton when she was seven or eight years old. Her father moved the family back to Ohio where he married Anna Griggs in 1866[3], and the next year Laura had a new step-sister Carrie.[4] The 1870 Census shows Isaac as still being a hotel keeper, but there was also unfinished business back in Paxton which, by chance, echoed Matteson activity in Michigan. Posted in the *Paxton Record* in June 1875:

CHANCERY NOTICE.
STATE OF ILLINOIS, ss.
FORD COUNTY,
In Circuit Court to August Term, A.D. 1875.

Mary Ann Swinford,

vs.

Martin B. Thompson, Resin Randolph, Perry Randolph, George Randolph, Lucy Pierson, Roxy Salter, Rachel Martin, Elizabeth Bird, Arthur Shilling, Burt Shilling, Laura Shilling, Harry Randolph. In Chancery.

Affidavit of the non residence of Resin Randolph, Perry Randolph, George Randolph, Lucy Pierson, Roxy Salter, Rachel Martin, Elizabeth Bird, Arthur Shilling, Burt Shilling, Laura Shilling, Harry Randolph. Defendants above named, having been filed in the office of the Clerk of the Circuit Court of Ford county, notice is hereby given to the said parties last above mentioned, viz. Resin Randolph, Perry Randolph, George Randolph, Lucy Pierson, Roxy Salter, Rachel Martin, Elizabeth Bird, Arthur Shilling, Burt Shilling, Laura Shilling, Harry Randolph, that the complainant, Mary Ann Swinford, has heretofore filed her bill of complaint in said Court, on the Chancery side thereof, and that a summons thereupon issued out of said Court, against the above named defendants, returnable on the first day of a term of the Circuit Court of Ford county, to be held at the Court House, in Paxton, in said Ford county, on the third Tuesday of August, A.D., 1875, as is by law required and such is now pending.

Now unless you the said Resin Randolph, Perry Randolph, George Randolph, Lucy Pierson, Roxy Salter, Rachel Martin, Elizabeth Bird, Arthur Shilling, Burt Shilling, Laura Shilling, and Harry Randolph, shall personally be and appear before said Circuit Court of Ford county on the first day of the next term thereof, to be holden at Paxton, in said county, on the third Tuesday of August, A.D., 1875, and plead answer or demur to the said bill of foreclosure, the same and the matters and things therein charged and stated will be taken as confessed and a decree entered against you according to the prayer of said bill

532 n4   W WHITE, Clerk.

Gray, Swan & Patton, Atty's for Complainant.[5]

Mary Randolph Shilling's three children and her surviving siblings were listed as defendants. One of her brothers, Perry Randolph, had gained notoriety from the 1850s to the 1870s as a member of a counterfeiting ring. A brief biography of Randolph is included in *the History of Regulators of Northern Indiana*: "Perry Randolph emigrated with his father to Bath, Medina county, Ohio, about the year 1832, and although his father is reputed to have been a man of honest and industrious habits, his son Perry gave early indications of his inclinations to and genius in crime. The time of his emigration to Indiana is not precisely known."[6]

The publication also refers to confessions and points out, "The reader will readily perceive, from the foregoing confessions, that the house of Perry Randolph was a rendezvous and trading point in all the commodities of criminal commerce, for the whole fraternity of felons and counterfeiters, east, west,
north and south."[6]

The twenty years of national attention which her uncle had received as part of the counterfeiting ring could not have escaped Laura and her Shilling family:

The *Hillsdale (Michigan) Standard*, reported in January 1858:

IMPORTANT ARREST.—The Toledo Blade states that the notorious Henry C. Humphrey, better known as Hank Humphrey, who has long been famous in police annals as a consummate counterfeiter and horse-thief, was arrested in St. Louis, recently. He broke jail at Laporte, Indiana, about two years ago, and has been at large ever since. Humphrey formerly belonged to the famous Latta gang in Southern Michigan, and after old Latta was run off into Iowa, he joined Perry Randolph's gang in Indiana, just over the line. It is supposed that some of Randolph's men furnished him with tools through the grates, with which he sawed himself out.[7]

The *Wheeling (West) Virginia Daily Intelligencer*, also made reference to Laura Matteson's uncle Perry Randolph in July 1858:

Counterfeiter Arrested.—A few days ago, Perry Randolph, and another counterfeiter were arrested at Warren, Ohio, by officer Hague of Pittsburgh. One thousand dollars had been offered for the arrest of these men by the State of Indiana. A large quantity of counterfeit money, principally tens on the State Bank of Ohio, and fives on the Farmer's Bank of Kentucky, was found with the men arrested.[8]
A few days later, *The Hillsdale (Michigan) Standard* also reported on the arrest.

IMPORTANT ARREST.—The Cleveland Review of Monday states that officer C. P. Bradley, of Chicago, and officer Moon, of Pittsburgh, passed through that city on Saturday evening, having in charge Perry Randolph and Geo. Elmore, (or a similar sounding name) _____ men in the gang of counterfeiters which has so long infested Northern Indiana, and for the arrest and breaking up of which the celebrated "Ligonier Regulators" were organized. The two above named escaped arrest at the time, and Mr. Bradley was engaged in hunting them up. After a long search he found them in Mercer Co., Western Pennsylvania, and is now on his way to deliver them up to the proper Indiana authorities. They are represented to be wealthy farmers, and to have figured in former years in Summit county, Ohio, and vicinity.[9]

Perry Randolph was tried and sentenced by an Indiana court but apparently did not serve a lengthy sentence. According to the *White Cloud Kansas Chief*, White Cloud, Kansas, politics may have played a role in Randolph's release in 1860:

The Fort Wayne Times denounces Gov. Willard very severely for pardoning out of the Penitentiary one Perry Randolph of DeKalb county. Among the documents which secured the pardon is a letter from Henry Monroe, better known hereabouts as "Col." Monroe. The Col. says his pardon would be "entirely gratifying to his friends, of which he has many in this county, as him and his father are the leaders of the Democratic party in that county!" This ludic and patriotic appeal doubtless did the business![10]

Eight years later, after his pardon, counterfeit currency attributable to Randolph landed him on page one of *The National Republican*:

Counterfeit Greenbacks in the West. St. Louis, Dec. 6—A special to the Republican, from Kansas City, says large quantities of counterfeit greenbacks have been discovered afloat in the southwest counties of this State. Suspicion points to Perry Randolph, an old farmer living near White Water (White Pigeon), Michigan as being the principal vender. A detective, assuming the name of a tax collector, wrote to Randolph for $16,000, agreeing to pay $2,000 for it. Randolph replied he would bring it to Kansas City. He arrived on Wednesday, and was arrested, and confessed his guilt. In default of $10,000 bail he was committed.[11]

The Wheeling (West) Virginia Daily Register picked up the story of Perry Randolph two days later:

Perry Randolph, the Michigan farmer who was arrested in Kansas City, last week, for selling counterfeit greenbacks, says he was furnished with the bogus money by a book seller named Parker, who lives in Northern Indiana. Parker is an excellent engraver and made the plates himself. He was to furnish Randolph with $25,000 in fractional currency by the first of January.[12]

In 1969, Randolph´s release from prison once again made front page news in *The National Republican* reported on February 6, 1869, that Randolph had been released from prison:

Perry Randolph, of White Pigeon, Michigan, who was arrested in Kansas City, last December, for counterfeiting, was released on Saturday.[13]

The saga of Laura Shilling Matteson's uncle did not stop there. In 1870, the Philadelphia *Evening Telegraph,* reported:

A Novel Suit. Perry Randolph, who was arrested in Jackson county, in this State, some months ago, for passing counterfeit money, entered suit in the United States Circuit Court yesterday against Swift and Cowan, lawyers of Kansas City, for $20,000 damages. Randolph alleges that he had paid Swift and Cowan $7500, for which they were to procure bail for and defend his case, which they failed to do, and kept his money.[14]

Finally, in August 1876, the *Chicago Daily Tribune,* wrote one of the last reports concerning Laura's uncle.

PARDONED.

Special Dispatch to The Tribune.
ST. LOUIS, Mo., Aug. 12—*Perry Randolph, a United States prisoner sentenced Sept. 9, 1871, to ten years imprisonment for having in his possession counterfeit money, was pardoned by the President, and started for his home in Michigan this morning. Randolph is an old man, and is said to have stood well in the community where he resided, having a large and interesting family. He was arrested in Kansas City about the year 1868, having in his possession $22,000 in counterfeit money, and was let out on bail, which proved to be straw, and used by the Secret Service men as a stool-pigeon to draw into the net the band supposed to be engaged in distributing the queer. Not proving a success in this particular, he was recaptured and brought back to Jefferson City, and tried for the offense and sentenced as above. The evidence being that the prisoner had been sufficiently*

punished, and the officers of the Court recommending it, a pardon was granted as stated.[15]

Between the publicity about Laura Shilling's uncle and the decade-long publicity involving his own problems of mortgage foreclosures, fraud, forgery, and even murder, Milo Matteson must have been eager to turn the page, for himself and his wife; and after the two-decade long nationwide attention that her counterfeiting uncle had received, Laura Matteson must have welcomed a restart to their lives as well.

Even though newspaper articles of the time described the perils of a new frontier, the couple likely decided on the course of their new start in life by reading such accounts as:

To the shrewd, persevering, energetic ones, come along, for there is plenty in Colorado to reward the brave and energetic. . . . Mining is, beyond all question, the foundation of the growing greatness of the State, and it is most interesting to learn from an elaborate calculation, coming recently from a reliable source, that after making full allowance for the labor of all the men employed from the beginning, and all the money sunk, the residue shows a better return than any other investment in this country.[16]

Mining in the West was the siren song for many, but the Shilling family saw their future fortune in another market. The seed that was taking root in their minds had appeared in the 1870 Census. While still in Ohio, Laura's brother Arthur Shilling was listed as a "Clerk in Clothing Store."[4] The 1880 census listed Chicago's Isaac Shilling as "Salesman in Cloak House", and both brothers Arthur and Charles as being in the occupation of "Sales in Notions."[17]

Regardless of whether the driving force was pure entrepreneurship or putting the past behind them, Milo and Laura Matteson and the Shilling family members forged plans in the summer of 1881 to face the challenges of the new frontier together as "Matteson & Shilling", and by October of that year had decided "elsewhere" would be Gunnison, Colorado, where they received a welcome from the local press:

A CHICAGO FIRM WHO THINK GUNNISON IS THE PLACE FOR BUSINESS

Mr. I.W. Shilling, of the Chicago firm, Matteson & Shilling, has been in Gunnison for the past week to determine if it were worth while to settle in the place and establish a business. He left Chicago a few days before with the intention of deciding between Pueblo and Gunnison; and after thoroughly examining the town has made up his mind that this is the place to work in.

A car load of dry goods, fancy goods, men's furnishing goods, boots and shoes, left Chicago last Tuesday, and will soon be in Gunnison. The store which Mr. Shilling has selected to drive his trade in is in the stone building on Main street above Georgia avenue. He has already given the contract for putting in counters and shelves and has leased the store for six months.

Matteson & Shilling will start with a ten thousand dollar stock, which they will increase to suit the demands as high as fifty thousand dollars. An examination of the town and its wants has convinced Mr. Shilling that carpets and curtains are much needed by the citizens; therefore he has ordered a fine and full stock of these articles.[18]

Gunnison

7

A NEW BEGINNING

While Little Prairie Ronde, despite all its hardships, conjured up few images one associates with the American frontier, Gunnison, Colorado, fit the picture of an American frontier in every possible way with its numerous ties to Western legends.

The land was inhabited by the Utes when the white settlers first arrived. They were a nomadic native people, having been introduced to the horse by the Spanish, and much like the Plains peoples, their camps consisted of teepees, allowing mobility in pursuit of game. Specifically, the Gunnison and Uncompahgre River valleys were home to the Tabeguache Ute tribe.

Ironically, the white man who would ultimately speak for these Ute people was none other than Kit Carson. Between trapping along the Santa Fe Trail in the 1820s and guiding John Fremont along the Oregon Trail and on to a still-Mexican California in the 1840s, Carson had had many encounters with native tribes—the Blackfoot, Crow, Navajo, and Apache being some he categorically hated and fought.[1] Dime novels were printed back East exaggerating Carson's "heroics" to the point that he had taken on entire villages single-handedly and although Carson had gained fluency in multiple Indian languages during his trader years, he was actually illiterate and could only dictate his memoirs to John Mostin in 1856.[2] In them, however, he neglected to mention that his first and second of three wives had both been native Americans.

Whether it was either of his first two wives or due to his advancing age, Carson did show a soft spot toward the Utes and in 1868, just months before his death, he accompanied Chief Ouray and a delegation to Washington D.C. to meet with President Andrew Johnson. Ouray was reluctant to cede more land to the settlers, but was pragmatic. In one of the annual reports of Indian affairs, Ouray was quoted as saying, "Long time ago, Utes always had plenty. On the prairie, antelope and buffalo, so many Ouray couldn't count. In the mountains, deer and bear everywhere. In the streams, trout, duck, beaver, everything.... White man came, and now Utes grow hungry a heap.... White man grow a heap, red man no grow—soon die all."[3] So Ouray and 47 other Ute chiefs signed a treaty with the U.S. government, moving their lands west of the 107th meridian, assuring them that much of the entire western Colorado slope would be their new home—yet again the government breaking the promise President James Monroe had made 70 years earlier: "As long as water flows, or grass grows upon the earth, or the sun rises to show your pathway, or you kindle your camp fires, so long shall you be protected by this Government, and never again removed from your present habitations."[4]

The Denver Public Library, Western History Collection

Despite the availability of land and the relative security that the Treaty of 1868 provided, a Gunnison cow camp failed to develop into a frontier community throughout the 1870s. But two events brought an abrupt change: first, Congress passed the Bland-Allison Act in 1878, authorizing silver coinage; and second, silver was discovered at Leadville, Colorado, in 1879. The gates had been opened to settlement, and as one correspondent wrote to the *Colorado Daily Chieftain* in May 1880, "One would think there must be an end to this procession, but the end is not yet, for far away on the Saguache Road, there is a long line of white wagon covers."[5]

Prospectors were not the only ones drawn to the Gunnison River Valley. The Silver Boom led to an infrastructure fed by anyone with an enterprising idea. According to C.E. Hagie's description of Gunnison that was printed in *The Colorado Magazine*,

During the rush days of 1880 two hundred houses were erected between May fifteenth and August fifteenth. The town was wide open—with everything that the term signifies, or did signify in the frontier days. Every kind of business sprang up and flourished. The Niehl and Fritz Brewery stood out as the big business at one extreme of the "necessities" scale with Stone and Phillips Grocery at the other. In between were livery barns, a school house, while a daily newspaper served the interests of all. Between 1880 and 1882 two banks were organized, stage lines were put into operation for freight, passenger and mail service and eastern capitalists were vying with each other for a major "finger in the pie".[6]

Two enterprises which literally raced to be part of the Gunnison Boom were the Denver & Rio Grande and the Denver, South Park & Pacific railroad lines. Both companies wanted part of the pie, and speculation was so high as to which line would be completed first that Gunnison developed a western side along New York Avenue in anticipation of a D&SP roundhouse, while the newer eastern side of the town sprang up along Main Street, based on the arrival of the D&RG. Both lines were completed into Gunnison, the D&RG laying track through the Royal Gorge and arriving on August 8, 1881, a full year ahead of D&SP, which had opted for a shorter route but had been held up by the drilling and construction of the Alpine Tunnel. There was enough boom to be shared, however, and after servicing Gunnison, both companies continued on to Leadville.

The Rocky Mountains of western Colorado were attractive for the prospector, the entrepreneur, and the rancher, but the short growing season and sparse rainfall were not inducive to farming. The mountains, however, offered opportunity to one other line of work as well—to the outlaw. The mountains provided a place to hide out when, for whatever reason, it was necessary to escape one's past and weather the storm. Such was the case with Wyatt Earp, whose activities and acquaintances in Dodge City, Deadwood, and Tombstone were legendary. After the Gunfight at OK Corral, the murder of brother Morgan, and Wyatt's subsequent vendetta ride, Earp headed for the mountains of Colorado with a group of men, including Doc Holliday and Bat Masterson. Earp settled in Gunnison in May 1882, camping outside the town along the river. He was generally viewed as being on the bad side of good, but the local sheriff weighed the risk in confronting his men and decided an uneasy truce was the better choice. At first the gang was only occasionally seen in town buying supplies, but later Wyatt ran a faro table in Biebel's Saloon. Although Earp's gang avoided any trouble which might gotten them extradited to Arizona, Wyatt was involved in a gold-colored brick scam he had pulled in 1878 in Texas, when he sold a German tourist fake gold for $2000. Whenever Doc Holliday had too much to drink, the gang would whisk him away to avoid trouble, and it was Bat Masterson, whom Earp asked to help save Holliday from extradition back to Arizona. Masterson, who had become sheriff of Trinidad, Colorado, traveled to Denver on Holliday's behalf and convinced Governor Pitkin to refuse the extradition.[7]

Wyatt Earp   Doc Holliday   Bat Masterson

George A. Root describes the community which the Shillings and Mattesons had chosen for a new beginning in *The Colorado Magazine* of November, 1932: "Gunnison was probably no worse than any other frontier Colorado town, but it so happened that in the first nine months after I arrived (October 20, 1881) there had been no less than six shootings and murders, all of which ended fatally, one lynching and one legal hanging."[8]

Library of Congress, Geography and Map Division

59

8

BUSINESS AND PLEASURE

One can only speculate what hopes the Mattesons and Shillings attached to their new lives in a new community. For the Shillings it is fairly clear that father Isaac and both sons, Arthur and Charles Herbert, with their experience in clothing and notions, saw the opportunity that retail business would provide during a mining boom. Initially, the company was the joint family venture "Matteson & Shilling's" and was advertised in The Gunnison *Daily News Democrat*. The November 11, 1881, edition publicized the opening of their store:

Demand for what the store offered was evident, as announced by various papers. In December the arrival of Isaac's son, Charles Herbert, was announced in *The Free Press*: "Mr. C.H. Shilling, of Chicago, reached here on Friday last. He will remain here in the employ of Mattison (sic) & Shilling, dry goods men."[1]

And the Gunnison *Daily News Democrat* reported on new shipments to the store. On December 16, the paper announced: "Some choice patterns in Lace Curtains just received at Matteson & Shilling's. The latest novelties in Ladies Neckware, Silk Handkerchiefs, &c., at Matteson & Shilling's."[2]

And a new shipment on December 21st: "A fresh invoice of carpets and rugs just received, at Matteson & Shilling's."[3]

As for Milo Matteson, whether his main interest in Gunnison was a share in Shilling's dry good business, in mining, or in just shedding his past and making a new start deep in Colorado, is impossible to say. But the wish to improve his fortune, by whatever means, had long been one of Matteson's driving motives.[4]

As for Laura Shilling Matteson, the question arises as to what would motivate a 26-year-old woman, with a toddler not yet one year old, to relocate to the edge of the frontier. Pregnant women in the nineteenth century did not show themselves in public, so it is safe to say that Laura would have seen the warnings about the frontier *The True Northerner* printed prior to her son's birth in Decatur in November 1880: "A rumor has reached Denver of the massacre of twenty-five prospectors by the Indians in the Lower Gunnison country. No particulars are given."[5]

And on October 29 another article told of a potential Indian outbreak: "The Gunnison country of Colorado has called on Gov. Pitkin to send arms and ammunition immediately, as an Indian outbreak is inevitable. The Utes are running off horses in droves."[6]

Nevertheless, Laura willingly accepted the risks to herself and to her son and accompanied her husband and family to Colorado. Having been connected with cut-throat mortgages, counterfeit rings, and ultimately murder, the Matteson couple had suffered a decade of ill feeling in Michigan. Records from the next four years show Laura not being as involved in her family's retail business but in building a more cultivated reputation than she had enjoyed in Decatur. Only two months after the Mattesons arrived in Gunnison, Laura landed at the top of the "everybody who is anybody" list in The Gunnison *Daily News Democrat:*

A CHRISTMAS BALL GIVEN BY THE VENERABLE ORDER OF ODD FELLOWS

The members of Gunnison Lodge No.89 of the Independent Order of Odd Fellows gave a grand ball at the Tabor House last night. It was by many odds (or rather by many Odd Fellows) the largest and most successful ball of the year. The spacious dining-hall of the hotel was cleared for the feet of the dancers. An excellent string orchestra, consisting of four pieces, furnished the music. Dancing was begun early and lasted late. There was nothing slow about the affair. The attendance was sufficiently large to fill the floor in all the dances, and the floor was constantly filled.

At one o'clock supper was served. It is perfectly safe to say that such a supper has never before been served at any public hall in this city. The tables, half a dozen of them, were works of decorative art. In Chef Hays Mr. Cuemin has found a cook who is unquestionably familiar with the getting up of sumptous [sic] repasts.

As the Odd Fellows constitute one of the largest social organizations in the city, nearly everybody who is anybody was present. It is of course impossible to mention the names of all who graced the scene. The following is, however, a partial list of the ladies, and what they wore:

Mrs. Matteson, seal brown silk with steel and amber trimmings, white lace fiehu, and diamond ornaments.

Miss Head, black velvet, with garniture of natural flowers and point lace.

Miss Cass, white satin en train, trimmed with valencienes lace.[7]

Ten more stand-out ladies and their elegant outfits followed in the list of "everybody who is anybody" in Gunnison.

Matteson's one-year-old son DeForrest was even thrust into the spotlight at the Christmas Fair when a Roman Afghan was to be awarded "to the prettiest baby", and according to the report, "as all parents think their baby the prettiest, there is likely to be a lively contest over this before the matter is settled. Last night the vote stood: Baby Upperen, three; Baby Wallingford, twenty-five; Baby Hinkle, thirteen; Baby Gid, one, and Baby Matteson, five."[8]

By February 1882, according to *The Gunnison News-Democrat*, both Milo and Laura were establishing themselves as pillars of society by helping organize "the event of the season":

A Grand Mardi Gras Ball will be given on the evening of the twentieth of February, in the store room formerly occupied by Messrs. Sells & Co., corner of Main street and Tumitchi avenue. The proceeds are to be used in paying for the lots for the Episcopal Church. The invitations will be issued immediately. Price of tickets, including carriage for ladies, $3.00. Spectators, who will not take part in the Mask Ball, $1.00.[9]

Thirty-five Gunnisonites were then listed as organizers of the grand ball, among them M.D. Matteson on the Committee of Arrangements and Mrs. M.D. Matteson working with the Committee on Reception.[9]

Indeed, a day later "the event of the season" was front page news and was reportedly beyond compare for the young mountain community:

MARDI GRAS.
THE CARNIVAL SEASON FINISHED WITH A GRAND BALL LAST NIGHT

Oscar Wilde Interpreted by a Western Mayor, and Numerous Other Incongruities

If anything was needed before last night to prove that Gunnison is a metropolis, that want was supplied at the Mardi Gras ball. There have been a good many very successful dances given in this city, but never before was there one given which was in every respect such a glowing success. On the eve of the Lenten season, and acknowledged, as it was, to be the winding up of the long winter festivities, it was only fitting that the affair should have been given for so deserving an object as the building fund of the Episcopal church.[10]

Mayor Kubler dressed as "the sweet aesthetic ass" Oscar Wilde and was "too utterly utter", according to witnesses, along with monks and nuns, kings and Russian peasants. Mrs. Matteson chose to be an artist, her brother a sailor, and Mr. Shilling appeared as a Puritan "in a very handsome white costume with hat and plume."[10]

The Puritan, however, was back to work the following day according to the Gunnison press:

Mr. Shilling, of Messrs. Matteson & Shilling, left yesterday for Chicago to purchase his spring stock. The firm has done remarkably well since it was established here, and proposes to put in an immense stock of fine goods this spring. The members of the firm are wide awake and enterprising, and just the sort of men to succeed in this western country.[11]

The year 1882 was presenting opportunity for Matteson and Shilling, "just the sort of men to succeed."[11] The Mattesons had found their place in Gunnison society and now needed both a fitting residence and an imposing place of business to reflect their status. Milo wasted no time developing both.

Messrs. Parks & Co. are at present employed at work on a building for M.D. Matteson, on the corner of Wisconsin and Ruby Streets. The house is a frame structure, containing eleven large rooms, closets &c, also a bay window. The house will, when completed, be as handsome as any in the city. This firm have made plans for a number of other buildings, both residences and business blocks, but the parties contemplating building, are undecided as to whether the structures shall be brick or frame, among these buildings, is one of three stories, for Matteson & Shilling; and another for a Denver party, two stories, both business blocks.[12]

The M.D. Matteson house, photo from The Gunnison Historic Walking Tour

BREAKING WITH THE IN-LAWS

With the family residence at Ruby and Wisconsin ready to receive Gunnison's finest, Milo turned his attention to a representative place of business for Matteson & Shilling. By June 1882, the *News-Democrat* unveiled his plan:

THE BUILDING BOOM

Upper Main Street To Have Another Fine Brick Business Block

Mr. M.D. Matteson, of Messrs. Matteson & Shilling, yesterday sold a half interest in the lot just north of the Preston building on Upper Main street, to Mr. D.F. Hopkins for $1,750, cash. This lot was purchased during last January by Mr. Matteson from Green & Powell for $2,600, including a building worth from eight to nine hundred dollars which then stood upon it.

It is the intention of Messrs. Matteson & Hopkins to at once begin the erection of a brick building on it, twenty-five by eighty feet in size and two stories high. The front will have iron columns and plate glass windows, and the building when completed, will cost from eight to ten thousand dollars. The work will begin the early part of next week, and the contractors say they can have the walls up within a month.

The first floor will be used by Messrs. Matteson & Shilling for their dry goods business. If a satisfactory arrangement can be made with the Masons and Odd Fellows the rear sixty feet of the upper floor will be thrown into a hall for their use. If not, the whole floor will be cut up into offices and sleeping rooms. Altogether the building premises to be a decided addition to that part of the city.[1]

Weekly reports in the *News-Democrat* followed the building process with "The work of laying the foundation for Matteson & Hopkins' new building on Main street was commenced on Monday,"[2] followed only a week later by "The brick work on the new Matteson & Hopkins building was commenced on Monday morning."[3] But by July 1, Matteson had changed his mind and bought back Mr. Hopkins' half, deciding to make his building even more imposing than originally planned. The second floor would house the proprietors, leaving a third floor for offices, rooms, or a community hall. The Gunnison Daily *News-Democrat* described the building plan in detail:

The Matteson Building

Mr. Matteson Wednesday completed the purchase of Mr. E.R. Hopkins' interest in the new building in course of erection, on Main street. The original plan of the building was for two stories, but Mr. Matteson has fallen in with the popular idea and proposes to add a third story. The third floor will be arranged for offices in front and a hall in the remaining portion back. The front of this building will be finished with the Golden fine pressed brick and the roof covered with tin. All modern conveniences, such as gas, water, etc., will be placed in the building. Messrs. Krueger & Morrison have obtained the contract to do the plumbing work. Fire escapes will extend from the second and third floors to the ground. This building when finished will add materially to the general appearance of Main street.[4]

The reports continued throughout July with "The iron colums placed in the Matteson building on Monday were cast at the Gunnison foundry."[5] and "The Matteson building is now under roof. It's a dandy."[6]

By August, the living quarters on the second floor were finished, and as the Mattesons were settled into their own home, one might have expected the Shillings to live above the dry goods store. Only a month earlier the Gunnison newspapers had announced the arrival of the Shilling women: "The wife and daughter of I.W. Shilling arrived here several days ago, and are at present guests at M.D. Matteson's. They will remain here all summer."[7] Then on July 29, "I.W. Shilling and family will move in their new home on Taylor street in a week or so. The building is owned by W.F. McIntire who talks of erecting several more on adjoining lots."[8]

When the much-anticipated three-story landmark was finished, the top level bore signs on either side of the building which could be read for miles. However, the sign did not read "Matteson & Shilling Dry Goods", but rather 'Shilling & Co. Dry Goods and Carpets".

The friction between the two families seems to have been created from an incident that arose during the construction of the building. According to the Gunnison Daily *News-Democrat* in May 1882:

BURGLARS AT WORK.

The Daring and Altogether Remarkable Robbery of a Dry Goods House Last Night.

Mr. Shilling went to the Methodist church sociable last night to see Mrs. Jarley's wax works. Mr. Matteson, Mr. Shilling's partner, however, did not, and neither did Mr. Hamlin, his rival in trade. These latter two gentlemen, on the contrary, went to the Globe theatre. Before doing so, however, they proceeded as they expressed it, to "put up a job on Mr. Shilling." The latter gentleman is somewhat nervous at the idea of robbers, so the two worthy gentlemen named above, thought they would play a practical joke, and 'have some fun with the old man.'

To this end they forced in the back door of the store, and having gained admittance, proceeded to 'rob' the store in the most approved style. The silks were taken from the shelves and hid, and the cash drawer was emptied of its cash. This done the two gentlemen went to the theatre.

An hour or two later Mr. Shilling came home, and with his usual prudence and caution entered the store to see that all was right. He was not long in discovering the absence of the silks, and soon after found that his cash drawer was empty also. Mr. Shilling is not a gentleman who would let the grass grow under his feet under such circumstances. The store had been robbed, that was apparent. But who did it? That was something for the officers to find. The police were notified and a messenger was dispatched for the sheriff.

The officers came in hot haste. They entered the store, examined the doors and windows, found where the thieves had entered and then set about discovering some clue that would aid in the discovery of the thieves.

All this time the authors of all the mischief were quietly seated in the theatre a few doors away, chuckling to themselves at the thought of 'how the old man would take it.' Then they thought they would visit the store and see. When they arrived there, they found the place in the hands of the officers. Policemen with lanterns were looking for footprints outside, while each was giving his theory of the daring burglary. This was a little more than the jokers had bargained for, so they proceeded to give their theory. When they had done speaking the sheriff looked at Mr. Shilling, and that gentleman looked at the sheriff. The policemen looked at nobody. They had business down on Tumitchi Avenue, which required their immediate presence.

Mr. Shilling made a few remarks, and so did the late lamented sheriff. The jokers tried to explain, but the explanation was a sorry failure. Somebody was very angry. It was not Mr. Matteson or Mr. Hamlin. They went back to the theatre, and Mr. Bowman went home. It is safe to say, however that neither Mr. Matteson nor Mr. Hamlin will attempt any more practical jokes, at least for a day or two.[9]

The following day, Matteson had revised his account:

Mr. Matteson explains that he and Mr. Hamlin did not break into the store on Friday evening for the purpose of playing a joke, but to look after a lighted lamp which was flaring up in a dangerous manner. Some of the neighbors had noticed the lamp, and called their attention to it, and, as Mr. Shilling had the keys, they were compelled to break in the door. After they were inside the joke which they afterwards played suggested itself to them.[10]

The anger resulting from the incident apparently did not dissipate within a day or two, and on June 6 the dissolution of Matteson & Shilling was announced:

NOTICE OF DISSOLUTION
The firm of Matteson & Shilling is this day dissolved by mutual consent, M.D. Matteson retiring. All bills will be paid and collected by Shilling & Co.
M.D. MATTESON
A.B. SHILLING
GUNNISON, June 5, 1882 [11]

One day later the *Free Press* addressed the question as to what new interests Milo Matteson might pursue.

The firm of Matteson & Shilling was dissolved on Monday, Mr. Matteson retiring. The business will hereafter be carried on by Shilling & Co., A.B. Shilling of Chicago becomes junior member of the firm. In their new departure we

70

wish them success. Mr. Matteson will give his entire attention to personal business.[12]

The History Colorado Collection

Mr. Matteson's personal business would not be the money-loaning he had engaged in in the past. Banks were established for that purpose, even in Gunnison. But there was rent income, both from the original store property at Main and Georgia plus the new three-story showplace on North Main.

Throughout 1882, despite speculation concerning the "break-in" and the ensuing dissolution of Matteson & Shilling, the Mattesons continued to make a name for themselves in the Gunnison community. The generous floor plan of their recently completed residence offered an opportunity to entertain scores of people, so while Wyatt Earp and his gang were camped along the Gunnison in tents and running faro games at Biebel's Saloon on the west side of town, grand receptions were being orchestrated on the east side at the new Wisconsin Avenue residence:

Details of one such reception made the front page of *The* Gunnison *Daily News-Democrat* in July 1882:

A PLEASANT PARTY

The Delightful Reception Which was Given to Rev. Mr. Loder and His Bride Last Night

The reverend A.L. Loder, pastor of the Tabernacle Presbyterian church, returned from the east yesterday, accompanied by his bride, and in the evening a reception was given at the residence of Mr. and Mrs. Matteson, on Wisconsin street, in honor of the newly wedded couple. The large and elegant parlors of the Matteson residence were crowded with the friends of the groom, of whom fully one hundred were present.

Mr. and Mrs. Loder received their friends standing in front of the bay window off the back parlor. In the recess behind them was arranged a bank of flowers and plants, while over their heads was suspended a beautiful floral horseshoe.

Mr. and Mrs. Matteson and Mr. and Mrs. Jones stood on either side and introduced the guests as they came up. The formal reception lasted an hour or more, and the company then broke up into little groups and gave themselves up to enjoyment in various ways.

In the dining room an elegant lunch was spread consisting of strawberries, ice-cream, cake, etc. The table was also beautifully decorated with cut flowers artistically arranged.

In the front parlor those present were treated to some excellent music, both vocal and instrumental. Among those who favored the company in this way were Mrs. Matteson, Mrs. Jones, Mrs. Dunham, Miss Bennett and Mr. Stephens. Altogether the reception proved the most successful ever given in Gunnison. Mrs. Loder expressed herself as well pleased with her new home. The lady is a petite brunette, and was dressed in some light colored material. As the list of those present included nearly all the prominent society people of the city, it will not be necessary to mention names. The reception lasted until after midnight. Mr. and Mrs. Loder will at once go to housekeeping in their residence on upper Iowa street. Miss Loder, who went east with her brother, returned with them.[13]

In addition to lavish receptions, Laura Matteson did not shrink from displaying her musical talent on various occasions. In February 1882, when Gunnison's first postman, Alonzo Hartman, made a trip back East and returned with a bride, his friends surprised the newlyweds with a reception, banquet, and grand ball at the Mullin House. The Gunnison *Daily News-Democrat* reported on February 24, "During the evening, Mrs. Matteson, Mrs. Lindauer and Mrs. Davis favored the company with a number of songs and instrumental pieces."[14]

Later, in May 1882, Mrs. Matteson's performances continued:

AN ARTISTIC SUCCESS

The Entertainment Given at the Tabernacle Last Night for the Free Reading Room

The musical and literary entertainment at the Presbyterian Tabernacle last night was an artistic but not a financial success. The audience was a very small one, not over sixty people being present. What the people lacked in members, however, they made up in enthusiasm and, notwithstanding the discouraging drawback of a small house, the entertainment proved a most delightful one.

The first number was an organ voluntary by Mrs. Oliver. Then followed an opening chorus by a male quartette composed of Messrs. Chisolm, Whittlesey, Abercrombie and Eaton. Mr. Stevens sang two tenor solos, "My Dearest Heart" and "Just Touch the Harp Lightly." Major Mann also sang "The Man-o-War's Man" and "The Yeoman's Wedding Song." Mrs. Matteson and Mrs. Jones sang "O'er the Hill and O'er the Dale," and Mrs. Matteson and Mr. Abercrombie sang the duet "Wilt Thou Begone, Love," from the balcony scene of "Romeo and Juliet."[15]

One of Gunnison's most significant events of 1882 was the completion of the water works. Prior to this, water was drawn from the river and sold in town at exorbitant prices. But by June 1882, a main pipe had been laid up Virginia Avenue to the corner in front of the *News-Democrat* office and there branched off in eight directions, not only making water less of a luxury for the townspeople, but also offering a safeguard against fire, which could wipe out entire blocks of stores and dwellings. The *Free Press* called attention to the need for firefighters in a June 6 article, "Months have elapsed since anything was heard of the engine company organized here last winter. There may be a time when Gunnison will be in need of firemen, and now is the time to have men drilled for active service."[16]

Gunnison heeded the call and two firefighting companies were established, and when the water company had to test its new system, both companies were present. George A. Root describes the occasion in the November 1932 issue of the *Colorado Magazine*:

When the systems were completed, the water company gave the fire companies a chance to test the water pressure. On the appointed day picked squads of Company No. 1 and the E.A. Buck Hose Company, rival organizations, met at the intersection of Main and Virginia avenues and, attaching a length of hose to fire plugs on opposite sides of the street, they turned the water on one another. For about half an hour they heroically and stoically stood their ground until one side was drowned out. The water company demonstrated that water could be thrown more than twice as high as the highest building in that vicinity. The test was a success and furnished plenty of fun for the onlookers.[17]

It seems that Milo Matteson was involved in one or both of these companies, as a picture survives of the above-mentioned occasion:

The description of this photo reads:

The Buck Hose Company, Gunnison Volunteer Fire Department, financed by Elisa Buck, Gunnison businessman, on Main Street and Virginia, in front of the First National Bank, Gunnison, Colorado. The long line of fire fighters in uniform stand with hosecart, harness and fire hose. Identifiable members include left to right: J. Miller, T.J. Kane, Mase Block, Fred Leon Leonard, M.D. Matteson (on horse). Business signs read: "Abercrombie & Karr Lawyers," "Western Union Telegraph Office," "Meat Market," "Bakery," "Gunnison Brewery," and "Dry Goods & Carpet."

The sign on the towering building in the background, in fact, read "Shilling & Co. Dry Goods & Carpets", emblazoned on the Matteson Building for all to see.

The Denver Public Library, Western History Collection

Unfortunately, while the images of the firemen in the photo are relatively focused, Milo Matteson or his horse apparently moved during the exposure, resulting in a blurred two-faced effect.

The year 1882 had been very kind to the Mattesons. Their new house on North Wisconsin was stunning, and the 3-story brick building that towered over Main Street was a Gunnison landmark. Laura Matteson had entertained and sung her way into Gunnison's polite society, and Milo was making connections necessary to continue his business ventures. Perhaps part of his networking was becoming part of the fire fighter organizations of Gunnison, and by August 1882, his image had become one of a responsible citizen—being elected as 2nd vice president of the Firemen's Association.[18]

RISE AND FALL OF GUNNISON

Think of it, you sleepy, old fogies of the east: Gunnison, only three years old, with a population of 5,000; Iron and Steel works to be built at a cost of $5,000,000; a new hotel, nearly completed to cost $200,000; gas and water works that have cost $200,000; two new blocks of buildings to go up, to be heated with steam, at a cost of $75,000; two railways connecting with the east; a street railway to be built at once; a thoroughly organized fire department; a telephone exchange; a smelter; two banks; three brick schoolhouses; six churches; steam planing mills; foundry and machine shop; wholesale business houses; an opera house; and last, but not least, two daily and weekly newspapers.[1]

The boasts printed in the Gunnison *Review-Press* in the spring of 1883 may have coincided with the climax of Gunnison´s prosperity. On March 31 of that year, the Gunnison *Daily Review-Press* had devoted nearly a whole page to Gunnison's luck in attracting a five-million-dollar steel works to the area. Upon receiving the news, an impromptu celebration on March 30 made way for a procession the following day, organized by Milo Matteson.

Attention Firemen:

The members of the Loudon Mullin Hook and Ladder company, the E. A. Buck Hose company No. 1, and the Gunnison Hose company No. 2, are requested to meet at their respective houses at seven o'clock sharp, to participate in the parade to-night. By order of

M.D. MATTESON,

Chief Gunnison Fire Department[2]

As Chief of the Gunnison Fire Department, Milo was assured of a prominent spot in the procession and being elected marshal, the *Review-Press* listed him up front:

Let everyone turn out this evening for the procession and demonstration in honor of the good news for Gunnison. The procession will consist of carriages, horsemen and footmen bearing torchlights. There should be a good representation from every business house in the city. The hour set for the procession is a convenient time, being 7:30 o'clock sharp, and will enable the procession to make its tour of the city before a late hour.

A number of citizens met at the First National Bank last evening, and selected a committee to make arrangements for a procession, and make up a programme for to-night. The committee appointed Mr. M. D. Matteson to act as Marshal and Mr. M. Rush Warner as Assistant Marshal. The procession will form on upper Main street at half-past seven o'clock sharp, and will be made up in the following order:

Marshal and Aids
City Officers,
Police Department,
Gunnison Band,
Gunnison Fire Department,
Torchlights,
Citizens in Carriages and on Horseback.[3]

Building a population of 5,000 in only three years, the expansion of Gunnison was inevitable. Wyatt Earp and his brother Warren had not camped down by the river by themselves. Hundreds of tents housed prospectors waiting for reservation lands to be opened, allowing them to stake a claim. The 107th Meridian would not hold settlers back for long.

As always, the Mattesons and Shillings continued to keep their eyes open for opportunity. Isaac Shilling had already voiced his opinion in May 1882 concerning a bill held up in Congress, according to The Gunnison *Daily News-Democrat*: "Mr. Shilling favored holding a meeting on Monday night and thought it would be well to let the Colorado delegation in Washington know that the people of this part of the state are getting tired of waiting, and that unless something was done regarding this Reservation business at once the lightning might strike when least expected."[4]

The bill to open the Ute Reservation for settlement was finally signed in late July 1882, much to the relief of some prospectors and farmers who had not waited for Congress to act. Gunnison was no longer the end of the line. The railroads moved on, the prospectors moved on, and Milo Matteson, while keeping his showplace home on Wisconsin and Ruby, saw fit to end his activities with the fire department. According to the Gunnison Daily Review Press in June 1883:

GOOD WORK DONE

By a Full Board of the City Fathers Last Evening

For accomplishing much in a short space of time, the meeting of the council last night was a commendable illustration. It adjourned in one hour after the mayor called the session to order. Following the customary reading of the minutes of the last meeting the question of the resignation from M. D. Matteson, as chief of the fire department was introduced. It was accepted.

Gunnison, Colo., June 21, 1883[5]

Perhaps it was the idea of a five-million-dollar iron and steel works which diverted Milo's attention away from fire-fighting in Gunnison. By July The Gunnison *Daily News-Democrat* revealed Milo's new venture to get in on a portion of the steel works pie:

A company has been organized this week for the purpose of putting in extensive sampling works at Quartz, three miles above Pitkin. The company consists of M. D. Matteson and D. R. Hopkins of this city and Fred M. Hausling, of Pitkin. These gentlemen returned from Quartz yesterday evening where they have been since Saturday looking over the camp and selecting a site for the works. They determined upon a location just about the "U" at Quartz where excellent water power can be secured with a twenty-five-foot-fall in a very short distance. The location of the mill is most favorable. It not only affords convenient market for the ores of upper Quartz district, but also the Tin Cup district. The company will put in works which, if occasion demands, can be readily extended to a capacity of a hundred tons a day. These three men will take active charge of the works and devote their entire attention to the business.

When Mr. Matteson returned to Gunnison last evening he received a telegram containing the news that his wife was dangerously ill in Chicago which made it necessary for him to start immediately for her bedside. But for this unexpected delay the machinery would have been ordered this week and the mill running by the tenth of next month. As it is Mr. Mattison (sic) could do nothing but ask the remainder of the company to wait until he could send them word from Chicago as to the length of time he would likely be detained. Mr. Hausling went to Denver to-day with Mr. Mattison (sic) where he will wait a telegram from Chicago as to further movements.[6]

Laura Matteson's condition forced Milo to leave for Chicago, hampering his involvement in the Quartz Mill project. On August 3, however, the Gunnison press reported Laura's chances of recovery were good: "A letter just received from Mr. M. D. Matteson states that Mrs. Matteson is still low, but improving under the excellent medical care she has had. If she continues to improve they start for Gunnison in two weeks."[7]

It seems that Milo missed out on the development of a Quartz Creek mill, so his attention turned in a different direction, southwest of Gunnison and deeper into the Rockies. According to The *Review Press* in November 1883: "M. D. Matteson left for the placer diggings on the Dallas this morning. He recently invested several thousand dollars in some of these claims and is going to look after the work. A large ditch is being taken out for the purpose of carrying water to the claims, and everything being put in readiness for working the property to its full capactiy."[8]

The *Silver World* also reported a week later:

The prospective building of the D.&R.G. railroad from Montrose to the Dallas has started a new town scheme. The Denver Times says: 'There have been filed with the secretary of State the articles of incorporation of the Dallas Town company. The capital stock is $50,000 and is non-assessable. The company is organized to locate and plat towns in Ouray and Gunnison counties, but more especially to prepare a townsite at the junction of Dallas creek and Uncompahgre river. The directors for the first year are A .J. Bean, Charles D. Gage, A. J. Spengel, Thos. C. Brown and M. D. Mattison.[sic] The principal office of the company will be located at Gunnison City.'[9]

The Dallas Town Company directors had a more pressing motive than just establishing a new stop along the D. & R.G. railroad. A large ditch was being dug and the quest was gold. In September 1884, the *Colorado Daily Chieftain* named M.D. Matteson as superintendant of the Dallas Placer Mining Company:

THE NEW TOWN OF DALLAS

Sinners' Home was the euphonious name given the stage station (at the point where the Dallas enters the Uncapahgre river) by Charlie Diehl, of the great mercantile firm of Buddeke & Diehl, of Montrose, but a Gunnison company got hold of the locality last year and laid out a town and appropriately named the place Dallas.

Dallas is the dinner station on the stage line and the Placer hotel is a model in its way. It is kept by Mr. C. D. Gage, a veteran placer miner, and he is ably assisted by Mr. E. Helfer, a gentleman who thoroughly understands his business. The best the markets afford is not too good for the guests who are generally in condition to enjoy a good dinner after the twenty mile stage ride from Montrose. The Placer is a favorite hotel and a bar which contains the best of cigars and other refreshments is kept in connection with the hotel. Mr. Gage is interested in the Dallas Placer mining company, which is the biggest thing of the kind in Colorado. The officers of the company make headquarters at Mr. Gage's hotel.

T. C. Brown, of Gunnison, is president; A. J. Spencer, secretary; M. Coppinger, treasurer, and M. D. Matteson, superintendent of the company. They have a capital stock of $65,000, and have already expended $26,000. They have a ditch over five miles long, which carries 1,500 miner's inches of water and will have 300 feet pressure at the lower end. There is 8,500 feet of fluming on the ditch. The main hydraulic pipe is fifteen inches in diameter and the gravel will be handled entirely by water power. The company owns 1,200 acres of placer land in this locality. A test was made of the gravel last year by Mr. John H. Martin, with a small hydraulic apparatus and he cleaned up $157, in gold, after three days' washing. Mr. Martin is the inventor of a great labor saving hydraulic machine, and is now superintending the erection of the works which will be in operation sometime in October.

A new hotel is about completed at Dallas which will be kept by Mr. Samuel Jay, the old popular hotel keeper, formerly of Sargeant, the eating place west of Marshall pass. Mr. Jay knows how to keep hotel, as those who have visited Sargeant in times past can testify.

The Dallas post office is kept by Mr. Max R. Krausnick, who keeps a nice stock of groceries and provisions, and is stage and express agent at Dallas. He is a tip-top good fellow and an A 1 business man. His better half assists him in the post office when business is rushing.

Mr. George W. Cobb also keeps a grocery store and saloon at Dallas. He is one of the old timers of the valley and is postmaster at Portland.

Mr. Preston Hotchkiss, of the Hotchkiss Brothers, merchants, keeps the Portland post office, in the absence of Mr. Cobb, who has a good business at Dallas.

Dallas is building some and has a number of business men whose names I do not recollect. It is rightly located for a smelting point, good coal being plenty in the vicinity, and it must be a railroad junction in the near future, for here is where the road for Telluride and Rico must leave the Uncapahgre valley.[10]

The destructive effect placer mining would have on the environment when hydraulic pumps moved tons of silt down previously clear

The Denver Public Library, Western History Collection

streams and rivers was not a subject in 1884. Even so, not all voices spoke favorably of the Dallas Placer Mining Company.

In February 1884, *The Sun* had described Daniel Day's dissenting voice in *The Solid Muldoon*:

The Gunnison town-site and placer sharks who are re-staking agricultural land down the valley, are liable to get rounded up in great shape when their trespassing begins to vex the grangers. Ouray county is not by any means a paradise for that class of robbers. — Solid Muldoon[11]

The directors of the Dallas Placer Mining Company, however, persisted in their quest for gold, albeit in vain. If the Dallas Town Company was hoping for the same degree of boom Gunnison had experienced, it certainly was in for a disappointment. Gunnison's own prosperity was beginning to wane. The building boom was all but over. The opera house Frank Smith had opened in January 1883 would be reposessed in 1884, but not before the recuperated soprano Laura Matteson appeared in the title role of Bradbury's *Esther, the Beautiful Queen*. The following appeared in the *Review-Press*'s review, March 1884:

Mrs. Matteson won new honors last night. Her voice was much stronger than on the previous evening, and her acting natural and impressive. In the difficult solos she has to render, she sustained the character of the queen to the delight of everyone.

Miss Loder was evidently the favorite and was frequently interrupted by the plaudits of the spectators. In answer to the repeated encores at the close of the mournful scene of 'The Galling Defeat,' the curtain arose the second time for the tableau at the close.

The Choral Union will never want for an audience in any public entertainment they may present in the future.

This appreciative report of the second night's performance is not to be construed as a criticism of the first performance, but I can confidently confirm the judgment of the reporter in calling it a marked improvement, for I know from personal experience that we all felt more the spirit of the real characters. We forgot ourselves and the story almost played itself. I recall how anxious Mr. Matteson was about his wife succumbing to the emotion of the play. He said, 'Be careful about allowing her to feel too deeply her tragic part. She is a bundle of nerves and I am afraid she might faint.' She made the audience weep in sympathy as she pleaded for her people.[12]

Only three weeks after her triumph as Queen Esther, the *Review-Press* reported that Laura and Milo had left Gunnison for the summer, presumably going to Dallas: "Mr. Shilling has moved into Mr.

Matteson's house in the north end of town. Mr. Matteson will be away all summer and Mrs. Matteson most of the time, and they prefer to have the house occupied by careful parties than standing empty."[13]

Milo Matteson seems to have remained with the Dallas Company venture for some time, as newspaper reports him driving between Gunnison and Dallas again in July 1886: "M. D. Matteson started for Dallas yesterday with his pony and buckboard. He will be absent a couple of weeks."[14], then followed by "Mr. M. D. Matteson returned from Dallas and Ouray this morning. He reports business in Ouray more than ordinarily good. Every day several stage-loads of passengers arrive and the camp is filled with strangers."[15]

But by late July 1886, the dreams of gold were in fact exhausted, and the Solid Muldoon announced "The Dallas placers will not resume this season."[16]

The Denver Public Library Special Collection

Dallas remained more village than town, chiefly a stagecoach stop and a transfer station for the D. & R.G., and in September 1888, the *Colorado Daily Chieftain* reported the community's demise:

Burning of Dallas, Colorado

Ouray, Col., September 10. – This morning at 2 o'clock a fire started in the kitchen of Jay's hotel at Dallas, a village twelve miles north of here on the Denver

& Rio Grande, and the transfer station for Telluride and San Miguel, and in two hours' time the entire business portion of the town, consisting of seventeen substantial houses, was a smoking ruin. The loss will reach fully $50,000, with only about $10,000 insurance in Denver companies.

Your correspondent reached the scene about noon and found the business men, though slightly disfigured yet still in the ring, and the most of them filling out orders for lumber to erect new buildings.[17]

As for the five million dollar steel works project of Gunnison, according to *The White Pine Cone* on January 20, 1888 it was still a half-finished pipe-dream:

THE OUTLOOK

The Cone has reliable information that the Gunnison Steel Works Company is meeting with extraordinary success in raising the money needed to put in the plant. The stock was put on the St. Louis market a short time since, and is selling rapidly. Fully half the funds needed has been obtained, and in sixty days more, it is more than probable, that the entire amount will be secured. This insures the success of the Works at Gunnison; will close the sale on the Contact Mountain iron claims of this district; and secures to White Pine a branch of the D.&R.G. railway.[18]

There would be no gold in Dallas and no iron and steel works in Gunnison. The boom had run itself out within a decade. The miners had moved on, and by 1890, Gunnison's population had plummeted from 5,000 to only 1,000. The opportunities the West had presented in the early 1880s became more and more limited. While the Shillings chose to adapt and find opportunities elsewhere in Aspen and Cripple Creek, Milo Matteson decided to sell his holdings, among them the showplace home on Wisconsin and Ruby and the 3-story brick Matteson Building on North Main which later became known in Gunnison as the Webster Building, housing Herman Webster's own dry goods business. And so it was that the Matteson family left the mountains of Colorado behind to pursue new ventures back East.

11

BACK EAST AGAIN

Oddly, although Milo had remained close to his parents in Chicago, he chose Kenosha on Lake Michigan, with its population of approximately 6,000, for his family to reenter life back East. Once dubbed Southport, Kenosh was Wisconsin's southernmost natural harbor and the closest point to Chicago outside of Illinois. The draw to Kenosha was perhaps the deal his father Almanson had made, according to *The Daily Inter Ocean* in February 1887: "Mr. Eli Runals has about closed the sale of 200 acres of fine land on the south side of Prairie avenue, to Mr. A. M. Matteson, of Chicago. Consideration, $20,000, which is considered low for so valuable a piece of property."[1]

A new home followed as the newspaper reported in January 1888: "Mr. M. D. Matteson moved into his new house on Prairie avenue on Tuesday."[2] And once again, the Mattesons proved that they had a nose for opportunity. According to *The Daily Inter Ocean* in April 1888:

A real estate boom seems to be extant in Kenosha. Mr. Matteson, of Chicago, bought a tract of land of E. G. Runals last year, and this spring has sold a portion of it at such a profit as nets him about $20,000 on the investment. Purchasers of the thirty-two acres, Messrs. Tuttle and Frost. Orders to purchase from Chicago capitalists are on file in agent's offices, and prices are advancing rapidly.[3]

By the fall Laura Matteson had recommenced her entertaining, a subject reported on the society pages in September 1888: "Mr. and Mrs. Arthur Schilling and son, of Aspen Col., Mrs. Annie Matteson and son, of Chicago, and Miss Grace Chadwick, of Decatur, Mich., have left the pleasant home of Mr. and Mrs. Matteson, leaving Miss Dimp Chadwick to console the hostess for a few weeks."[4] And then in December: "The social events of the week have been in the form of small companies, among which may be mentioned the meeting of a club of young married people at the beautiful residence of Mr. and Mrs. Charles Allen, on the park, on Saturday evening, and a reception at the residence of Mr. and Mrs. Matteson on Tuesday evening."[5]

This last event was particularly noteworthy, as the Mattesons were expecting their second child, when it was the custom for 19th century women to generally shutter themselves away during pregnancy. But on March 26, 1889, the Matteson's second son, Randolph Warren, was born. The mother had help, 21 year-old Dell Chadwick remaining with the family in Kenosha until June 1890: "Miss Dell Chadwick, who has been with Mr. and Mrs. M. D. Matteson in this city the last year and a half will return to her home in Decatur, Mich."[6]

A move was necessary for Miss Chadwick at any rate because, according to *The Daily Inter Ocean* a month later, the Mattesons had sold their new home in Kenosha and moved on to Chicago: "It is still a mystery what the purchaser of the Matteson property is going to do. It is reported that a new manufacturing establishment will be erected there."[7]

By January 1891, however, *The Daily Inter Ocean* revealed what was to become of the rest of the 200-acre Kenosha purchase: "The Matteson property on Prairie avenue has been platted and subdivided into town lots."[8]

Chicago would prove to be the last station for the Matteson family. The city was still rebounding from its loss of 18,000 structures in the Great Fire of 1871. Despite 100,000 people being left homeless, the population increased threefold to the million mark in only 20 years. The city was vibrant, having just secured the Columbian Exposition (World Fair) to mark the 400th anniversary of Columbus's trip to the New World. This was fertile ground for Milo's real estate dealings, and after only 11 eventful years of Decatur scandal and Gunnison frontier, Laura would return to a world in which she could revel in her pursuits of the fine arts and entertaining.

12

GILDED CHICAGO

Celebrating the 400th anniversary of Columbus's arrival in the New World, The World's Columbian Exposition of 1893 opened a year late, but it ushered in the Golden Age of Chicago. The Great Fire had left 18,000 acres open, a playground drawing architects from across the country to redesign a city center in styles ranging from the beaux-arts "White City" of the Exposition to America's first skyscrapers. Traveling across the country with her companion Katharine Coman, Katherine Lee Bates was so impressed by the Exposition architecture that she included "alabaster cities" in her poem "America the Beautiful."[1]

The Columbian Exposition, 1893   Public Domain

A visit to the Exposition must have been thrilling for the Mattesons, who, according to The Gunnison *Weekly Republican*, had traveled to New Orleans for the World's Fair in 1884.[2] A challenge had been issued by the exposition's organizers in Chicago for engineers to design a landmark to outdo the Eiffel Tower, built especially for the Paris

International Exposition of 1889. George Ferris heeded the call and traveled from Pittsburgh to pitch his idea of a giant rotating wheel to "out-Eiffel Eiffel".[3] The observation wheel would contain 36 cars, each accommodating 60 passengers, and it would revolve twice every twenty minutes, providing breathtaking views of the exposition grounds, Lake Michigan, the 12 skyscrapers of the financial district, and even Buffalo Bill's Wild West Show. The show was situated directly adjacent to the exposition grounds, its participation having been denied by the organizers, but every twenty minutes, 2,160 wheel passengers were treated to views of cowboy and native American activity, boosting the show's popularity as it had on its European tours.[4]

The Original Ferris Wheel, Chicago, 1893

Coincidentally, after the exposition ended, the Ferris wheel was reconstructed in Milo Matteson´s neighborhood on the north side of Chicago. The Mattesons had settled on Dunning Street (later renamed Altgeld) near the Lake View district, the area where Milo and Laura would live out their lives. In Chicago, Milo Matteson was a smaller fish in a larger pond, but in addition to real estate transfers, building activity, and society news, the Matteson name would appear in more noteworthy contexts.

Early on during this period, the subject of the Morris murder resurfaced. What started in the summer of 1891 as a case of slander back in Decatur between two neighboring brothers evolved into assault and Tom Parsons stabbing his brother Kit. Then by December, when Tom accused Kit of abetting Milo Matteson's brother James in the Morris murders, Milo was forced to publish a statement in the Chicago *Herald* on December 3:

SAYS HE IS NOT A MURDERER

M.D. Mattison (sic) Denies All Connection with the Little Prairie Ronde Crime

M.D. Mattison (sic) makes a general denial of any connection whatever with the mysterious double murder near Little Prairie Ronde, Mich., twelve years ago, the account of which appeared in yesterday morning's issue of The Herald, accompanied with the intimation that developments were about to occur showing who was responsible for the killing of Mr. and Mrs. Charles H. Morris. Mr. Mattison (sic) lives at 1403 Dunning street. He said last night: "That telegram from Paw Paw, Mich. was evidently inspired by some of my old friends. To explain the animus of the story, as furnished in The Herald, I must acknowledge that there is no good feeling existing between the Morris faction and myself. In 1873, I was tried for forgery on charges preferred by his brother, Amos Morris, and was acquitted. I went to that part of Michigan when a young man, and began business as a money loner, taking a great many chattel mortgages. Naturally there was a prejudice created against me among the farmers as I had to make many foreclosures. I never held any mortgage on the farm occupied by C. H. Morris.

At the time of his murder I was in Decatur, Mich. on business, but [because of] rumors connecting me with the affair I gave up my residence in Chicago and moved to Decatur. I lived there for two years for the express purpose of clearing myself of any suspicion, and to afford every chance for legal investigation. I was never summoned to appear at the coroner's inquest, and there was no trial. The story that my brother James Mattison (sic) killed Morris is based on mere rumor. I saw him for the last time one year prior to the murder here in Chicago, and he was not with me in Decatur at the time the crime was committed. Since that time he has been arrested and adjudged insane at Mayville, N.Y. but escaping from the asylum soon

93

after he has not been heard of by me or his parents. The charge that I paid "Kit" Pearsons $800 for conveying my brother to the Morris farm for the purpose of killing Morris is so absurd that I do not know just how to deny it.[5]

Then, on December 4, The *Herald* followed with:

That Michigan Murder.

M. D. Mattison, who, it was intimated, knew something of the Morris murder at Little Prairie Ronde, Mich., some years ago, said yesterday that he, not Floyd Smith, had once held a mortgage on the Morris farm. His brother, he said, had been adjudged insane one year before the crime was committed and he had not seen him since. The brother had never been an outlaw in Texas, M. D. Matteson said, though he had met with business reverses there.[6]

Although Milo's statement that he had never held a mortgage on Henry Morris´s farm was false, the articles seem to have been satisfactory as no evidence that the matter was pursued any further appeared in Chicago newspapers.

During the 1890s, and even until he died, Milo was occupied with one particular investment his father had made in 1886, according to *The Daily Inter Ocean* on November 28, 1886: "A. M. Matteson bought of Louis Gathmann for $18,000 197 feet on Lake View avenue, north of Fullerton avenue, east front."[7]

This piece of land, with its views of Lincoln Park and Lake Michigan, was prime property even in the 19th century and certainly one of the best investments Almanson Matteson ever made. He lived until December 1897, having drawn up a will in April 1894. In it, his wife Eunice was to inherit a third of his considerable fortune and son Milo the rest. No mention was made of son James, but a codicil was added in June 1897, willing James' son Ralph a two story and basement flat building at 1409 Dunning Street.[8]

As Milo had been at the hub of activity in Decatur, sharing office space with the law firm Foster & Coleman, he set up an office in the Unity Building, one of the original skyscrapers from which exposition visitors could gaze at from the exposition's Ferris Wheel. A 17-story building, once the tallest in Chicago, it had been built by the politician

John P. Altgeld, who served as Governor of Illinois from 1893 to 1897. He had been the first Democratic governor of Illinois since the 1850s and had lost reelection in a particularly brutal campaign in which no other than Theodore Roosevelt said Altgeld "would substitute for the government of Washington and Lincoln a red welter of lawlessness and dishonesty as fantastic and vicious as the Paris Commune."[9]

Unity Building

John P. Altgeld

In 1897, when the news broke nationally that embezzlement had led to the Globe Savings Bank failure, Altgeld's name arose as bank vice president, providing the post-campaign press with sensational fodder. But Altgeld was able to avoid arrest with a series of clarifications. The Rockford *Republic* reported on April 30:

THE GLOBE FAILURE.

Ex-Governor Altgeld Explains His Connection with the Institution.

Chicago, April 30.—Ex-Gov. John P. Altgeld made a statement yesterday regarding his connection with the Globe savings bank, his knowledge of Charles W. Spalding and other matters with which his name had been coupled during the last few weeks. The ex-governor said:

"I never got any benefit, directly or indirectly, from the Globe savings the bank I believed it to be all right in every way. I got into politics in 1892, and, finding that I would be unable to give proper attention to the bank withdrew."

"The idea that I was a very heavy borrower of the Globe savings bank is a mistake. I borrowed of the large banks here during the last ten years. I built six of the largest buildings in Chicago, the Unity block being one of them. During that time I borrowed heavily of most of the large banks in this city."

Mr. Altgeld denied positively that he recommended Spalding for treasurer of the Illinois university.[10]

However, according to *The St Paul Globe* on April 14, Altgeld must have been aware of some illegal activity:

Another section of the amended bill says that Spalding, Edward Hayes, Charles J. Ford and John W. Lanehart, deceased, the latter either for himself or ex-Gov. John P. Altgeld, purchased a tract of land of eighty acres in Cook county, and Spalding, it is alleged, paid for his share of this property out of the funds of the Globe Savings bank, and, it is also charged, that Ford, Lanehart or Altgeld knew this. Of the sum of $103,000, which the state auditor ordered charged to the profit and loss account of the Globe Savings bank, it is represented $17,000 was an indebtedness of John P. Altgeld, and that $5,000 was an indebtedness nominally due from John W. Lanehart. It is charged, however, that the last amount was in fact a loan to ex-Gov. Altgeld. It is also claimed in the bill that ex-Gov. Altgeld has been transferring his property with the intention of keeping it from the creditors of the bank.

President Spalding, Vice President Averill and Cashier Churchill, of the bank, put in an appearance today in the court of Justice Hall and gave bonds for their appearance April 19 to answer the charge of embezzlement preferred by Adolph Edelman, one of the depositors in the bank.[11]

On the same day, *The Chicago Record* named Milo D. Matteson as being one of three men receiving land transfers from Altgeld, proving that he had played a more active role in the Unity Building than just renting office space:

Charges Against Altgeld.

The bill also sets up that since April 1 John P. Altgeld has transferred several pieces of property without valuable consideration, with the knowledge that he was indebted to the Globe savings bank, and, it is alleged, with the intent of placing his property beyond the reach of the receiver. The property was transferred, the bill states, to James H. Clark, William E. Schlake and Milo D. Matteson, and the court is asked for a restraining order to prevent further sale or conveyance of this property.

Injunctions are asked for to prevent transfer of the lots in Ford's subdivision in which Spalding is alleged to be interested and to have used the money of the bank to purchase his share. Ford was enjoined from assigning this real estate, but it is charged that in face of the injunction Spalding conveyed to Ford 267 lots and that after the injunction the complainant contends the insolvent bank has an interest in this property. The complainant also states that of the $103,000 charged off the books of the bank to profit and loss $17,000 was an indebtedness of John P. Altgeld and $5,000 an indebtedness of John W. Lanehart, but the bill alleges the last was really an indebtedness of John P. Altgeld.

Altgeld Declines to Talk.

John P. Altgeld declined to discuss the Globe Savings bank affair or his connection with that institution as charged in the supplemental bill filed by Cashier Churchill yesterday. "I have said all I intend to say on that matter," was all the reply the ex-governor would make to a request for an explanation.[12]

By July 1898, according to *The Topeka State Journal*, Matteson had reverted to legal defenses he had employed for a decade in Michigan:

Chicago Judge Sharply Reprimands Tedious Lawyers.

Chicago, July 23.—Wearied by the reading of long reports of testimony taken before a master in chancery in the Globe Savings bank case, Judge Tuley lost patience with the attorneys and censured them for the waste of time and money caused by the examination.

After Attorney Tyrrell had turned page after page of typewritten matter and gave no indication of finishing, the court interrupted and exclaimed:

"Is there no end to this interminable testimony? Won't you ever finish? If I had the power I would make counsel pay the expense incurred in taking this unnecessary matter. Hurry with it and get it out of the way."

The case on hearing was that of Milo D. Matteson, who, in his petition, asked the court to restrain the receiver of the Globe Savings bank from disposing of a note put up as security for another note, and also to prevent the receiver from prosecuting as indorser. The court dismissed the petition. Thus far none of the score or more similar ones has been allowed.[13]

Altgeld managed to convince the courts of his innocence, the focus being squarely on bank president Charles W. Spalding, who among other gifts, had deeded his stenographer $100,000 worth of ranch land in Idaho.[14] Spalding was sentenced to five years of prison in 1898. The *Kimball Graphic* reported: "Charles W. Spalding, one year ago president of the Globe National bank, Chicago, treasurer of the University of Illinois, occupant of a brown stone mansion on the Lake shore and a well-respected financial magnate, has begun a sentence of several years at Joliet. His last request before leaving Chicago was for a brief interview with his former typewriter girl. It was on her that he squandered much of his stealings."[15]

The century was coming to a close. On the one hand, Milo Matteson had maneuvered himself back into the thick of things, and he was litigating in the courts again. Alamanson had passed away and left his son a fortune. With this kind of security, what did the new century hold in store for the Matteson family?

13

MORE TRAILS OF FRAUD AND FORGERY

First and foremost, the Matteson family had always been entrepreneurs. At times they were listed as farmers, but it had been money loaning combined with real estate foreclosures that had made them wealthy. From the days of being represented by Foster & Coleman in Decatur, they had relied heavily on litigation and occupying courts at length, testing the patience of many a judge, as Judge Tuley had demonstrated in 1898.

The twentieth century, however, produced a new turn in events. In 1902, a member of his own family filed charges against Milo D. Matteson himself. According to *The Chicago Daily News* in 1902, the complainant was Milo's nephew Ralph DeLeo Matteson, a law student at the University of Michigan:

FIGHT OVER MATTESON ESTATE

Nephew Accuses Uncle of Causing Former's Disinheritance.

Embodying the incident used as the basis of the plot in "Richard Carvel," a bill was filed to-day in the Probate court accusing an uncle of scheming to deprive a nephew of his inheritance by poisoning the mind of the boy's grandfather against him. It is a bill in equity brought by Ralph D. Matteson, son of the late Merritt James Matteson, against the latter's brother, Milo, who is a real-estate owner and agent in the Unity building.

The plaintiff, Ralph D. Matteson, who is now a student in the law department of the University of Michigan, alleges in his bill that his uncle succeeded "by wicked and malicious scheming" in causing the collegian's disinheritance by his grandfather, Alamanson M. Matteson. The uncle is charged with posing as the friend and adviser of the young college student, at the same time filing false schedules of property to show that Ralph possessed one-third of the grandfather's estate.

In the unromantic verbiage and stilted phraseology of the legal document filed by Attorney Edwy Logan Reeves, is recited that the grandson of Alamanson Matteson, who died leaving a will said to dispose of $200,000, received only real estate valued at $4,500 as his share in the division of the estate under his grandsire's *will and was later induced by his uncle to trade the property—a house and lot at 1409 Dunning street, renting for $20 a month—for an untillable fruit farm in Michigan.*[1]

When Alamanson Matteson's will was first recorded in April 1894, his fortune was split with one-third plus their home in Arlington Heights going to his wife Eunice and two-thirds to his son Milo. Neither his son Merritt James nor his grandson Ralph were mentioned in the document.[2] However, in June 1897, a codicil naming Ralph D. Matteson was added to the will:

The circumstances as to why grandson Ralph had been left out of the will in 1894 are unclear. His parents had married in Decatur in 1872, but after some erratic behavior, the Mattesons had urged his mother Annie to divorce James, as the *Daily Inter Ocean* reported in 1878:

"DIVORCES.—1,941. Annie Matteson from Merritt J. Matteson; for adultery."[3]

However, there are indications that Annie, even after the divorce, was still in contact with the family at various times in Gunnison and Kenosha. But as there is no follow-up to Ralph's charges and Milo's building project at Deming Place and Lake View Avenue continued, it seems that attorneys once again came to his aid. Even the negative press did not stick as Laura was back to entertaining in grand style in early 1903. *The Chicago Daily News*, March 3:

NEWS IN POLITE CIRCLES.

Large Entertainment by North Side Hostesses—Minor Affairs.

Mrs. Milo D. Matteson, Mrs. Matilda A. Randall and Mrs. Tabor Randall are holding a large reception this afternoon between the hours of 3 and 6 o'clock at the home of the former, 1843 Wellington street. About 400 guests call and the hostesses are assisted in receiving by.

Mesdames—
Albert J. Hester, Philip C. Dyrenforth,
Julien Hequenberg   R.A. Bauer,
Fuerst   Donald C. Merrill,
MacGrew,   H.R. Stoddart,
Horace Goodrich, W.C. Pease,
Louis Ritching.

At the tea tables, Mrs. Allen T. Haight, Mrs. Lorin Wells, Mrs. Von Glahn and Mrs. Daniels preside. An orchestra stationed in the hall gives a programme of music. Mrs. Matteson is gowned in white French boutonne with point de venise and opalescent lace, and Mrs. Matilda Randall wears black lace, over red. Mrs. Tabor Randall is in tan voile with trimmings of Irish point lace. The house decorations are elaborate. White hyacinths bloom in the drawing room and the reception hall is beautified with palms and American beauty roses. Pink is the color scheme in the dining room. This evening the hostesses will entertain two distinct companies, the one at cards and the other with dancing, the dance being the last of a series of ten similar affairs. The ballroom will be decorated in Japanese effects.[4]

The name Milo DeHart Matteson had become synonymous with forgery and fraud back in Michigan in the 1870s. After the Morris trials he had freed himself of such accusations. The nearest he had come to comparable charges was being named in his nephew's suit in 1902.

However, on August 20, 1903, the Matteson name reappeared in connection with forgery and fraud, this time gathering nationwide attention from Washington, D.C. to Montana. In the Providence, Rhode Island *Evening Bulletin*:

EXTENSIVE FRAUDS UNEARTHED AT CHICAGO:

Practiced on Special Assessment Rebates and Large Sums Are Involved.

Chicago, Aug. 20—As a result of the arrest of Attorney Frederick A. Sawyer the city law department believes it is about to unearth extensive frauds in connection with special assessment rebates, of which $1,000,000 awaits claimants who have disappeared or are forgetful.

Sawyer is charged with forgery in collecting a rebate warrant for $250 on which he is said to have signed the name of A. N. Mattison (sic). Sawyer is said to have cashed more than 100 warrants. He also is said to have three offices in the downtown district and to have close relations with City Hall employees who know the amount of all rebates credited to property owners in the last 20 years.[5]

More accurately, the signature in question was A. M. Matteson, Milo's father, who had died nearly six years before. Besides declaring F. A. Sawyer as a suspected forger, the name of W. H. Madden was also called into question. The two men had dealt in real estate and advertised in The Chicago *Eagle* every week from the end of 1897 to the beginning of 1899.

W. H. MADDEN.   F. A. SAWYER,

MADDEN & SAWYER,

REAL * ESTATE.

Estates Managed. Taxes Paid.

500 Oxford Bldg., 84-86 La Salle St., Chicago.

6

As it turned out, the person accusing W. H. Madden of fraud was none other than Milo D. Matteson. On August 20, the Chicago *Daily News* provided a more detailed and dramatic description of Milo's entrance into the courtroom:

ON TRAIL OF FRAUDS
Arrest of Alleged Forger of Assessment Rebate Warrant Arouses Officials.
BROKERS' COMBINE HINTED
Former Clerk in City Hall Implicated by Story of Milo Matteson—F. A. Sawyer Arrested.

New figures appeared to-day in an inquiry growing out of the alleged forgery of a special assessment rebate warrant and city officials intend to find out at once how far such operations have gone. One thing likely to be investigated is a statement that several rebate brokers have pooled their interests and work in combination. That extensive frauds may be found is more than intimated, although Comptroller McGann declares the special assessment is strongly safeguarded.

City detectives are searching for William H. Madden, a former city hall employee, who they believe can throw some light on the forgery charge preferred against Frederick A. Sawyer, a rebate broker.

Sawyer was arrested late yesterday afternoon in a saloon at 132 Washington street by Detectives Thompson and Gallagher on the charge of forging the name of A. M. Matteson to a rebate warrant calling for $257. Madden was formerly connected with the special assessment bureau as the special assessment clerk and was accused of being one of the principals in the alleged looting of the famous "Fund W."

Associated with Madden was another man—an attorney who has since disappeared. Sawyer's case was called before Justice Prindiville this morning and at his request was continued for one week. He later admitted to a reporter for The Daily News that A. M. Matteson's name was not signed to the warrant when he got it. He could not explain, either, how it got there. Acting Corporation Counsel Colin C. H. Fyffe was satisfied to grant a continuance, as he and Comptroller McGann will begin work at once to examine several thousand like warrants, expecting to trace similar alleged forgeries.

Takes His Arrest Coolly.

Sawyer appears to take his arrest coolly. He displayed no sign of annoyance until he learned that "Andy" Craig, who had supplied a $2,000 bond for him last evening, had surrendered him and would not supply a new bond. The defendant was taken immediately to the coilroom in the Harrison street station, where he will remain until he finds a bondsman.

It did not develop until to-day that there was any hope of connecting Madden with the affair, although Sawyer admitted that he and Madden were associated for several years in caring for special assessment rebates, securing permission from the holders to carry the collection of them through the courts. While Sawyer was waiting in Justice Prindiville's court a well-dressed man wearing a pointed beard walked quietly into the courtroom and stood a short distance from Sawyer. He scanned Sawyer's features closely, shook his head in the negative and walked over to a corner where stood Assistant Corporation Counsels Beckwith and Hoyne talking with Acting Corporation Counsel Fyffe and Detectives Thompson and Gallagher.

This man was Milo D. Matteson, son of A. M. Matteson, who died in 1898. Mr. Matteson had been trying to identify Sawyer as the man who visited his office and sought his permission to collect a rebate voucher, calling for $257, which the stranger said was due A. M. Matteson.

Story Implicates Madden

"That is not the man," said Milo D. Matteson, "but let me tell you who it was. I met the man on the street yesterday after Sawyer was arrested. I followed him and learned his name was Madden and that he dealt in special assessment rebates. To-day I learned his initials were W. H. He is the man and he visited my office in 1901 and asked my permission to collect the rebate of $257 on a commission or a percentage. I informed him then that I knew of no rebate due the estate of my father and that I as trustee would surely know if any money was due from the city. I thought no more of the subject at the time, but later called on Comptroller McGann and learned that the city had issued a rebate voucher and a warrant on it. On or about April 31 (30), 1902, I met at the county building the stranger who had visited my office and I asked him about the affair. He said: "There is nothing to that. You have no claim against the city. I looked into it and found that much out and quit."

"It was not until recently that I learned the city warrant had been paid off on April 31 (30), 1903."

The detectives were immediately instructed to locate Madden and learn his story. He was never prosecuted for his alleged looting of "fund W." When William D. Kerfoot was the city comptroller he ordered an investigation, but was unable to discover any evidence that brought the alleged offense within the statute of limitations.

When Sawyer was interviewed at his cell he expressed an unwillingness to talk of his case. "I am the victim of spite on the part of the city officials," he finally said. "I have given out information about how things are conducted at the city hall in the special assessment department and the city hall officials are 'sore' on me."
When asked if A. M. Matteson's name was a forgery and if he had forged it he said: "No, I am innocent."
"Was Matteson's name on the warrant when you got possession of it?" he was asked.
"No, his name was not on it when I got it," he replied, "and I don't know how it did get there."

Explanation of Sawyer

"I handle so many of these things," he continued, "Why, I have secured over $40,000 in judgments against the city in the last eight months and I can't recall this affair clearly. I got the paper through an order of court and I will stand the consequences, as the court is back of me."

Acting Corporation Counsel Fyffe says Sawyer's talk about having got possession of the warrants through an order of court is "bosh." Sawyer says he is from a good family and he does not want the disgrace to fall on it. Before entering the police court to-day he removed two Masonic emblems.[7]

Detectives Thompson and Gallagher and Milo D. Matteson.
(The latter is standing at righ .of group.)
MAN CHARGED WITH REBATE PLOT. CHIEF WITNESS AND OFFICERS IN CASE. 7

F. A. Sawyer.

It is difficult to say whether F. A. Sawyer or W. H. Madden, or both, were involved in the rebate scandal. Their names had appeared prominently as real estate partners for over a year in the press. Furthermore, as their office was on LaSalle, on the west side of City Hall, and Milo Matteson's office was in the Unity Building on the east side of City Hall, it seems unlikely that the paths of these three "strangers" had never crossed in those five years, especially considering that they were competitors in Chicago real estate.

In addition, W. H. Madden's name had arisen in the Fund W scandal in which funds left over from public improvements were not returned to property owners but rather juggled to pay salaries of city employees. And although Milo Matteson served as a witness for F. A. Sawyer, instead deflecting attention onto Madden, it was Sawyer who was involved in more questionable affairs. According to *The Chicago Daily News* the very next day:

FIND MORE REBATE FRAUDS

Special Assessment Records Disclose Forgeries of Dead Man's Name

New evidences of fraud in connection with the collection of special assessment rebates came to light to-day in connection with the investigation following the arrest of Frederick A. Sawyer.

C. W. Parker told Acting Corporation Counsel Fyffe that he had seen on the records two forgeries of his father's signature, committed by some person presumably who had collected rebates due to the father.

"My father died in 1883," Mr. Parker told Mr. Fyffe. "The rebates were due in 1884, and not before, so that he could not have authorized any one to collect them for him. The signatures, besides, were nothing like his handwriting."

The father's name was T. L. Parker. The son lives at 182 51st street.[8]

Then on November 12, *The Chicago Daily News* reported Sawyer had been found guilty of forgery:

FINDS SAWYER GUILTY

Former City Employee Declared by a Jury to Be a Forger

Frederick A. Sawyer, formerly a city employee and later engaged in the business of collecting special assessment rebates, was found guilty of forgery by a jury in Judge Clifford's court to-day. Sentence was not passed and arrangements were begun by counsel to provide bail for the young man pending a motion for new trial.

The specific charge against Sawyer was that he had forged the name of A. M. Madison, deceased, to a special-assessment rebate warrant and secured the money, amounting to $200. He admitted that the name of Madison had been signed to the instrument, but claimed that the signature had been placed there by a clerk in his employ and under his authority. He also admitted that this method had been pursued in other cases and said he acted on the advice of his lawyers.[9]

However, according to a 1905 article in *The Daily Illinois State Register*, Sawyer had fled to New York in March 1904 and was wanted back in Illinois:

DIDN'T HAVE MONEY ON DEPOSIT

Yet Frederick A. Sawyer, it is Said, Issued Check on New York Bank.

Governor Deneen to-day issued a requisition on the governor of New York for the return to Illinois of Frederick A. Sawyer, who is wanted in Chicago on the charge of working a confidence game and obtaining money under false pretenses. He is under arrest in New York city.

It is alleged that on Dec. 18, 1902, after banking hours, Sawyer entered the business house of Fremont B. Malcolm at 153 Washington street, Chicago, the two men being well acquainted, and secured $700 of Malcolm, giving him as security a check signed by himself and payable to Malcolm's order at the bank of Foreman Bros. Banking company. The check, it is alleged, was deposited with the Metropolitan Trust & Savings bank, who returned it to Malcolm with the information that Sawyer had no funds with Foreman Bros. Banking company, nor had he any on Dec. 18, 1902. Malcolm charges he told Sawyer of this, and that the latter promised to pay him the amount immediately, but has never done so, and that on March 24, 1904, Sawyer left Chicago and has never returned.[10]

There are no indications that Milo Matteson was involved in the rebate forgery or fraud charges of 1903, although forgery had certainly been a recurring theme in his life. At the least, in the case of Madden and Sawyer, it appears that Matteson backed the wrong horse. Frederick A. Sawyer and William H. Madden both died in Chicago, in 1913 and 1915 respectively, and Milo Matteson spent the last ten years of his life building, prospering, and positioning his family as pillars of polite society.

14

COLLIDING WITH THE TWENTIETH CENTURY

When the first Pinkerton detective stepped off the train at the Decatur station in 1879, the day after the Morris bodies had been discovered, the station master described Milo Matteson as "a man who would do anything to make money." The last decade of Milo's life indicates that his long pursuit of wealth had indeed paid off. The $75,000 apartment building which he had started in October 1902 at Deming Place and Lake View Avenue was being advertised in the Chicago *Daily News* by August 27, 1903:

North Side. FOR RENT—NEW 5,6 and 10 room apartments at 161-165 Lake View-av., between Wrightwood-av. and Deming-pl.; come and see the large light rooms; hot-water heat; porches overlooking Lincoln park; gas grates in all bathrooms; modern   MILO D. MATTESON, owner.[2]

Furthermore, his mother, Eunice Bentley Matteson, had passed away that year, leaving her son the remaining third of Alamanson's fortune. Her obituary appeared in *The Chicago Tribune*: "MATTESON—Eunice Matteson, March 15, aged 77, wife of the late Alamanson M. Matteson and beloved mother of Milo B. Matteson. Funeral from late residence, 167 Howe-st., Tuesday at 2 p.m. Burial private."[3]

Chicago was happily preoccupied with its Exposition when the first decade of the twentieth century brought the automobile to the forefront, starting in 1901 with the Chicago Automobile Shows.[4] The days of Milo Matteson posing for a photo atop a horse were over. By 1909, and probably earlier, he had turned to the horseless carriage to travel from Lake View to the "Loop", an area created by the elevated train.

On January 9, 1909, he was driving south on Lake Shore Drive, accompanied by his wife Laura and his daughter-in-law Margaret. As they approached Schiller Street, their attention would have undoubtedly fallen on the Palmer Mansion, the largest private residence in the city, occupying the entire block. Potter Palmer had completed the castle-like structure in 1885, after making his fortune in the dry goods business, then selling it to Marshall Field, rebuilding State Street after the Great Fire, and presenting his bride Bertha the luxurious Palmer House Hotel as a wedding gift. He had even developed the very Lake Shore Drive on which the Mattesons were driving and turned Frog Pond into the Gold Coast.[5]

Bertha Palmer

The Matteson ladies might have been trying to sneak a glimpse of Bertha Palmer. She was Chicago's most prominent socialite, a widow who also maintained homes in London and Paris and moved comfortably among European society, having attended Czar Nicholas's coronation, and after Potter's death in 1902, had become a trusted friend of King Edward VII. Or perhaps the Matteson ladies were reminded of the Palmers' extensive collection of works by Monet, Renoir, Pissarro and Degas which they might have seen lent to the Columbian Exposition, now back in Bertha Palmer's private picture gallery again. Or they might have been anticipating a visit to Marshall Field's, which had become the world's largest department store with its five-story Great Hall and Tiffany glass ceiling, completed only two years earlier. At any rate, passing the Palmer Mansion that day, they all must have been dazzled by the sheer wealth the castle exuded. The same, however, might have applied to George Hoyt, a chauffeur turning out of Banks Street onto Lake Shore Drive.

According to The Chicago Sunday Tribune:

WOMAN THROWN TO STREET IN *AUTOMOBILE COLLISION:*

Her Machine Strikes an Electric Vehicle—Carried to Hospital in Mrs. Potter Palmer's Car.

Mrs. Matteson, wife of Milo D. Matteson, a real estate dealer, was thrown from an automobile yesterday afternoon at Banks street and Lake Shore drive by a collision with an electric machine owned by Julian L. Yale, 9 Ritchie place. Yales's machine was driven by George Hoyt, a chauffeur.

Mrs. Matteson was taken to the Henrotin hospital in Mrs. Potter Palmer's automobile, which was secured from the Palmer garage by Park Policeman Schiberg. In the evening she was removed to her home, 161 Lake View avenue. In the machine with Mrs. Matteson were Mr. Matteson and their daughter Margaret.

Hoyt was turning out of Banks street into Lake Shore drive when the Matteson machine, driven by Mr. Matteson, was coming south. The Matteson machine struck the other squarely in the center, throwing it some distance.

The impact threw Mrs. Matteson to the road, cutting her head and hands and badly bruising her body. Hoyt was more scared than hurt and took the machine to the garage. The Matteson machine was badly damaged, necessitating its removal to a repair shop.[6]

No lasting injuries resulted from the collision, however, as the Mattesons continued their motoring outings into the summer of 1910, reported by *The Chicago Daily News*:

Mrs. Milo D. Matteson Entertains Niece, Miss Lois Shilling; Events Planned.

By Florence Brooke.

Mrs. Milo D. Matteson of Deming place is entertaining her niece, Miss Lois Shilling, who arrived Thursday from Colorado Springs. Miss Shilling is a Wellesley girl and talented in a musical way, having a beautiful soprano voice. Mrs. Matteson's friends are already planning to give her visitor a pleasant time and she will pass the entire summer with her relatives, going later with them to Delavan lake. Mr. and Mrs. Matteson will not be away from the city any length of time, but will take motor trips for the week-ends. They are planning to pass July 4 in St. Joseph, Mich. with a party of friends who have leased a hotel for the celebration. Miss Esther Edwards gave a theater party yesterday in honor of Miss Shilling.[7]

Rather than motoring to St. Joseph, the Matteson party might have taken the 4-hour steamship trip from Chicago to St. Joseph, where, for a penny, they could take the moving staircase directly behind the ferry landing up to the prestigious Hotel Whitcomb with its beautiful view overlooking Lake Michigan and well-known for its mineral baths.

1910 Postcard   Public Domain

Automobiles and building remained Milo Matteson´s interests. Perhaps the bone-jarring drives to Delevan Lake in Wisconsin encouraged him to invest in George W. Kitterman´s pneumatic and cushion tire.

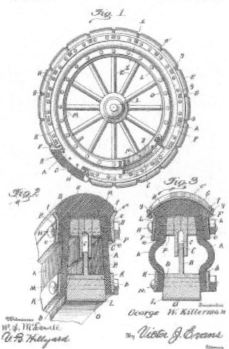

As for building, in addition to the $75,000 apartment building which had been constructed on Deming Place, Robert S. DeGolyer, a renowned Chicago architect, was enlisted to design an enjoining luxury apartment complex facing Lake View Avenue. This building, The Marlborough, with its semi-private entrance halls and spectacular views of Lincoln Park, would be the Matteson family's luxurious home for the next forty years.

Courtesy of Chicago History Museum

AN END FOR THREE MATTESONS

The next forty years would not see Milo DeHart Matteson motoring down Lake Shore Drive past the Gold Coast, or summering with his family at Delevan Lake, or just living the good life overlooking Lincoln Park and Lake Michigan.

In February 1912 Milo's cousin Frank died at the early age of 46.[1] True to Matteson form, he had been engaged successfully in real estate in the Buffalo, New York area along with his 88-year-old father James. Frank was divorced and childless, so since James' brothers John and Alamanson had both passed away in 1897, and since Frank had been James' only child, it is not a far reach to imagine that his uncle's inheritance might have been on Milo's mind when he traveled to Buffalo in March 1912. His uncle James was failing and would indeed not survive the year, but died as well on September 28, coincidentally on the anniversary of the Morris murders.[2]

FRANK H. MATTESON.   JAMES MATTESON.

Historical and Biographical Sketch of Cherry Creek, Chautauqua County, NY [3,4]

But as chance would have it, Milo did not survive the trip back East either. He was found dead in the Genesee Hotel in Buffalo on March 29, 1912. *The Chicago Examiner* reported on April 1:

MILO D. MATTESON DIES

Real Estate Dealer Expires in Buffalo; Heart Disease Believed Cause.

Milo D. Matteson, wealthy contractor and real estate dealer, whose home was at 2618 Lake View avenue, died suddenly at Buffalo, N.Y., in the Genesee Hotel. An attack of heart failure is believed to have caused death. Mr. Matteson had gone to the New York city to visit his uncle, James Matteson. At his home in Chicago last night it was said that he had been subject to heart attacks. His son, DeForest H. Matteson, has gone to Buffalo and is expected to return with the body tomorrow. Mr. Matteson is survived by a widow and two young sons besides DeForest, who was in business with his father.[5]

And in The Chicago *Tribune*: "MATTESON—Milo DeHart Matteson, beloved husband of Laura A. and father of De Forrest A. and Randolph W.; born Cherry Creek, 1845; died Buffalo, N.Y., March 29. Funeral services Tuesday, April 2, 2 p.m. at residence, 2616 Lake View av. Burial private."[6]

But back in Paw Paw, Michigan, the newspaper which had invested so much ink and space in Milo´s activities throughout the 1870s fumbled both his name and the information with "It is rumored that Hart Madison, formerly of Decatur and well known here, died in Chicago last week. *The True Northerner* has been unable to get details or verify the rumor."[7]

In the following issue, however, Milo was given a send-off, the likes of which he had been avoiding for over 30 years:

NOTED FORGERY BROUGHT TO MIND

Death of M. D. Matteson in Chicago Recalls Famous Criminal Trial.

In the last issue of The True Northerner appeared a rumor of the death of "Hart Madison" at the city of Chicago. The correct name of the deceased party was Milo DeHart Matteson. He was not only well known in Paw Paw, but elsewhere throughout the county and state. It was he that was defendant in the most famous criminal trial that ever occurred in Van Buren county, the Morris-Matteson forgery case. Matteson was a money loaner in Decatur during the 70s, and figured in 28 cases in the circuit court of the county between 1871 and 1889. Three of those cases were criminal cases in which Matteson was charged with forgery of certain notes and mortgages against the Morrises. The celebrated criminal lawyer, John Van Arman, was employed by the county to assist the prosecutor, the late Judge D. E. Comstock, in the trial of the cause, which lasted for four weeks and resulted in a verdict of guilty. The matter of an appeal to the supreme court was pending, but before it was perfected, the presiding judge, Hon. Charles R. Brown, unexpectedly resigned his office, which action on his part prevented such appeal being perfected and paved the way for a new trial of the cause. Feeling ran high against Matteson and the case was transferred to St. Joseph county. The second trial which was conducted on the part of the people by hon. B. F. Heckert and John Van Arman, resulted in an acquittal, a proceeding that was regarded in Van Buren county, to put it in the most favorable light, as a Scotch verdict. It was not long after this that Henry Morris and his wife were foully murdered. The murderer was never apprehended although the county offered a large reward for his capture. James Matteson, a brother of Milo D., disappeared immediately after and has not been seen nor his whereabouts been known, by Van Buren county people since that time. There were strong suspicions that there were some connections between the Matteson-Morris affairs and the assassination of Mr. and Mrs. Morris. It was known, however, that Milo DeHart Matteson was not at the scene of the murder, as he was at the village of Decatur when the crime was committed. Had Jim Matteson been arrested, and he would have been if he could have been found, he might not so easily have proven an alibi.[8]

In the end Milo was laid to rest in the prestigious Graceland Cemetery, north of Lincoln Park, where many prominent Chicagoans were buried. Closest to the Matteson family plot there is a monument marking the grave of John Peter Altgeld, the ex-governor who at one time had transferred properties to Matteson. Besides Altgeld, this northern portion of Graceland surrounding Lake Willowmere reads like a Who's Who of Chicago society and enterprise: Marshall Field, Cyrus McCormick, Charles Wacker, Henry Honoré, George Pullman, and on a bluff overlooking a small lake, the mausoleum of Potter and Bertha Palmer. Even Alan Pinkerton, whose agency investigated Matteson's role in the Morris murders, is buried in Graceland Cemetery. Here, lying next to his parents, Milo found the end of a trail from Cherry Creek to Decatur and from Gunnison to Lake View.

Who was Milo DeHart Matteson? Although not on the grand scale of a Potter Palmer, he had nonetheless been an accomplished and wealthy man in his own right. Over the years, any implied connection to the Morris murders had been successfully deflected, and his alibi on that day in 1879 was unshakable. But in 1880, the cross-examination in the foreclosure case conducted by the C. H. Morris estate posed some very uncomfortable questioning, and at least circumstantially, gave an insight into Milo Matteson's alleged thoughts. The attorneys for the Morris estate had collected incriminating statements from a series of witnesses, excerpts of which follow:

Q. Do you know Elliott Vincent heretofore of Marcellus, Cass Co, Mich?

A. I do.

Q. Did you at Decatur or near there not long after your forgery trial at Centreville in a said conversation with Vincent referring to some mortgages mentioned in your testimonies here use language in substance and effect as follows: "I will collect those mortgages if I have to kill Morris?"

A. I never made such a remark to any one.

And later

Q. Did you not while on your visits at Grand Rapids, shortly before your Paw Paw trial in conversation there with Mrs. Geo. W. White use language to this effect — "If the old lady, meaning Henry's mother, was out of the way I would have but little trouble to collect the mortgage."

A. I don't recall any such conversation.

Q. Did you not on said visit there at Grand Rapids in a conversation with Mrs. Geo. W. White use language to this effect — "I met her, meaning Henry Morris's mother one day near the Amos Morris place driving her horse and carriage and I had a good mind to strike her horse and make it run away and kill her."

A. My answer is the same as to the next preceding question.

And just before further cross-examination of Matteson was adjourned until April 5, this question:

Q. Do you know a Mrs. Springer and a Miss Eckler who there boarded at the Decatur House in Decatur?

A. I do.

Q. Did you not say in their presences at the Decatur House soon after you were so detained for a night in said jail words to this effect — It will be a dear night for the Morrises if it takes me twenty years.

A. I recollect saying that it would be a dear night for Morris and not Morrises as I expected that I could sue him for false imprisonment. Just who was present I am unable to state, but such remarks I know I made referring to Amos Morris as it was he that caused my arrest.[9]

How uncomfortable must this line of questioning have been for Milo to settle for only fourteen percent of his claims and to pay his own costs, when he had reportedly told a number of witnesses that if he lost these cases, he would not be worth a dollar?[9]

Although Milo D. Matteson was clearly not the murderer, a number of witnesses attested to him expressing a motive. If there is to be any chance to solve this mystery, one must turn to the loose ends, leads, and untimely deaths left behind in the Matteson and Morris wake.

Loose Ends, Leads, and Untimely Deaths

16

ASSASSINATED

Perched atop a wooded knoll in the Cherry Valley Cemetery, overlooking the road leading to and from Rockford, Illinois, an obelisk bears the following inscription:

MARSHALL S.

PRITCHARD

ASSASSINATED

Jan. 24. 1879

AGED 34 Ys.

11 Ms.

The murder of Marshall Simpson Pritchard falls squarely under the three categories of loose ends, leads, and untimely deaths. Just as the unsolved Morris murders would occupy Decatur for decades, the residents of Cherry Valley and Rockford would speculate about their own local mystery for years to come.

The Chicago Daily Tribune reported:

Rockford, Ill., Jan. 20—This community was horrified yesterday morning about 7 o'clock on hearing that an atrocious murder had been committed in the north part of the city, well towards the West Side Cemetery. The deed, as near as can be learned, was committed between the hours of 11 and 12. A pistol shot was heard in that vicinity at that hour. No attention was paid to it, as no outcry was made by the victim, who proved to be Marshall S. Pritchard, Town Collector of Cherry Valley. It appears he had been drinking freely during the day, but left Mapes' saloon alone at 8 o'clock. From this hour as yet no definite clew (sic) can be ascertained where he went. The murderer evidently suspected he had considerable money in his possession, as one pocket showed evidence of being rifled, but in his hurry to escape he missed one containing $100 and a watch. The ball entered the skull a little above the left ear, passing right through the skull, shattering it in a horrible manner. A large revolver laid close to the body, evidently to convey the idea of his having committed suicide. No cause can be assigned for such a course, as his

Although Marshall Pritchard had been raised in Illinois and had served with the infantry during the Civil War, he had spent some time thereafter visiting his uncle who lived in Charleston, Michigan, just west of Little Prairie Ronde. It was there that Marshall met Emma Hathaway, the widow he would leave behind and daughter of Grandma Hathaway who had informed the natives that "White bread costs money." The Hathaways, like the Morrises, had been among the first settlers of the area and, according to Benjamin Hathaway's obituary in 1896, the family had lived on the "prize farm of Cass County." In the same article, the *Marshall Statesman* reported, "The farm itself was a poem. Every nook and corner had its trees and flowers." Emma's brother Benjamin, a prolific author, was known as the "Prairie Poet".[2]

It is uncertain how long the Pritchards lived in Little Prairie Ronde, but they were married there in the fall of 1867, and their son Guy was born there in the summer of 1871. No record has been found indicating where the Pritchards made their home during these years, but they might have lived with the Prairie Poet, who had no children to help on his farm just across the road from Samuel Morris's. Or perhaps they lived with Emma's sister Jane Hathaway Copley, whose farm faced Amos Morris's land on one side and Charles Henry Morris's on the other. Marshall Pritchard knew the Morrises, and the connection was pursued twice, once in *The True Northerner* in 1879, and again in *The Rockford Journal* in 1880.

In an 1879 report dealing with Floyd Smith's arrest in the Morris Murder case, *The True Northerner* reported:

It will be recollected that on the 24th day of January last Marshall S. Pritchard was murdered near Rockford, Ill. It is claimed that he was a friend of C. H. Morris and that he was in possession of facts which would make him a valuable witness in the mortgage case. It is also claimed that he had been followed and shadowed for some time previous (sic) PRIOR to his death. All these matters are shrouded in a good deal of mystery and serve to keep up a feverish state of public sentiment.[3]

Then on November 20, 1880 the Rockford *Journal* followed with:

THE PRITCHARD MURDER

Facts which Unquestionably Connect his Murder with Michigan Parties.

An Important Witness, and he Must be Got Rid Of.

Three Murders Believed to have been Committed by the Same Parties.

Saturday morning, January 29, 1879 the citizens of Rockford were startled by the report that the body of a murdered man had been found in North Main Street, near the north limits of the city. Investigation proved the story to be true. Stretched on the crisp snow, surrounded by a pool of frozen blood lay the cold remains; by the side of them lay a soft felt hat with a bullet hole through it, byside (sic) him also lay an empty six shooter, a few pennies and silver dimes lay scattered near him in the road as if jostled out of his pocket when he fell, and in his pocket was a silver watch and a wallet containing over $100. A bullet hole square through the brain showed that the work was

COOL, DELIBERATE MURDER.

An examination of the remains developed the fact they were those of Marshal S. Pritchard, Collector of taxes for the town of Cherry Valley, Winnebago county. The whole city and surrounding country was intensely excited. An examination was at once commenced, before a Coroner's Jury which continued through a number of days. A thorough and exhaustive examination of persons and circumstances were had, to fix, if possible, the crime on the guilty person. Suspicion pointed strongly to several parties in Rockford, but it was only suspicion, and nothing was developed to fix the least shadow of guilt on any one on whom suspicion rested. Yet, notwithstanding this, the suspicion still lurked in the minds of many that the guilty parties were Rockford men, and there are still men in Rockford who retain this belief and think the Coroner's Jury failed in its duty in not getting to the bottom facts in the case.

The facts surrounding the case as developed during the investigation were few and simple. Mr. Pritchard, a man of about 35 years of age, with wife and child resided at Cherry Valley. He had been employed in a grain ware house in the village of Monroe, Ogle County, on the C.&P. rail road, some 8 miles south of Cherry Valley. In order to attend to his duties as town collector, he had left Monroe the Thursday before the murder, and returned to Cherry Valley. He started to make the journey on foot but when about two miles on the road he was overtaken by a farmer, with whom he rode to Cherry Valley. Instead of going to his home he took the 7:30 p.m. train on the C.&N.W.R.R. and came to Rockford, bringing with him the town collector's book in a leather case, such as each town is provided with, an old six shooter, rusty with age, and without a cartridge in either chamber. That night he stopped with Christian Henry, Restaurant and boarding house keeper, East State Street. In the morning he visited two or three saloons and drank considerable and between 8 and 9 'clock went to the saloon of Fred Mapes, West State street, where he remained all day. About 6 o'clock he went to the saloon of R. B. Hefferan, also on West State street, and thence to that of Augustus Kauffman. South Rockford, where he was last seen alive, so far as witnesses could identify time at about 9:30 o'clock that evening—the night before his death, his dead body being found early the next morning one and one half miles from there laying (sic) where it had fallen, there not being a mark in the surrounding snow to indicate a scuffle, or any resistance, the great pool of frozen blood in which the body lay indicating that the foul deed had been committed at that identical spot. The sound of voices in dispute followed by a loud pistol report heard by a family occupying a house within 70 feet of where the body lay, also indicating that the murder took place there. It was further developed during the examination that the deceased had on several occasions stated to his wife and twenty-three other persons that he believed he was followed or shadowed by someone, but he did not know who did it, why, or for what purpose; but knowing himself to be innocent of any offense against any one he paid but little attention to it, other than to express a sense of annoyance at it.

These facts, and the further one that none of the valuables on the person of the murdered man were disturbed, his money, watch and pistol all being intact surrounded the entire affair with an air of impenetrable mystery.

For some months, the JOURNAL has been in possession of facts which closely connect the murder of Pritchard with two other murders in Van Buren County,

Michigan. We have refrained from making these public until now, from prudential reasons, as the winds of justice might be defeated thereby.

One Sunday night during the last of September 1879, nearly eight months after the murder of Pritchard, Charles H. Morris, and young wife were brutally murdered at their home in Paw Paw, Van Buren County, Mich. It would seem that both had retired for the night, when Morris was called to the door. As he stepped out, he was shot down, and as if to make perfect work of his crime, the assassin then stood over the prostrate form of his victim and fired a second ball into him, the ball passing through the body and down through the floor of the veranda on which it lay. It seems the young wife, alarmed by the firing, had jumped up, and taking her husband's revolver, which he always kept under his pillow, had gone to his relief. At the door she was met by the assassin, who commenced firing on her (as the bullet marks in the wall indicated) he followed her through several rooms, firing as he went. In the parlor one ball took effect in her arm, scattering her blood over a marble top dresser and burying itself in one of the drawers. She finally took refuge in a closet where she received a fatal wound and fell. To make sure of his hellish work, as in the case of her murdered husband, the ruffian stood over her and fired another shot at her, it passing through her body and down through the floor into the earth in the cellar bottom. The murdered couple were found the next morning lying as indicated, cold and dead with only their night clothes on.

Although there was a large amount of jewelry, some valuable watches, and considerable money in the house nothing was taken. Not a thing about the premises had been disturbed or touched save a valuable and fast going saddle horse which was taken from the barn from among a half dozen other horses. This horse was found the next day, running loose in a pasture in Indiana some 40 miles from the scene of the dreadful murder. The selection of the well known animal indicated that the deed was committed by some one knowing the premises and the animal, and the fact that nothing of value being taken, also indicated, as in the Pritchard murder that the terrible act was premeditated and done for other causes than gain. The only indications as to time of night when done was the fact of a young man returning home about 11 o'clock at night from a Sunday school concert meeting a masked man on horseback riding rapidly and coming from the direction of the Morris mansion.

Of course this horrible crime caused intense excitement, and large rewards were offered by the families of the murdered pair, for the apprehension of the murderer, but so quiet and stealthy had been the work, that like the Pritchard murderer, the guilty man left no trace by which he might be discovered. Suspicion rested on various parties, but it was only suspicion, but it became so firmly fixed in the minds of the people of that vicinity that with many of them it amounts to a conviction.

The only clue, if clue it be, which throws any light on the cause of this crime is this: Charles H. Morris, the murdered man, and his brother Amos Morris, were left large landed property by their father; some time after the property came into their possession, mortgages to the amount of near $20,000 was recorded against the lands purporting to be given by the Morrises, and running to one Milo D. Matteson.

On three of the mortgages on the land of Amos Morris, suits were brought to foreclose and were contested in the courts and one of them was finally carried to the Supreme Court of the state of Michigan where it was held to be a forgery and set aside by a decree of Court. A short time after this, Milo D. Matteson discharged the other two of record. In the mean time it was believed that M. D. Matteson was the forger and he was prosecuted criminally and after spending some $20,000 to defend himself, our informant tells he "only escaped on a technicality." This settled the mortgages so far as Amos Morris was concerned, but two suits for foreclosure were still pending against Charles H. Morris, the murdered man, and were to be tried soon. Defense was made against them the same as on those with his brother just decided as forgeries.

Now, right here comes in the connection of the murdered Pritchard with these last cases. Pritchard formerly lived in Paw Paw, his wife also formerly lived there, he married her there and her family still reside there. He was intimately acquainted with the Morris brothers, and particularly so with the murdered one, Charles H., and was expected to have been a witness in favor of Charles H. Morris in the mortgage suits soon to come off, and here seems to be the motive for his murder brought to light by subsequent events, for our informant, a gentleman well posted says: "it was understood that he (Pritchard) might be a valuable witness in the case of the murdered Charles H. Morris, and if produced, might reveal some ugly facts." Hence it would seem that Pritchard was right in his surmises and statements to his wife that his footsteps were dogged by a "shadow," and that he was finally led away, and his valuable testimony and damaging facts were forever silenced in death. The further fact, that the patient and exhausting researches of the Coroner's jury by which they hunted up the whereabouts of every suspicious person in Rockford on that Friday night of the murder, and their failure to connect any one with the murdered man later than 9 or 9:30 o'clock, when he left the South Rockford saloon are strong corroborative circumstances favoring the theory advanced from Michigan that he was such a "valuable witness" that murder was resorted to get him out of the way and that the same parties and motives prompted it, as prompted the murder of Morris and wife.

Those most intimately acquainted with all the facts do not now hesitate to weave a net work connecting the murder of Pritchard and Morris and wife with the forged mortgages of Matteson, and believe that one be guilty of all the crimes, but who he is what still puzzles the authorities.[4]

The inference that the Morris and the Pritchard murder mysteries were connected and that Milo Matteson was involved seems to have died with this 1880 Rockford *Journal* article. Arba Moulton, who edited *The Decatur Republican* from 1897 to 1951, recognized the interest the Morris murders aroused, printed and reprinted the story, from time to time adding old timers' reminiscences and letters sent to him, but strangely, as he never mentioned Marshall Pritchard or Milo Matteson, both names were all too soon forgotten in Michigan.

In Rockford, however, Marshall Pritchard's name did crop up a few years later. In the aftermath of the Pritchard murder, a $1,000 reward had been offered statewide for information leading to the killer. The first of two accusations emerged in April 1884 and involved the former Rockford saloon keeper Harry Hillman. Since 1877 fourteen Rockford saloons had been operating without a liquor license when a man entered Hillman's saloon and ordered a beer. According to an article entitled *"Hilarious Harry"* in *The Rockford Journal*, Hillman, mistaking the patron for a detective who would "squeal on him", sprang over the counter and beat him so badly, the police had to be called to break up the fight.[5] Charges were filed, but they apparently did not stick, as by the following year, Hillman had become a member of the Rockford police himself.[6]

The accusation, that Harry Hillman was Marshall Pritchard's killer, came from a man named Charles Rundell, a cousin of Marshall Pritchard's, in April 1884:

Last Friday, he stated, he met one George DeMunn, learning that Rundell was a relative of Pritchard, told him the following story: On the night Pritchard was killed he (DeMunn) was at Alice Hardy's notorious house on North Main Street, in this city. Just as he was coming away he heard the noise of quarreling and saw three men approaching in a cutter. He recognized Harry Hillman, (another party) and Marshall S. Pritchard. The quarreling continued and finally Pritchard and Hillman jumped out. Pritchard then struck Hillman once or twice. Hillman then whipped out a revolver and shot Pritchard dead in his tracks.[7]

By the time this accusation surfaced, Hillman had resigned his position with the police, becoming "a fully accredited advance agent of Balabrega, the wonder worker" in March 1879[8]. But after his engagement in Rockford, the great Balabrega took his travelling magic show to New England, and for a while, Hillman was working as an auctioneer in Iowa. But when Hillman saw his name connected with DeMunn's accusations, he wasted no time travelling to Belvidere, Illinois, to confront DeMunn. In an affidavit signed on April 28 before a notary public, DeMunn stated "that he never heard of the abovementioned Harry Hillman until his name was mentioned that day by Charles Rundell; never saw Harry Hillman to know him, and would not know him if he should see him; and further states he was not acquainted with the said Marshall S. Pritchard." In the same affidavit, DeMunn states that Rundell told him of the $1000 reward involved and offered him half for swearing that he had seen Hillman shoot Pritchard.[9]

With Rundell's word against DeMunn's, the trail to Marshall Pritchard's killer turned cold once again, but six months later *The Daily Register* revealed that James Banta, confined to the penitentiary in Joliet for forgery, had "a knowledge of the entire facts of the murder", and had testified extensively before a grand jury in Rockford, implicating Gideon Cooper and William Larson in the killing.[10] However, after 4 days of the parties levelling accusations at each other, the grand jury found no reason for indictment in the Pritchard murder, Cooper and Larson were released, and Banta was returned to prison in Joliet. Banta even went as far as to pen a confession to Rockford's sheriff in July 1885:

Sir:--I take my pen in hand to let you know something that has not become known about me as yet. It is this. On the 24th day of January, 1879, Saturday night, I did shoot and kill Marshall S. Pritchard of Cherry Valley, a tax collector. The crime was committed in the north part of town, near the watering trough on North Main Street. This has been preying on my mind ever since it was done, and now I am ready to fully confess and let the law take its course. I think there is a reward of $1,000 out, but you will know best about that. Now you know what to do in this matter, and when that is done I will tell all. I am now in jail here, as I suppose you know. Do as you think best about letting the papers know this.

I am, sir, yours most respectfully,

James Banta alias C. T. Warren[11]

In the same article, however, *The Daily Gazette* declared Banta to be "a crank in the first order," and his confession, although once again garnering nationwide attention, seems to have been perceived as a further lie. His prison sentence for forgery was up in October 1885, but by November 17 he was back in court pleading guilty to a new charge of forgery. While awaiting his sentence in jail, he finally divulged that his murder confession had been a myth.[12]

Although serving out his second forgery sentence in Joliet, Banta was good for at least one more surprise. According to *The St. Paul Globe* in 1886:

Joliet, Ill., March 7.--A novel wedding occurred at the penitentiary this evening, the bride being Lizzie Conners and the groom a convict named James Banta. Miss Conners arrived in this city about 2 o'clock this afternoon. She proceeded at once to the prison and was allowed an interview with her former lover, James Banta. After talking over matters for some time the prisoner said he was willing to marry the woman if he would be allowed to do so. He made an affidavit to that effect, and, armed with the instrument, the woman went to the county clerk's office to get a license, but did not have the money to pay for it. The clerks took up a collection to raise enough for the license, and presented her with a marriage certificate. With these in her possession she returned to the penitentiary, where the marriage ceremony was performed this evening in the reception-room by the chaplain, Rev. J. J. Walters, quite a crowd of officials and visitors being witnesses. The groom was sent to the prison from Jo Daviess county on a ten years' sentence for forgery, and was received Nov. 22, 1885.

Both Rundell and Banta seem to have been driven by the $1,000 reward offered for information leading to the Pritchard killer. Apparently, the reward was never collected, as the murder of Marshall Pritchard was never solved and remained a mystery. The sole reminder today is an obelisk in the Cherry Valley cemetery with the inscription "Assassinated."

Cherry Creek Cemetery   Photo by author

MILO'S FACTOTUM

Because leads as to the Pritchard murderer, however contrived, took several years to surface, the Morris murders were immediately associated with Milo Matteson, or someone he had hired. As already stated, the Pinkerton detectives believed Floyd Smith to be a crucial source of information and worked undercover for weeks to gain his confidence.[1]

Dana P. Smith (no relation to Floyd) published his memories and insights in a *Decatur Republican* article in 1936 dubbed *"The Tragic Story of Floyd Smith"*. He described the lynching of Smith and how he had been strung up twice and let down, each time maintaining his innocence despite his unusual agreement to intercept all of Matteson's mail immediately following the murders.[2]

According to the article, Floyd Smith had been raised on the Wilkins farm, about two miles straight north of the Dolphin Morris homestead. In fact, Leland Wilkins was married to Floyd Smith's sister, Mary, whose family lived just across the road. Wilkins did not speak highly of Floyd Smith to the Pinkerton agents, saying "that he is a very bad man, and that when Smith swore in the interest of Hart Matteson that he saw Amos Morris going down the valley road, he swore to a lie, for he (Wilkens) knew that Smith was not at home on that day."[1]

"Factotum", the Latin combination of *farcere* ("to do") and *totum* ("everything"), is the term *The Saginaw Herald* chose in December 1879 to describe Floyd Smith and his alleged role in the Morris murders:

The Morris Murder Demonstration.

On December 17th, Riley Huntley, who was the hired man of the murdered Henry Morris, made a complaint before Justice Haynes of Decatur, charging Floyd Smith, the general factotum of M. D. Matteson, with complicity in the Morris murder, and a warrant was issued and served by Constable Botsford. The latter effected Smith's arrest about 9 p.m., and while on the way with him to Decatur a band of ten or fifteen masked men suddenly presented themselves before Botsford and bid him release Smith. He did so, and was then told to "go home," a thing he performed expeditiously. In the meanwhile the rescuers or releasing party paid their attention to Smith, and by making ominous threats of hanging and burying "right there and then" they induced him to disclose some facts touching the mystery of the Morris murder. It is understood that Smith at first denied all knowledge of the matter, and was swung up a few times until finally he "allowed" he had received letters intended for M. D. Matteson, but directed to himself. What else, if anything, was said by him is not "on the street," and no one knows who constituted the masked party. It is just a touch of the lynch law awakened in one of the most quiet and law-abiding communities in the world over the mystery, or rather over the inability to solve the mystery by the regular law proceedings of the horrible tragedy enacted in the Morris homestead mansion last September. Smith is at large.[3]

The same week *The True Northerner* detailed the arrangement between Smith and Matteson concerning incoming mail:

Smith's examination was commenced on Tuesday, as mentioned above. Constable Botsford was called to the stand and testified substantially as follows, as reported it us by one who was present: When he arrested Floyd Smith the first time, he was met by a party of unknown men who halted them on the road and forcibly ejected himself and his assistant from the cutter, and after securing Floyd Smith, put him back and told him to "git," which he did. He had no knowledge of what occurred after that and to the time he made his second arrest on Friday last, except what Floyd Smith told him. He also testified that Smith further said that Matteson came to him (Smith) the day after the murder of Morris, and said that they would detain and examine his mail at the Post Office and to avoid that he (Matteson) had caused his mail matter to be addressed to him (Smith); that Matteson's mail came thus addressed with a private mark on one corner of the envelope to distinguish it from any that might be designed for Smith; that he thereafter received Matteson's mail— some through the Decatur office, some through the Lawrence, Breedsville and other surrounding offices; that Matteson's outgoing letters were delivered to him to be mailed through different offices, and were so mailed. This went on until Smith's wife became alarmed when Matteson's correspondence was turned over to some one else. At this point the case was adjourned until Tuesday, the 30th inst. At nine o'clock in the forenoon. We learn that an immense crowd was present and that the excitement was intense.

The examination of Floyd Smith commenced this morning at ten o'clock before Esq. Haynes. Officer Botsford testified of having conversation with Smith. The latter told him that about three days after the murder of Morris, Matteson came to him and wanted him (Smith) to allow his (Matteson's) mail to come in his name; that a pencil mark on one corner of the envelope would show the letter to be for Matteson. Smith also stated that his wife put a stop to the proceedings. The examination was adjourned to one week from to-day.[4]

But by January 9, the accusations against Smith had been dismissed, according *to The Kalamazoo Gazette:* "Floyd Smith, who was arrested near Decatur, for complicity in the Morris murder, has been discharged because there was no evidence implicating him with the transaction."[5]

The fact that Smith had worked for Charles Morris and that the farm he had moved to bore a Matteson mortgage upon it certainly lent significance to what role, if any, Smith played in the Morris murders. However, as Dana Smith related in 1936, "In my acquaintance with Floyd Smith, while he never brought up the subject, he never seemed to shrink from answering questions about his experience. He maintained that he was innocent, and suspicion to the contrary never ripened into proof."[2]

For Floyd Smith, however, the years left for him to maintain his innocence were not many, and for his young wife, even fewer. He had married 18-year old Alice Rutner, who Dana Smith described as a "frail girl" and "so affected by what had happened to her husband that her health failed and in six months she died at the age of 21 years and 8 months."[2] The 1880 census cites the cause of death as consumption. Her grave in Chamberlin Cemetery, Lawton bears the name "Allie", her death date of June 3, 1880 and interlocking wedding rings. Certainly, at 21 years of age, hers was an untimely death.

Whether it was among the property Milo Matteson disposed of or not, Floyd Smith seems to have lost, or given up, the mortgaged farm in Hamilton Township, for in January 5, 1883, *The True Northerner* reported in its column *Hamilton Correspondence*, "Floyd Smith has been on a holiday visit to some of his old acquaintances here."[6]

By November 1 of the same year, he had landed a new job in Lawton: "Floyd Smith of Decatur, is gathering in the boys' nickels at a new shooting gallery in the old National saloon."[7] But his employment was short lived, according to *The True Northerner*, which reported only three weeks later: "Floyd Smith has left and the shooting gallery is closed."[8]

Floyd Smith did not survive the year. Dana Smith reported that "Floyd Smith lived alone in poor health for five years. His neck troubled him greatly and was chiefly the cause of his death. He passed away in Paw Paw in a building that formerly stood where the National Bank building is now."[2]

Ultimately, on October 30, 1884, *The True Northerner* reported: "Died, at the residence of J. W. Emery, Esq., in this village, on Wednesday, the 22d inst., Mr. Floyd Smith, a brother of Mrs. Emery. He was buried on the 24th inst. In the township of Porter, in the Weldin (later Chamberlain) cemetery."

Only 35 years old, Floyd Smith certainly had suffered an untimely death when he was laid to rest next to his wife Allie. Any undisclosed secrets.

18

JENNIE'S ACCOUNT

As already described, the first person to discover the bodies of Charles Henry and Esther Morris was their hired girl, Jennie M. Bull. She was the daughter of Henry Bull who lived 80 rods west of the Morris homestead, and at the time of the murders she was 24. Her testimony was printed and reprinted many times in numerous newspapers, but according to "A Scrapbook History of Decatur, Michigan", one of the oldest versions of her testimony was reprinted in *The Decatur Republican* in 1903:

Recalling Morris Murder

(The story of the Morris murder as published in the Paw Paw Free Press and Courier of October 2, 1879, was completed with testimony before a coroner's jury and the jury's verdict. The paper is faded and worn in creases and difficult to read, but Operator Howe has done a good job of deciphering and has here preserved the manuscript which otherwise would have been lost to the world.)

The Testimony

Jennie M. Bull, (a girl who had worked several years for the family) testified – "I went away to Geo. Reits' at Charleston, yesterday about quarter past eleven; came home about 4 o'clock; found the house locked; I went home to father's then came back about half past six. They (Mr. and Mrs. Morris) told me they went away about noon to John Gould's in Porter; they had a horse named "Raish" and single buggy. The clock struck 8 as I blew out my light before retiring. They were both at the barn feeding colt when I went up stairs. There was no one around here when I came home. I heard them talking after they came back from the barn; don't know when they retired. I walked to Charleston alone. I heard no noise in the house during the night, but a jar. (She explained that she did not know what it was or suspect anything wrong and went to sleep again.) I slept over the dining room, just over the door where Henry was found on the stoop. My stair door was shut but not fastened by a catch—was ajar. The inside lock on the porch door was fastened by a catch for fastening the bolt of the lock. While we were eating our lunch, Mrs. Morris said, "Jenny, did any one bring you home?" I said no. She said, "there are buggy tracks that turned up the lane from the east", but nothing more was said about the buggy.

When I woke this morning my arms were numb. I awoke and saw the sun up, and wondered why I was not awakened and got up this morning about half past six o'clock. I came downstairs and saw Henry lying on the porch as I went by the door. The door was open, but the screen door was shut. All the rest of the doors of the house were locked.

I went out at the woodshed door and went to Mr. Gillitt's, in the tenant house. The hired man was not there. Mrs. Morris while at lunch told me she thought he would not be here tomorrow on account of the sickness of his wife. His name is John Klinger and did not see him when he came. I was at Gillitt's. It was about an hour before I came back.

I ran to my father's from Gillitt's, and came back again with my mother after a little while, for I was afraid to come back alone, and found John Klinger, Mr. Rosewarne, Charley Rosewarne, and my father at the barn and Elias Morris and wife in the house. They came out as soon as I got back. There have not been any strangers here for several days or weeks.

No one working for Henry but Johnny Klinger, he has been here six or seven weeks. Before him Riley Huntley worked for him nearly four years. Johnny came to work Monday and Riley left Tuesday afternoon. Levi Reits worked one month with Klinger. When Reits left here he went to his fathers. He lives on the Goble place, now owned by Austin Charles.

Riley quit working because Henry did not like his drinking, but parted good friends as far as I know.

Mrs. Morris always kept her jewelry in the right hand drawer of the bureau and always locked the drawer when she went away. When I have made the bed I have often found the revolver under his pillow, but sometimes saw it on the washstand, to the right of the door as you enter, after the bed had been made. He generally slept on the front side of the bed next the door. I have been here with them 4 or 5 years, and was intimate with them, so much so that Mrs. Morris would tell me to be sure and lock that drawer if I went away. I guess they hid the money about the bureau but I do not know.

He sold I think $122 worth of hogs at Decatur on Wednesday. "(She did not know whether he got the money."¹

Jennie Bull Phillips 1855–1924

Photo courtesy of her great-granddaughter

139

Two deviations crop up in this testimony compared to other versions. Jennie uses Henry's given name while using Esther Morris's surname. In addition, as opposed to other versions, she does not say that her door was blocked by a trunk, but rather ajar. Despite the fact that so many shots had been fired, that a chase had ensued through the house, and that it would have been difficult to imagine Esther Morris not screaming for help, no wrong-doing on Jennie's part is implied. On the contrary, there are no indications that she was ever considered a suspect in the murders.

Jennie Bull married Fred Phillips in Marshall, Michigan in August 1881. She lived in Kalamazoo and, within 10 years was mother to one son and three daughters. The 1910 Census, listed her as a pastry cook in a Kalamazoo hotel. Fred left Jennie and his family, remarrying in Mishawaka, Indiana, in 1919. Jennie died on April 11, 1924, in Battle Creek at the age of 68 and was buried in Riverside Cemetery in Kalamazoo, Michigan.

19

THE LITIGATORS

Of the army of attorneys employed by Milo Matteson to conduct his business, three should be highlighted: Newton Foster, Jerome Coleman, and Arthur Brown, all subjects of untimely death.

Matteson seems to have had a keen sense as to where to position himself to maximize his influence. Just as he would set up his office in the Unity Building near Chicago´s City Hall later in life, he had opted for the back of Newton Foster´s office in small town Decatur. A simple partition separated him from all the legal proceedings which passed over Foster´s desk.

Newton Foster had studied law after serving in the war effort and had a practice in Decatur with Oscar Field until Field suffered his own untimely death before his 35th birthday in 1874. *The True Northerner* reported:

The Decatur Republican of January 22d, in speaking of the death of Oscar W. Field, says:

Oscar W. Field, Esq., died at his residence in this village this morning, between four and five o´clock. His age was 34 years and 11 months. He has long been a sufferer from lung disease, and for some months has been confined most of the time to his house.[1]

Jerome Coleman had completed his law studies in Ann Arbor and joined Foster in place of the failing Field. Milo often employed Foster and Coleman to witness acknowledgements of mortgages he held, and in the much-publicized Matteson-Morris forgery case testimony, it became clear what degree of care, or lack thereof, was taken, according to *The True Northerner* in December 1873:

NEWTON FOSTER SWORN.

Questioned by the Court.

(Witness shown mortgage in question.) That is my signature, all I remember about it is one day was taking testimony in my office and was requested to witness a paper

by Mr. Matteson, I stepped into his office, Morris and Matteson were there, Matteson said „there is Morris' signature, I want you to witness it,“ my attention was called to the amount of the consideration. I did not see Morris sign it.[2]

In his ensuing testimony, Newton Foster stressed that he was called away from the testimony he was taking and only briefly stepped into Matteson's office. He admitted to having done considerable business for Matteson, but did not socialize with him.[2] Still, the following year showed that there was interaction between them when Foster and Matteson traded properties, according *to The True Northerner* in March 1874: "The Decatur Republican says: 'Newton Foster has bought the Matteson place on the corner of Phelps and St. Mary's streets, giving his former residence on Wheeler avenue in part payment.'[3]

(Author's note: remarkably, the Matteson house stood on the very lot cleared in the 1950's to make way for the Webster Memorial Library. It was here in its Genealogy Room that the author discovered the article with the boldly printed „M.D. Matteson is the Murderer“.)

Whereas Coleman's testimony would prove problematic, Newton Foster's was credible and without doubt, and in August 1877, *The True Northerner* reported that Foster was still representing Matteson in an appeal:

The case of Matteson vs. Morris has reached another point in its course. On the 24th and 25th of July the case or cases now pending between them and growing out of the forgery of mortgages, was argued before Judge Coolidge at Niles; the lawyers preferring to accept the hospitality of the judge and do their work at Niles in his spacious library, where he gave to them and the cases all proper and patient attention.

These cases are attempts to foreclose the mortgages dated Feb. 14 and Feb. 28 by Matteson. The suits are brought in the name of James Matteson, and the bills set up the making and delivering the notes and mortgages and their transfer for value to James Matteson, and then alleges that Morris pretends they are each and all forgeries but in truth they are not forgeries and Morris did sign and execute them at Decatur on the days specified, and then interrogates the defendant calling for his answer on oath whether he did not sign, deliver and execute the papers, but not a question about consideration is put to him. Morris answers that it is true that he pretends they are forgeries—in short, they each and all are forgeries, and if the signature is genuine it was obtained by some fraud or deceit upon him perpetrated in some manner unknown to him.

Besides the notes, mortgages and assignments, the complainant put little testimony in the case. That little was to prove by one witness that Morris was in Decatur Feb. 28: also there Feb. 14, `73; and the testimony of three experts living in Chicago that the forged signatures were just like some Morris showed to them.

The defendant put the sworn answer and a lot of testimony that Morris had no use for the money alleged to have been let him,--was not at that time using any considerable amount, and that when informed that those mortgages were recorded went directly to work to remove them. Also put in proof that Matteson had been proven the holder of other fraudulent notes which, when disputed, were compromised or destroyed. Also a large number of witnesses that the signatures were not his by persons who had seen him write. He also had these signatures enlarged by photograph, showing marked departures from his natural way of writing.

The cases were argued by Mr. Foster for complainant and Mr. G.W. Lawton for defendant. Messrs. Beebe, Bacon and Orville Coolidge were in the case. Judge Coolidge has the cases now under advisement.[4]

Only two months later on October 12th, the newspaper published Newton Foster´s obituary:

DECATUR LOCALS.

From Our Own Correspondent.

At six p.m. yesterday (Sunday) Newton Foster died at his residence in this place. He had an attack of bilious fever at Niles last week, and his wife went there to care for him, but he recovered sufficiently to return home Friday afternoon last. Sunday afternoon at about four o´clock he had a sort of fit, and Dr. Keebles was summoned, but as Mr. Foster had recovered, or apparently so, the doctor returned home. He had hardly reached home when he was summoned again, and when he arrived he found Mr. Foster dead. It is a sudden and severe shock to the entire community. The immediate cause of his death is supposed to be heart disease.[5]

Newton Foster was only 41 when he died. He left a widow and 4 children under the age of 13 surviving him, and was another victim of an untimely death.

Newton Isaac Foster (1835-1877)
Don Foster (1863-1865)

Alleged Photo of Newton Foster   Public Domain

Jerome Coleman, on the other hand, spoke freely of his social contact to Matteson according to his testimony reprinted in *The True Northerner* in 1873:

JEROME COLEMAN SWORN

Questioned by the Court.

(Shown mortgage in question); the signature as a witness is mine, also the signature to the acknowledgment; on June 21st the Sunday School had a picnic, and I left the office at 10 o'clock, played croquet till dinner on the picnic grounds with the little girls, after dinner played with older people, in the afternoon Matteson came and called me to do some business for him, we went to Decatur in a buggy.

BY ATTORNEY FOR THE PEOPLE

We went up stairs and Matteson, after some search, said Morris was not there but he would bring him. I went into my office where they were taking testimony, went from there to the printing office, heard talking and tramping and found the people leaving my office, sat down and wrote, then Matteson and Amos Morris came in, Morris ahead, Matteson threw down the papers and asked me to take Morris' acknowledgment. I asked Morris if that was his signature, he said it was and that the amount $5,018 was right, I signed the acknowledgment on June 21st, between 4 and 5 o'clock, left the picnic between 3 and 3 ½ o'clock, it was a long half mile from the village, was at the office a long half hour before I took the acknowledgment, found several persons in my office, they were still taking testimony. Mrs. Granger was being sworn, saw Morris first in my office, he came in just before Matteson, Matteson came out ahead. Matteson said he wished I would witness the amount, there was no one but Morris and Matteson present, heard the shuffling of feet while I was in the printing office, when I went out of the office I went down in front of the office, went into the printing office to pass away time, was told that Morris was over to Upton's office, it is across the street and about 100 feet, don't know how Morris and Matteson came in together, saw the folded paper, but did not have it in my hand and never saw it before I took the acknowledgment, only read the consideration, heard no conversation between the parties, I asked Morris if the consideration and signature were correct, he answered affirmatively. It was a warm sunny day, think he had a coat on, don't know that he said a word except to answer my questions. Matteson asked where Foster was, said he wanted him for a witness. Foster was not in his office, he had not yet witnessed it, the people had not been gone *from my office to exceed 5 or 10 minutes, went to the picnic about 10 o'clock afoot, a lady went with me, Mrs. Tarnell. Foster is also Notary Public, did not leave the picnic till Matteson came, he came about an hour after dinner, we dined about 1 or half past, have known Matteson 5 or 6 years, in Decatur, his business was money loaning. I did business for him taking acknowledgments, and when Foster was away consulting with him, I have drafted papers, the firm was retained by him, we received $80 for counsel fees if we did outside service we received only our expenses; after taking the acknowledgment I went down on the street and conversed with Mrs. Sherman; Matteson then took me back to the picnic grounds and played croquet. Matteson was not there when I stood upon the walk, don't know where Matteson was, did not see Foster during the time, was near my office it was not sundown, think Matteson was looking for Foster, he left me in the office; Foster and I have talked considerable about the matter, have told him what I have testified to, have talked to others about it, don't know of any money passing between Matteson and Morris, see Morris only occasionally, never had any other business with him, have conversed with him, can't tell the circumstance. He came to Decatur frequently, I see him perhaps 15 times a year, I know the Morris place on the prairie, it is about 4 miles from me. I have been to the house on his place to see the party who resides there, Mr. Jerome Smith, to see what he knows of Morris being to the place to get a load of hay; I have worked hard to get testimony in the case to prove this mortgage genuine, and that Morris was in Decatur on the 21st of June, know that Matteson had conversation with Mrs. Northrup, that they left the picnic grounds together, after he took me back: can't say whether Smith's father followed me to Decatur or not, did not see him there that night, saw him a few nights afterward; had conversation with him, had no talk about the mortgage with him, Smith did not say to me it was wrong to take those children's statement, besides I don't believe Morris ever had the money, I was making a fight for my own personal safety.*[6]

By the next year, however, Coleman was accused of perjuring himself in the course of the forgery case, as *The True Northerner* reported on September 18th:

The examination of Jerome Coleman, charged with perjury committed in the Matteson Forgery case, was had on the 11th inst. before Justice Galligan, and he was held for trial at the Circuit Court. His bail was fixed at the sum of one thousand two hundred dollars.[7]

Apparently, the perjury charge did not hold, but in the summer of 1879 *The Kalamazoo Gazette* reported that he had been arrested again:

Our readers are probably yet familiar with the celebrated Matteson-Morris forgery cases that occupied the attention of the courts so much a few years ago since and that were recently settled. Jerome Coleman, of Decatur, was Matteson's main witness, who testified that he acknowledged the mortgages given by Morris to Matteson. This man Coleman was deacon in the Presbyterian church and his evidence had great weight in the case. Coleman has now been arrested by the government Pension Agent for alleged crookedness in procuring a bounty for a widow. He was taken before the United States Court, at Grand Rapids, and put under bonds for his appearance. S.N. Thomas, of Decatur, an uncle of Matteson's, going his bail. The amount of pension recovered was about $1,500, and it is claimed that Coleman retained half of it for his services, when the law declares what the fees of lawyers shall be in such cases. Coleman's bonds, we believe, are fixed at $3,000.[8]

The True Northerner described Coleman's arrest in greater deal:

MR. COLEMAN'S ARREST.

No mention was made in the Republican last week of the arrest of out townsman, Jerome Coleman, on a charge of taking more than lawful fees for prosecuting a pension claim, because the facts were such that we felt inadequate to the task of explaining them satisfactorily, although we were satisfied that Mr. Coleman had done nothing wrong, unlawful or ungentlemanly in the matter. But a very erroneous and libelous article in the last issue of the Northerner prompts us to say a few words in Mr. C.'s defense.

Nine years ago the attempt was made for Mrs. Lewis to procure a pension from the loss of a son in the army, and, although the claim was known to be a rightful one, after prosecuting it energetically for four years, the call for evidence was of such an exacting nature that the outlook for furnishing the required evidence was very doubtful, and Mr. Coleman having furnished all the money up to that time, refused to proceed further unless she would furnish money to pay expenses. Matters stood thus for some years, Mrs. Lewis calling upon him from time to time, to see what could be done about the matter, and was told by Coleman that if she would furnish the money to pay expenses he would do all he could to get her claim allowed. Finally, in 1878, she, accompanied by her son J.H. Lewis, came to Coleman and prevailed upon him to proceed in the matter at his own expense, offering to enter into an agreement to give him one-half of the first money paid her by the Government, in compensation for what he would advance and the risk he would take, she stating that her relatives, friends and neighbors had been earnestly appealed to, but would not help her to a dollar, and that she would prefer half a loaf to none. This was finally agreed to, and Mr. Coleman then commenced the work—a sort of leap in the dark. If he was successful he would make quite well; if not he would lose all. No one objected to this arrangement so as Mr. Coleman was doing the work, paying expenses and taking great chances on everything; but when the claim was finally allowed and the amount forwarded and paid over according to agreement, then it was discovered that Mrs. Lewis had plenty of friends and relatives who were greatly interested in her welfare, and ready to pronounce the old lady imbecile and the whole matter a fraud.

COMMENTS ON ABOVE.

As we understand the case Mrs. Lewis' claim for a pension was on the ground that an eighteen-year-old son had died while in the army, and that said son was her sole dependence for support. The war closed fourteen years ago, and Mrs. Lewis had a husband who was active and industrious, (so it is said) for a period of twelve years since the close of the war, and who sickened and died but two years ago.

By reference to the above it will be seen that Mrs. Lewis still has a son J.H. Lewis, whom we understand is not by any means a pauper; and beside it is said that she has a daughter, or daughters, who are also above penury, and who would doubtless do something for the old lady.

Well may Mr. Coleman, in the above defense, say that „the call for evidence was of such an exacting nature that the outlook for furnishing the required evidence was very doubtful.“ Probably the government did not understand why and how the old lady Lewis was so entirely dependent on the dead son for support, while she had a husband in robust health, and other sons and daughters alive and healthy, and with her and in her immediate neighborhood.

From the above defense, it would seem that the article in the TRUE NORTHERNER of week before last was not so „erroneous and libelous“ after all.[9]

In fact, Jerome Coleman's guilty plea was reported in The Grand Rapids Evening Leader in March 1880:

United States Court.

Hon. S. L. Withey, Judge

Friday March 19.—United States vs. Jerome Coleman. For charging an excessive attorney fee in procuring a pension. Pleaded guilty. Sentenced to pay a fine of $100.[10]

Although Coleman was disbarred by the Department of Interior on April 16, 1880, he continued to practice in Decatur until The True Northerner reported his death in July of 1884:

Mr. Jerome Coleman of Decatur, a member of the Van Buren County Bar, died at his residence on the morning of the 23d inst. Mr. Cole:man had been dangerously ill for some time past, and his death was not unexpected. The Decatur Republican gives the following brief biographical sketch of the deceased:

„Mr. Coleman was born in Tinmouth, Vermont, in 1833, and came to Michigan with his father, Harry Coleman, in 1836. He was a graduate from the law department of the university at Ann Arbor in 1871, since which time he has practiced law here, though ill health has compelled him to confine his practice mostly to office work, in which he has been quite successful. He leaves a wife and two children. "

His funeral took place at Decatur last Thursday afternoon. After the conclusion of the last sad rites, the members of the bar who were in attendance held a meeting at the office of Parkhurst, Fitch, and Blackman as a committee to draft resolutions, expressive of the respect in which the deceased was held by his professional brethren, and to present the same to the court, with a request that they be spread upon the journal thereof.[11]

Jerome Coleman only lived to be 51 years old, leaving a widow and two children to survive him, an equally untimely death.

Arthur Brown´s representation for Milo Matteson was briefer than that of Foster and Coleman´s, but in 1874, after the first guilty verdict in the forgery case, he argued for a retrial, and The True Northerner showed on May 1st there was no love lost between the Kalamazoo attorney and the citizens of Van Buren County:

There is nothing so very strange about Arthur Brown having a vision, during the time he was making his argument for a new trial in the Matteson forgery case, in which he saw „a lot of old women" attending the trial and „who were continually hissing and ready to hoot," or that the good people of this county appeared to him to be „semi-savages and animals." Seeing that soon after the trial of the case he went into the vision business, in which all manner of creeping and hissing reptiles and serpents gave him infinite trouble by taking possession of his boots and otherwise annoying him.[12]

The newspaper sought more revenge on July 24th:

On account of the visions he saw when he was on it before, Arthur Brown didn´t wet his whistle so often on his late stay among us.—Well, if we can drive him from his cups, he may yet become quite a useful boy. We are glad to be able to chronicle any improvement in that direction.[13]

and again on December 11th:

The following from the Decatur Republican of the 3d inst. tells its own story sufficiently to be understood by all order-loving people.—The Arthur Brown mentioned is the same villain who traveled so far out of his way to insult the good people of this County by bestowing on them vile epithets, while addressing the jury in the famous Matteson forgery case last winter. People should treat him as they would a pestilence:

„Last Monday, before Justice Bennett, Fred. Carlton was on trial for selling liquor.—Mr. White of this place appeared for the prosecution, and Arthur Brown, of Kalamazoo, for the defense. After the preliminaries had been settled and a jury empaneled, it was found that the old game of secreting and „running off" witnesses had been renewed, and the suits were withdrawn. We dislike to speak of some circumstances connected with that trial, which are a disgrace to our town. We speak of the disregard of all rules of decency and order by many of those present. The action of Mr. Brown, in bullying, browbeating, and insulting a Justice, who was too timid to assert the dignity of the Court and stop such proceedings, and in sneering at and insulting the ladies present, was well supplemented by that of some of the crowd, who, encouraged by the presence of a ‚brave leader' from abroad, took occasion to exhibit all the low characteristics of a mob. One prominent Decatur man in particular, who is often conspicuous on such occasions, when the Justice remonstrated with him for noisy demonstrations at some peculiarly insulting language of the little

Justice court lawyer from Kalamazoo, saying to him that he should be compelled to fine him if he did not desist, told him, in a loud and insulting manner to ,Fine and be G—d d---d.' The Justice issued a warrant for him afterward and brought him into court to answer for contempt, but let him off without punishment, probably to glorify over his exploit and repeat it substantially on some future occasion. Whatever may be the opinion as to the merits of these liquor suits, there can be but one opinion among law-abiding and order-loving citizens as to the impropriety of degrading a court of justice by such proceedings. We hope never to see the like in Decatur again. And to those wholesale liquor dealers from Kalamazoo, who are so much interested in the affairs of our little burgh as to come here and assist their bluffing little attorney in encouraging a mob in our court rooms, and who it is rumored have raised a fund to be expended in Decatur in fighting the crusaders, we would very mildly suggest that Decatur can take care of its own internal affairs, and our citizens will not fancy the idea of having Kalamazoo ,forty rod' forced down their throats, whether they wish it or not."[14]

After the motion for a new trial, Arthur Brown´s attentions were diverted away from Van Buren County toward women, prosperity, and politics. Married to Lydia Coon in 1872, when Brown´s affair with Isabel Cameron, daughter of a powerful Michigan politician, became public in the late 1870´s, his wife divorced him.[15] He then invested in a mine in Utah, divorced Lydia and moved there in 1879, becoming active in the Republican Party, and when Utah became a state, he served as one of its first U.S. senators for the short term from 1896 to 1897. Marrying Isabel after his divorce, he had a son, ran a successful law practice in Salt Lake City, and seemed to have settled into a life of respectability. The exception was his 30-year younger mistress, Anne Madison Bradley, despite being married with three children herself. Arthur had met her in 1892, when she was 19. His wife Isabel hired detectives to follow them, resulting in much publicized adultery charges, but his wife refused to give him a divorce. The confrontations between the two women came to a climax when Isabel surprised the couple in an Idaho hotel and after Arthur and his law partner separated the two when Isabel tried to choke Anne, an all-night screaming match ensued. At dawn Isabel returned to her home, and Brown gave Anne a .32 caliber revolver to defend herself.

Isabel died from cancer in 1905, and although her death might have paved the way for Anne and him to legitimize their bond, Bradley traveled to Washington, D.C. where Arthur was conducting some legal work. She checked in as Mrs. A. Brown, took a room next to his, and persuaded a maid to unlock the adjoining door. There, she discovered letters which actress Annie Adams Kiskadden had written to Brown, indicating that their marriage was impending and, in a fit of rage, shot Brown in his hotel room with the very revolver he had given her to defend herself.[16]

Arthur Brown died six days later. At her trial, Anne pleaded temporary insanity, saying that she had woken from a trance when the gun discharged. Powder burns on Arthur´s hands indicated that there had been a struggle. Anne testified that, for years, Arthur had promised her he would divorce Isabel while fathering two sons by Anne. Several wedding dates had been scheduled, but always postponed. In his will, drawn four months prior to his death, Arthur had written, „I have never married Anne Madison Bradley and never intend to", renouncing her sons as well.[17]

Anne was found not guilty, never remarried, and died in Salt Lake City in 1950.[16]

Anne Madison Bradley   Arthur Brown   Isabel Cameron Brown

At 63 years of age, if Arthur Brown´s death was not untimely, it was most certainly unseemly.

One other untimely death should not go unmentioned, that being Arthur B. Thomas. Although not an attorney, Thomas was in the office with Jerome Coleman and Alamanson Matteson the day that one of the Amos Morris mortgages was allegedly witnessed. According to Alamanson's account to Arthur Brown, there was some question as to who should witness the document. Milo Matteson initially did not want his father to be the one, and Coleman suggested that a boy who was present might fill the role. In the account, Brown posed the questions and Alamanson Matteson answered:

Q. Who was this boy?

A. It was Mr. Thomas's boy in the hardware store there at Decatur.

Q. How old a boy was he?

A. I should think he may be 14 years old now.

Q. Was then.

A. No I should think not then.

Q. What is his first name?

A. Arthur I think.[18]

What followed was a tedious exchange of testimony in which Alamanson Matteson avoided providing any substantial information due to poor recollection. What is notable about this testimony is that the Thomas boy, whose first name Alamanson vaguely remembered, was his own nephew, the son of S. N. Thomas, who years later would cover Jerome Coleman's $1,200 bail after his perjury arrest.

Little else is known concerning Arthur B. Thomas, except that he clerked in his father's hardware, and like Floyd Smith and Jerome Coleman, also suffered an untimely death in 1884. He was only 26 years old, and as in the case of Coleman, the cause of death was attributed to Bright's disease.

STABBED IN THE BACK

To understand the possible connection the 1891 Parsons Brothers incident might have had with the Morris murders, it is necessary to return to Floyd Smith and his family. Dana P. Smith, in his 1936 piece for *The Decatur Republican*, maintained that Floyd Smith had grown up on the Leland Wilkins farm about 2 miles straight north of Dolphin Morris' homestead.[1] The 1873 plat map of Van Buren County verifies that the Smith and Wilkens families lived directly across the road from each other:

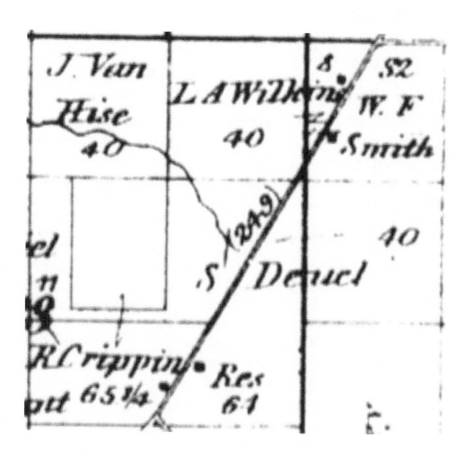

The Smith family consisted of:

Father William Smith and mother Prudence McMinn Smith and their children

Mary E. Smith (1836–1886) married to **Leland Wilkins**

Catherine Jane Smith (1840– ?)

Julia Mary Smith (1841–1920) married to Eden Engle

Jennie C. Smith (1842–1888) married to **John W. Emery**

Eunice Lenora Smith (1844–1925) married to Stephen Weaver

Delia Clarinda Smith (1846–1927) married to **James Christopher Parsons**

William F. Smith (1848–1884) married to Alice Rutner

William F. was listed in the 1850 and 1860 censuses as having been born in 1848., On the occasion of her brother Floyd's death in 1884, Mrs. John W. Emery published a note of thanks in *The True Northerner*[2], and it follows that the youngest in the family must have been William **Floyd** Smith.

J.C. Parsons, also known as "Kit" appeared several times in the local press, once in 1877 in a suit against his brother-in-law John W. Emery. Much later, however, they appear to have become allies, although not always legally, as *The True Northerner* reported in April 1889:

John W. Emery and Kit Parsons of Bloomingdale, were arrested last Saturday by Sheriff McFarlin, charged with a violation of the game laws in spearing fish. They appeared before Justice Mason Monday morning and, on their plea of guilty, were fined $1 each and costs, making a total of $10.55.[3]

The 1870 census shows J.C. still living across from the Wilkins farm in Decatur Township with his wife Delia and brother-in-law Floyd.

210	210	Wilkins L. A.	44	m	w	Farmer	2010
		" Mary E.	33	f	w	Keeping House	
		" Luella	10	f	w	Att, School	
		" Charlie	8	m	w		
211	211	Parsons J. C.	36	m	w	Farmer	2500
		" Dell	24	f	w	Keep House	
		" Harry	4	m	w		
		Smith Floyd	21	m	w	Farmer	2000

But by 1880 they had moved to Bloomingdale Township and lived next to Daniel and Rhoda Fowler.

1873 Plat map Bloomingdale   1912 Plat map Bloomingdale

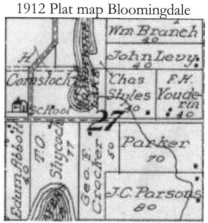

The only disturbance appearing to involve Parsons, that is, before his brother Thomas returned to Michigan, was an altercation in 1884. *The True Northerner* reported a curious assault on July 24 which might even have resulted in another untimely death:

The trial of those two men whom Kit Parsons had arrested for assault with intent to commit great bodily injury came off Thursday. The evidence before the bench

(Smith and Clement) did not warrant the holding of the accused, and they were dismissed on payment of costs. At the solicitation of one of the parties we concluded not to mention names.[4]

Then, in July 1890, the simple news item in *The True Northerner* could have been accompanied by rumblings and dark clouds approaching from the west: "Kit Parsons has a brother from California visiting him."[5] In fact, Parsons had two older brothers, Daniel and Thomas. All three brothers had joined the war effort, Daniel dying in the Andersonville prison camp in 1864, and Thomas, according to his own account, confined to Libby prison for sixteen weeks. In 1870 he headed for California where he spent the next 20 years.[12]

Shortly after Thomas returned to Michigan, *The True Northerner* announced the death of Parsons' 68-year-old neighbor Daniel Fowler.[6] His widow, Rhoda Savage Fowler, was left to fend for herself and run a farm, as their only child Francis, had succumbed to typhoid fever in 1874. So it was that in January 1891, at 61, she married Kit Parsons' 55-year-old brother Thomas.[7]

Whereas the brothers might have benefitted from having adjoining farms, matters between them quickly soured, according to *The True Northerner* in August 1891: "Thos. Parsons was before Justice Mason on the 30th ult., charged with assaulting his brother, J. C. Parsons, jury trial. Not guilty. Complainant paid the costs."[8]

Followed on September 2 by:

It seems that the Parsons Bros. are to have still another tilt in court. This time it is rumored that Tom is arrested for slander. That fellow has a bad tongue and seems determined to use it, whether in court or out. He opened a broadside on Postmaster Smith last week and used language that would cause a Fejee (sic) Islander to blush with shame.[9]

Then, by October, the animosity between the two brothers had escalated into a stabbing:

The Parsons brothers (Tom and J. C.) of Bloomingdale township have been in a continual jangle for a year or more past, and two or three lawsuits have resulted from their differences. Tom was recently released from jail on bail for this appearance at the circuit court to answer to a charge of slander preferred by his brother. Their farms are adjoining each other, and a few days ago some cattle belonging to J. C. got into Tom's fields and he shut them up as hostages for damage. J. C. went over to his brother's house, prepared to pay all damages and take his cattle away, but the occasion afforded too good an opportunity for a row to be neglected, and it was improved with a zeal worthy a good cause. Tom pulled a murderous looking knife from his sleeve and proceeded to cut and carve his brother after the most approved western method, inflicting two wounds in the back and another on the arm. Tom is in jail pending an examination Friday before Justice Mason. We are not informed as to the seriousness of the injuries inflicted.[10]

Within a matter of weeks, however, Tom Parsons managed to divert the attention from the assault to charges that his brother Kit had aided and abetted the Morris murderer. *The True Northerner* reported on December 2:

Any reference to the brutal Morris murder that occurred on Little Prairie Ronde over thirteen years ago is sufficient to attract immediate attention, hence the county papers are now all agog over a statement made by Tom Pearsons (sic), one of the actors in the stabbing affray at Bloomingdale last month. It seems that a suit for slander is now pending against Tom, brought by a man commonly called "Kit" Parsons, and that the former now tells a wonderful story of a confession made to him by Kit, in which the latter owned to complicity in the crime and said that the much sought for Jim Mattison (sic) did the killing. Though this is possible, it gains little credence from dispassionate judges, and we hardly expect to see this long talked of mystery unraveled.[11]

The sensational news, however, was not confined to county papers. *The Chicago Herald*, picked up the story on December 2 and ran Tom's detailed claims as front page news: (Author's note: The name Matteson is misspelled throughout the article as Mattison. Floyd Smith is referred to as Lloyd, and the Parsons name is misspelled as Pearsons)

MAY REVEAL A FRIEND.

LIGHT ON A MYSTERIOUS MURDER.

The Approaching Trial of the Pearsons (sic) Slander Suit Likely to Disclose the Author of a Hideous Crime Committed in Michigan Years Ago.

Paw Paw, Mich., Dec. 1.—The coming trial of a slander suit between Thomas and Christopher Pearsons, it is believed, will throw light on a mysterious double murder committed in this vicinity several years ago.

On the morning of Sept. 29, 1879, the people in the vicinity of Little Prairie Ronde, Van Buren County, were startled by the announcement that a young man of the name of Charles H. Morris and his wife were brutally murdered the evening before in their own house, which was situated about sixty rods from the public highway on a farm owned by Mr. Morris. Appearances indicated that the fiend who perpetrated the foul deed called Mr. Morris to the door and shot him down as soon as he responded to the call. His body lay on the porch just outside the door. His wife had evidently heard the shots and ran to see if she could be of any assistance to her husband, when the murderer turned and fired upon her. She ran through two large rooms, their bed-room, and into a closet, where she apparently hoped to immure herself from pursuit. Several bullet holes were found in her body.

A neighbor's boy met a white-faced horse, which he knew to belong to Mr. Morris, bearing a man swiftly away from the Morris residence. This horse was found at daylight the next morning in the streets of South Bend, Ind., foaming with sweat and overcome with fatigue. The fiendishness of this act created a fever of excitement throughout the whole community, which lasted for weeks. A man by the name of Lloyd (sic) Smith, who lived on a farm belonging to M. D. Mattison (sic) and who held a large mortgage on the Morris farm, was seized by a mob and nearly strangled to death by hanging, in order to make him divulge some clue as to who did the murder. The attempt was unsuccessful, and this poor fellow died some two years later, presumably from the effects of exposure and unjust treatment.

MAY DISCLOSE THE CRIMINAL.

The man Mattison above mentioned had been tried on a charge of forgery, in which it was alleged that he signed the mortgage against the farm belonging to young Morris, and after the murder was committed there were many rumors afloat concerning him. Detectives kept careful watch over all his movements, and the authorities intercepted his mail, to prevent which he had it come in the name of Lloyd Smith, hence the suspicion that Smith was cognizant of who committed the crime. It is still a mystery who did the fearful deed, but light may be thrown on the matter when a certain cause now pending in the Circuit Court for Van Buren County shall be brought on for trial.

A short time ago Christopher Pearsons, better known as "Kit" Pearsons, brought an action for slander against his brother Thomas Pearsons, the slanderous matter being, as alleged, that Thomas charged Christopher with having received $800 for his alleged complicity in the Morris murder. Thomas was given notice that on the trial of said charge he will justify those statement his version of the matter is as follows:

When Thomas was thirteen years old his mother disowned both of the boys, and both enlisted in the union army, serving throughout the greater portion of the war. Thomas was taken prisoner and bore the hardships of Libby Prison for sixteen weeks, during which period he was reduced in flesh from 170 pounds to ninety-six pounds. In 1870 he went to California and was there for twenty years, returning in June a year ago and went to visit his brother "Kit." The latter was very desirous that Thomas, who had brought about $1,000 in cash back with him, should make his home at their house. This Thomas would not agree to do, and as an inducement "Kit," as alleged, told him how he had made money without working and that he knew he could do it again.

He then went on to say, as Thomas declares, that he received $800 from M. D. Mattison for conveying the murderer of the Morris pair from his, Kit Pearson's house, to the scene of the crime, some twenty-five miles distant. He said the name of the person who did the shooting was James Mattison, a brother of M. D. Mattison, who had for many years been an outlaw in the State of Texas.

Some Corroborative Facts.

It is a fact that this James Mattison had been here some weeks previous to the murder a guest of his brother at Decatur, and that some two or three weeks before the murder was committed Jim Mattison disappeared, ostensibly returning to his home in Texas.

"Kit" says, as alleged by Thomas, that, instead of going to Texas, Jim Mattison came to his house in the night, where "Kit" secreted him until his departure should have been forgotten, and that he Pearsons took a double team and buggy and carried Mattison to the Morris homestead. Arriving there, it was agreed between them that "Kit" should stand guard outside the house and Jim Mattison should do the bloody work. If there was any suspicious movements or fear of being surprised in the act "Kit" was to give three notes of warning on a policeman's whistle, with one of which he was provided. After the shooting Jim was to go into the barn, take this white-

faced horse and fly for his life, and when he was ready to mount for his flight if all was well each was to give three whistles. According to the story told him by his brother, Thomas Pearson alleges that this was done and Jim Mattison made his escape. "Kit" then returned to his home near Bloomingdale, arriving there just before daylight Monday morning.

What gives plausibility to this story told by Thomas is the fact that the officers investigating the crime traced a buggy from the home of Kit Pearsons to the Morris place and back, that a distinguishing feature of the buggy was that one of the tires was fastened on with a wire, the track of this wire being plainly visible in the road, and also the fact that at the time the murder was committed Thomas Pearsons was in California and knew nothing of the crime until his return a year ago, when it was told to him by his brother.

Alleged to Have Received the Money.

Tom says that "Kit" told him he was to receive $400 for taking the murderer to the scene, and $800 if he should prove successful in putting Mr. and Mrs. Morris out of the way, and that because of the complete success he received the full amount, with which he purchased forty acres of land, which now constitutes half of his present farm. There has been bad blood between these two brothers for the past year, and at one time "Kit" had Thomas arrested for assault and battery, but Thomas was acquitted of the charge. Thomas is now in jail upon another charge preferred by "Kit" of assault with intent to do bodily harm.

Thomas Pearsons is rather a slender, sandy-complexioned man, fifty-five years old, of short stature, with a keen, determined gray eye; is of a nervous temperament, and impresses one with being a determined and, when aroused, a desperate man, and he swears that if "Kit" commits any further depredations upon him or his that he will surely and certainly take his life.

The result of this trial for assault is awaited with a great deal of interest, but it pales into dimness compared with the deep interest there is in the slander suit, and the public are breathlessly hoping that the case will develop some clues to one of the most atrocious deeds in the criminal history of Michigan.[12]

A part of Tom's story which lent it credence was the description of the 40 acres which Kit allegedly bought with the $800. On the 1873 plat map, two farms of 40 acres each lay adjoining the Fowler farm.

Parsons might have initially bought the George Gay farm, then added the E. Calkins' farm later with the alleged bonus.

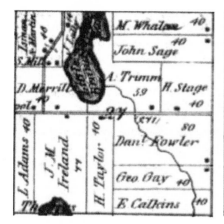 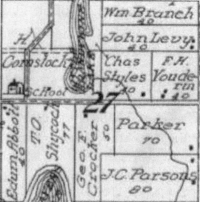

Whether fact or fiction, Thomas Parsons' description of the crime in a major Chicago newspaper was so detailed that Milo Matteson was forced to respond the very next day, his statement already included in Chapter 12 "Gilded Chicago".

By January 29, 1892, *The Muskegon Chronicle* reported that a three-day trial in Paw Paw had culminated in a guilty verdict for Thomas Parsons:

At Paw Paw the case of Thomas Parsons for stabbing his brother has been on trial in circuit court for three days. Yesterday the jury brought in a verdict of assault with intent to do bodily harm. The complaining witness was his brother J. J. C. Parsons. This was the case in which it was expected that some light would be thrown on the Morris murder mystery, but nothing was developed.[13]

The True Northerner then announced the sentence a week later: "The trial of Tom Pearsons (sic) for stabbing his brother Kit, which was on trial as we went to press last, resulted in his conviction. He was sentenced to four years at Jackson, to which place he was escorted by Sheriff Thomas on Monday."[14]

But in October of 1892, *The Jackson Citizen Patriot* reported that Thomas had been moved to the asylum in Ionia: "*John Garvey, Thomas Parsons, and Geo Wilson, demented convicts, were taken from state prison to the asylum at Ionia on Friday. Garvey was sent from Jackson, Wilson from Alpena and Parsons from Van Buren, the two former for theft and the latter for assault.*"[15]

Rhoda divorced her volatile husband of two years in January 1893[16] and lived only two more years, according to *The True Northerner* in October of 1895.[17]

The news of Thomas Parsons' removal to Ionia was his last known available record, but J. C. and Delia Parsons survived Thomas' accusations and lived on their farm until 1920 and 1927 respectively. During that time records show that their home remained open to family members. In 1896 Floyd Smith's brother-in-law died at the Parsons' farm, according to *The True Northerner*: "Mr. Wilkins died at Kit Parsons on Tuesday morning, of old age, being nearly 80 years old. He used to live between Lawton and Decatur. The remains will be interred in the Decatur cemetery."[18]

Only two months later, *The True Northerner* reported yet another death at the Parsons' farm: "Mrs. Grace Trim died at the home of C. Parson's last Thursday."[19] According to the certificate of marriage to Charles Trim in June 1894, Grace Laverne Smith's father was listed as Floyd Smith, her mother as "unknown", and her age as 18.[20] Oddly, she is not listed in the 1880 census with Floyd and Alice Rutner Smith.

But the family ties are significant as a daughter, Floy Laverne, was born to Charles and Grace Trim in 1895, only sixteen months prior to her mother's death, and censuses show that J. C. and Delia raised their grand-niece on the farm in Bloomingdale until her marriage to Leroy Belt in 1920.

James Christopher Parsons died on August 2, 1920, at the age of 76. Delia Parsons, last surviving sibling of Floyd Smith, died on November 27, 1927. The couple and memories of all that they had witnessed were laid to rest in Robinson Cemetery, Gobles, Michigan.

As for Thomas Parsons' revelations, there are three possible explanations. First, they could have been a product of Parsons' imagination and a scheme to divert attention from the assault charges he was facing. Or most simply, the claims Parsons made could have indeed come from his brother Kit's confessions. Or finally, the wagon track with the wire mark is so reminiscent of vigilante accusations concerning Floyd Smith, one must wonder whether Tom Parsons turned theories involving Floyd Smith into a case against Kit to even the score.

Whether Tom Parsons' version of the Morris murders holds water or not, what emerges yet again is the claim that James Matteson was Little Prairie Ronde's most famous murderer. Thus, the time has come to turn attention to the man whose own son described him as "the wickedest man he ever knew."[21]

21

THE WICKEDEST MAN

Although the initial community reaction in 1879 was that Milo Matteson had been behind the Morris murders, fingers quickly pointed to his brother James, because on the day of the murder, Milo and his wife had been especially visible in church and socializing at the Duncombe House. The Pinkerton investigation dealt extensively with James' whereabouts prior to the crime. The speculation only increased with the accusations Thomas Parsons brought to light in 1891. Even Milo's obituary in *The True Northerner* ended with "Had Jim Matteson been arrested, and he would have been if he could have been found, he might not so easily have proven an alibi."[1]

Merritt James Matteson was the older of the two brothers, born in Cherry Creek, New York in 1844. By 1865 he is listed in the U.S. Census as a "seaman on lake".[2] The lake referred to was likely nearby Chautauqua Lake, where, from 1863, steamships across the 17-mile lake between Mayville and Jamestown.

"Chautauqua": one of 15 steamships in service on the lake until her boiler blew in 1871.

While the 1870 U.S. Census shows the Matteson family in Decatur, Michigan, James is not listed[3]:

773	Matteson Q.M.	48	1/2	W	Logging Camp	3m	9m	New York
	"	41	3	W	Kuflg hohu			Ohio
	M.C.	35	4	W	Learning mom		675	New York

Whether he was still in New York or boarding with another family in Van Buren County, on August 22, 1872 he married 20-year-old Annie Robertson in Decatur. She was from Ontario, Canada, and lived with the family of her step-brother, Decatur physician William Ross. In the record of their marriage, James was listed as a "school teacher".[4]

One pupil who was subjected to Matteson's cruel teaching methods was Sarah Graham Norton who published her reminiscences in *The Decatur Republican* in 1928:

I will never forget my first experience at school. One morning mother let me go to school with Alice Smith and Elzina Perry. The teacher shut me in a closet because I could not remember a word. I was so frightened that I did not want to go to school again for a long while. When Cala Longwell came there to teach, I went my first term to her.

At that time they did not have school on Saturdays as the parents wanted the help of the larger children. In those days they hired men to teach the winter terms and lady teachers for the spring and fall terms.

When I was about old enough to go to school they began building the new school house which is the present East Decatur building remodeled.

The two Waters' children, Quinglas and Nettie, and my brother and I had some good times going and coming from school. We had a lot of different teachers as so many of them only taught one term, which might be of two, three or four months. A teacher seldom stayed a full school term.

The worst teacher or master we ever had, was Jim Maddison (sic). No matter what the weather was if we were not on the grounds when the last bell rang, we were not allowed to enter until recess or at noon. He became so cruel that the pupils all left school. The action school board tried to discharge him but he had his contract and claimed they could not discharge him, and he refused to go.

It was in the contract that he was to board around. Each family was to board him so many days or weeks, according to the number of children they had of school age.

He went to the school house each morning and built a fire and remained there all day alone, not a pupil came. He studied law until the end of the term and drew his salary the same as though the full quota of children were there every day.[5]

At times during the 1870s, however, James spent time in Texas. The Pinkerton agents quoted Milo in their investigation report:

"In regard to his brother Jim he said, he and his father had had a great deal of trouble with him, that Jim had been a wild boy, they had furnished him with $10,000 with which to go into business in Texas but he had never been successful, they did not know what had become of the money, he had been in business in Austin, Texas, but he had never been able to learn what had become of the money."[6]

The *Weekly Democrat Statesman* confirmed one of his business ventures in Texas in February 1875:

USURY.—A judgment has been obtained in the District Court of Travis county against Daniel A. James, in favor of one Mattison (sic), *which gives some idea of the blood-sucking power of money lenders. In September, 1873, Mattison loaned James $160 at ten per cent a month. Sometime thereafter $60 was paid upon the note, but a jury has now found James indebted to Mattison in the sum of $957. Who ever heard of such a result? Yet, it is so, and we feel almost ashamed to tell it.*[7]

Furthermore, only a week after the Morris murders, James Lucy, an Austin detective, provided William Pinkerton with more insight into James' time in Texas:

"Austin, Texas, Oct. 6, 1879

"Dear friend William:

"I received yours of the 3rd inst making inquiries in regard to one James Matteson. My information up to the present writing is as follows: M. J. Matteson was indicted by Grand Jury of this (Travis) county in the spring term of '77 in two or three cases for perjury and swindling; he gave bond, which he at once "jumped", and has not been seen here since. He speculated in notes, and was a money lender and pawnbroker on small scale, was a good horseman and pretended to be somewhat of a horse trainer and driver. I am also informed that he taught negro school in this

169

state; had a wife with him here, was embroiled in two or three law suits on account of his money lending proclivities. Was not a drinking man or a gambler while here, but exhibited a great desire to make money with little regard for the fairness of his transactions. When he jumped his bond here he was supposed to have some money probably four or five thousand dollars. In his money transactions he showed a desire to lend his money in "burnt proof" style, so that no one might be able to collect anything from him by garnishment or attachment, and would operate through a third party or loan in another name than his own, pretending to be simply an agent for some unknown party. His bond was forfeited here, but through some flaw or other the forfeiture was set aside by the court and bondsmen relieved. It is supposed that Matteson has money here now in the hands of a party that is operating for him. I have not been able to ascertain Matteson's present whereabouts up to writing, but have just learned that information may be had here that will locate him, which I will endeavor to get at once and notify you. I suppose that M. J. Matteson is the one you want beyond all question as he was the only person ever known here by the name of Matteson. There was a J. B. Matteson who lived here some four years ago, went from here to Rockdale, William Co. Texas, set fire to his saddlery shop and burnt it up for the insurance, for which he is now under indictment in William Co.; he is still in this state and can be found, but I am satisfied M. J. Matteson is the man you want, and I will take great pleasure in attempting to locate him which I think will be done in two or three days at the farthest and will notify you at once."

Signed, James Lucy[8]

The wife to whom Detective Lucy referred was most probably Annie Robertson Matteson, as son Ralph DeLeo Matteson was born in Austin on September 17, 1877[9], but whether James was still in Travis County at the time or had fled is unclear. By January 1878, however, *The Cedar Falls Gazette* announced the arrival of a new teacher M. J. Matteson: "Changes in Teachers—M.J. Matteson, of Minnesota, has been employed to take charge of the department taught last term by A. H. Nye."[10]

Once again, James Matteson found himself in a classroom situation, but this time it took less than four weeks for his volatile side to surface which *The Cedar Falls Gazette* described in February 1878:

On Wednesday morning of this week the excitement was intensified by an altercation between M. J. Matteson and T. L. French over a ferruling given Jesse French the day previous. Without entering into the particulars which led to the difficulty we may briefly state that on Wednesday morning Mr. French told his boy to go over to the school house and get his books. The boy said he would not dare to, when Mr. Fench said he would go with him. Arriving at the school house just before school opened, and meeting Mr. Matteson, words were exchanged that will not be justified nor excused. Referring to the use of his (French's) name on the day previous in an insulting manner before the school, Mr. French opened upon Mr. Matteson with very harsh language. Words followed words, when French started down the steps and Matteson started back in the school room. The latter soon reappeared and ordered French to leave, which he refused to do. French had arrived at the foot of the steps and Matteson was on the second step from the bottom, when hostilities again opened, and Matteson drew a large ten inch Colt's revolver, dealing a heavy blow that sent him reeling to the floor, at the same time inflicting a horrid gash over the left eye. Two other blows were struck after Mr. French got up. He is cut in the forehead, on the side of the jaw, and on the top of the head. We should here state that Mr. Matteson justifies his attack on the grounds of self defense, as he claims that Mr. French put his hand behind him and took an attitude as though he were going to draw a revolver. Mr. French states that he had no revolver with him.

A warrant for Matteson's arrest was issued at once on the charge of assault with intent to commit murder, the Board going his bail. The hearing will take place to-day before Esq. Knapp at 9 o'clock.

We cannot say how serious the wounds on Mr. French may prove. It is feared that serious results may follow, and that he may lose the sight of one eye.

We give only the facts as near as we can learn them. Of course there are statements and counter statements afloat, and there are many details which enter into this difficulty, which we omit. We await the result of the suit now pending, leaving our readers to judge for themselves whether the revolver is needed to enforce discipline in a civilized community, such as Cedar Falls claims to be.[11]

The *Buchanan County Bulletin* also described James' assault on February 8: "A school teacher at Cedar Falls, named M. J. Matteson, made a savage assault upon T. L. French last week, inflicting blows upon the head with a heavy revolver, which were deemed serious. The origin of the row was the whipping of French's boy by the teacher. French went over to see about it, and a war of words ensued between him and the teacher, which ended as above. Matteson was arrested on a charge of assault with intent to murder."[12]

M. J. Matteson was to be prosecuted for his actions, but by the trial date, according to *The Waterloo Courier* in October 1878, the defendant once again had disappeared: "State of Iowa vs. M.J. Matteson. This is the Cedar Falls school teacher who assaulted T. L. French. Defendant not being present, the bail was declared forfeited, but permission was given to produce defendant at next term of court, or prove his insanity. Particulars of his recent doing will be found in another column."[13]

A detail here which should not be overlooked was the phrase "or prove his   insanity."

Whether James' wife Annie needed any persuading or not, after the pistol-whipping in Cedar Falls, the Mattesons persuaded her to divorce him. The notice appeared in *The Daily Inter Ocean* in June 1878: "Divorces.—1,797, Alice E. Ives from Charles W. Ives; for cruelty—1,941, Annie Matteson from Merritt J. Matteson; for adultery."[14]

It is impossible to say whether adultery was actually behind her grounds for divorce or not. The Mattesons told the Pinkerton agents that they had encouraged Annie to do so. According to their report, she herself stated that "she obtained her divorce because James was insane."[15]

James' next caper warrants an element of skepticism. If insanity had to be proven in order for Jim to escape the Cedar Falls attempted murder charge, what happened on Chautauqua Lake on November 4, 1878 certainly filled the bill. As many national newspapers did, *The True Northerner* reported the incident:

A Life-Struggle with a Maniac.

On Saturday last a rather finely-dressed and well-appearing man landed at Fair Point, Chautauqua lake, and engaged board for a fortnight at the Palace Hotel. There was nothing unnatural in his appearance, nor did it seem at all remarkable when he attended church on Sunday morning and bowed in fervent prayer near the altar. People, noting his conspicuous position, looked with admiring wonder on the man who, regardless of the scrutinizing vision of the whole congregation, manifested his religious zeal in the most emphatic manner. On Monday morning the stranger strolled out near the lake, and there met Mr. George Irwin, a somewhat noted duck-hunter, who had just come in with his dog and gun. The stranger affably greeted Mr. Irwin, and asked to be allowed to examine his gun. Mr. Irwin unsuspectingly handed over the weapon, when the stranger carefully examined it, then cocked it, and, holding it toward Mr. Irwin, asked him how he would rather die—would he prefer being drowned to being shot? Mr. Irwin, regarding the question as a joke, replied that, if it was necessary to die right there and then, he preferred taking a turn in the water. It was then that the stranger's eyes glared with maniacal frenzy, and, dashing the gun upon the sand, he grappled with the now-terrified Irwin. The struggle was a desperate one. The maniac was a powerful man, and, with an iron grip, dragged the sportsman to the water's edge, when the struggle for life and death became even more desperate. Finally, they both went into the water, and, while floundering there, some men who stood at a short distance ran to the rescue and were scarcely able to release the victim from the maniac's clutch. His clothes were nearly all torn from his body, and he was terribly bruised by the brief and fearful encounter. Just about this time a small steamer came to the dock. It required four strong men to put the maniac on board. He was taken to Mayville and lodged in jail. He persistently refused to give his name, declaring as a reason for his conduct that it was necessary to sacrifice some life to the consecration of the Sunday-school ground at that place; that he had been chosen as the instrument of death. He seemed to talk sanely about the matter, and regarded Mr. Irwin as an unappreciative man, because, as he said, it was clearly in his power to shoot Irwin upon the spot, whereas he had given him his choice of death, and when about to yield his preference four worldly friends appeared upon the scene and interfered.—Erie (Pa.) Dispatch[16]

While the stranger refused to identify himself, Alamanson Matteson described the same incident to a Pinkerton agent in October 1879 as a sign of his son's insanity:

This same date in Chicago, the operative in the vicinity of A. M. Matterson's was approached by A. M. Matteson and asked if he was not looking for his son James, as he had noticed they had been watching the house for some time past. He said that it was a year since James had been around the neighborhood. He then began giving the operative a sketch of Jim's life. He said James disappeared once for a long time, and at last he received a letter telling him that his son was confined in the Insane Asylum at Dewittville, N.Y., and after he had been there about six weeks he made his escape. He said that once when James was going along the road some place in Iowa, he met a man, and taking from him his gun, gave in his choice either to be drowned or shot. The man preferred to be drowned, and so James threw him into the river, and he would have drowned had not assistance come. The old man said that James had been deranged a long time, and that it had caused much trouble to him and his family, so much so that he had advised James' wife to get a divorce.[17]

Even the Cedar Falls assault victim reached the Pinkertons in a letter dated October 18, 1879:

"I noticed your remarks about the Mattesons, and I am surprised to learn that his folks live in your neighborhood. I had been informed that he or his folks lived in Chicago, and have had some track of him since the occurrence at Cedar Falls. He undertook to kill a man in New York state last summer, at or near where the Champlin boys used to live. Who gave you your information, and what prospects are there that the detectives will get him? I do not know as I want him, but we don't want to forfeit his bail bond. I recollect of reading about the murder you speak of in Michigan, and if Matteson had the law suits and indictments against him you speak of, there can be no doubt but what he is the right man. Some of them pretend to say that he is crazy; that he is a terrible desperado there is no question, and I am only afraid he will come to my back sometime. He tried not to have me prosecute the indictment against him, and caused a letter to be written to me. This was in the summer of 1878. I do not want to meet him again, and hope he will soon be locked up as he is a dangerous man."

Signed, T.L.French, of Adams and French, Sandwich, Ill.[17]

Is it possible that James orchestrated his show of insanity to avoid the attempted murder charge in Iowa? If so, Chautauqua, New York would have been a perfect setting. The Chautauqua Assembly had

quickly spread across rural America since its beginnings in 1874 as a summer educational camp for Sunday school teachers. It became a form of entertainment which would later rival vaudeville for popularity. Choosing the Mother Chautauqua setting at Fair Point maximized visibility, and if James had indeed been a seaman on Chautauqua Lake back in the 1860s, he would have been intimately familiar with the Chautauqua-Mayville-Dewittville steamship triangle. From his fervent prayer near the altar on Sunday to the shoot-or-drown ultimatum on Monday, James would have been able to assure an immediate entry into the Mayville jail, and considering his behavior, an easy transfer to the Asylum for the Insane in Dewittville. If his father's account was correct, maintaining that he had escaped after only six weeks, then James had proven a plea of insanity and, by the onset of 1879, had regained his freedom.

As to Matteson's whereabouts prior to the Morris murders, the only indication found was in the 1891 Chicago *Herald* story of the Parsons brothers. The *Herald* wrote,

"It is a fact that this James Matteson had been here some weeks previous to the murder a guest of his brother at Decatur, and that some two or three weeks before the murder was committed Jim Matteson disappeared, ostensibly returning to his home in Texas.

"Kit" says, as alleged by Thomas, that, instead of going to Texas, Jim Matteson came to his house in the night, where "Kit" secreted him until his departure should have been forgotten."[18]

Kit Parsons' farm just south of Bloomingdale was about 20 miles north of Decatur. In Allan Pinkerton's report to Elias Morris on October 14, 1879, he described a peculiar confrontation about 10 miles west of Bloomingdale:

Tuesday, Oct. 14, 1879

K. met you at Dr. Broderick's house this morning, and heard about the same statement as above related; also that a man living in Decatur named Botsford, and who used sometimes to do dirty work for Hart Matteson had called at your house the other day, and said he had changed his mind in regard to Matteson and now thought that hart Matteson was concerned in the murder, and in speaking about the team that was met upon the road the night of the murder, he (Botsford) said that he believed that Floyd Smith was the man who drove that team, and that Smith took the murderer over to Henry's house, and leaving him in the vicinity drove back home again, and it was decided that K. should see Botsford and get his statement, as you thought he could be trusted although he used to work for Hart Matteson. It was also decided that K. should see Ed Arnold, a merchant who has been working hard on the case, and who you thought had some important information to give. Dr. Broderick brought in Mr. Arnold and the following is his statement.

Statement of Mr. Arnold.

On the 8th inst I went to Breedsville to fix the postmaster in regard to any letters that Hart Matteson might leave there or any that might come for him. The postmaster informed me that on the week previous a couple of letters were put in the night box of his office, and he is quite certain that the man who put those letters in the box drove a small black horse, but could give no further description of him, and could not remember to whom the letters were addressed, but the envelopes were a little larger than the ordinary size and of a reddish color. I arranged with the postmaster so that I will know of any letters that Matteson mails, or any that come for him. I went from Breedsville to Grand Junction and fixed the postmaster there also; and in conversation with John Wright, owner of a saw mill he related to me the following circumstance which happened at his house on the 6th inst.: Wright and his wife were away from home and left a servant in charge of the house. While they were about a stranger came to the house and inquired for Mr. Wright; the girl informed him that Mr. and Mrs. W. were not at home, but that Mr. W. would be in shortly, and invited him to a seat in one of the rooms. The stranger took a seat, and the girl went about her work; her duties were such as to cause her to pass the room door in which the stranger was seated. Once she looked into the room and could see nothing of him, she stepped inside, and as she did so the stranger got out from behind a safe that is in the room, where he had been crouched down as though hiding from someone; she wanted to know what he was doing there, and he replied "Oh! Nothing"; some other remarks passed between the two, and she went about her work again; and in passing the room again discovered, in company with another girl, that he was not there. She found him in the sitting room examining some books and papers that lay on the table. The second girl asked him if he wanted to see Mr. Wright. He said he did, and she advised him to go down to the mill where he might be, but the man said he would as leave wait where he was, and after remaining a while longer he went out and towards the town. When Mr. Wright returned the girl told him of the peculiar actions of the stranger, and gave him a description of the man. Mr. Wright went immediately down the street, and meeting the stranger, asked him what he meant by skulking about his house. The stranger put his hand to his hip-pocket as though to draw a pistol (and Mr. W. saw a pistol in his pocket) and stated that he was a physician and had called at Wright's house to see if he did not want some medicine. Wright informed him that he did not want any medicine and did not believe he was a doctor. The fellow then drew from his inside coat pocket a bundle of doctor's prescription blanks, and wanted to know how he would come by those things if he was not a physician. Wright allowed that anyone could get those blanks from any drug store. They bandied words for a while, and the stranger finally made out a prescription for Mr. Wright of which the following is a copy:

Fluid extracts of Dandelion -- $\mathfrak{z}i$
Golden Seal -- aa
Princess Pine -- aa
Buchen -- aa

Wahoo -- ff ½
Port Wine – ½ pt.
M. Leg. 1 tablespoonful 3 times per day ½ hour before meals.

The heading of the original prescription blank was M. M. Dale, druggist and apothecary, South Haven, Mich., and at the bottom the stranger wrote his name as Dr. G. M. Bates. Drs. Rose and Broderick assert that the prescription is not made out proper, and that no regular physician would have made it out as it is. K. has therefore written to M. M. Dale enclosing the prescription and asking for information regarding Dr. H. M. Bates. Mr. Wright stated to Mr. Arnold that while talking with this stranger he noticed something about his eyes that seemed familiar, and gave his description as being about 5 ft. 10 inches high, rather slim build, but broad shouldered, kind of hollow chested, had dark or sandy short burnside whiskers, and heavy mustache, and the points of the mustache extended across the face to the side whiskers. At this point in Mr. Wright's description, Mr. Arnold asked him if he ever knew Jim Matteson. Mr. Wright started suddenly, and bringing his hand down hard upon the box on which they were sitting, exclaimed, "By George, that was the man!" and said the man had dark eyes, and he knew Jim Matteson and was quite positive that this stranger was he, who said also, that he would visit a couple of small towns first and finally bring up in Kalamazoo. It is said that Jim Matteson is a very eccentric individual and the actions of this man at Mr. Wright's corresponded exactly with some of his former capers.[19]

In speaking with the Pinkerton agents, Alamanson and Eunice Matteson gave contradictory accounts, once claiming they had not seen James for about a year, and another time, for three months. The father, however, was well-versed on the incident at Chautauqua and the subsequent asylum escape at the end of 1878, although Matteson had declined to disclose his identity, and no names had been mentioned in the press. Mother Eunice even went as far as to say they had felt for four months that James was dead, but offered no evidence of this.

Acquaintances and neighbors attested to having seen Matteson after the murders. Allan Pinkerton reported:

"This date in Chicago, operative W. again saw the man Harris who lives in the vicinity of A. M. Matteson, and who thinks he saw Jim Matteson last Wednesday night (October 2nd). Harris said he knew through his brother William Harris that Jim Matteson had to get out of Texas for some trouble with a mortgage. Harris further said that A. M. Matteson had been in the habit of selling milk to the neighbors, but this morning he told the children who came after it, that he would not sell any more milk; this would indicate that he wished to keep people out and away from his house. The operative learned today from the neighbors of A. M. Matteson, that the morning after the murder he had gone around telling them that there had been two murders committed near where his boys lived, and it was thought the hired man did it, as he had had a quarrel with the murdered parties that same day. He also told them that he had a mortgage on the farm of the murdered man for $11,000; and that his son Hartman D. Matteson had written him that he did not dare to leave his place, the people were so excited about the murder, and thought that he knew something about it. Hart D. Matteson's wife also told one of the neighbors' wives that her husband was liable to be shot at any time for taking cut throat mortgages; the neighbors also say that when the Matteson boys come to their father's, they generally come and go in the night. Last night old man Matteson seeing the operatives around the house, and suspicioning what they were there for, got very drunk. Today the old man left with his horse and buggy about 11:30 a.m. and returned at 6 p.m."[17]

Another neighbor had seen James according to the report: "The operative then saw a Mr. Southwick who lives one door south of A. M. Matteson, who said that he had seen James around within three months."[17]

When the Van Buren County Board of Supervisors and the Morrises called off the Pinkerton investigation after a month's time, the Matteson name disappeared from the local press, as did James Matteson himself. His name appeared in only two instances, the Tom Parsons accusations in 1891 and Milo Matteson's obituary in 1912. The community had possibly seen enough litigation with the family and did not want to risk a slander law suit once again. Even Arba Moulton, the venerable editor of *The Decatur Republican,* having kept the story of the Morris murders alive in his readers' memories for more than 50 years, avoided printing the name. Toward the end of his career, he devoted an entire column to James without naming him. Even at such a late date, he danced around specifics, writing:

An incident which adds interest to the story relates that the man whom public sentiment aided by circumstantial evidence, at the time associated with the murder as the possible murderer, was at one time the teacher of the East Decatur school. At the beginning of the term he entered the school house with his arms full of law books and during the term, devoted more time to the latter than he did to the unfortunate children whom he punished so cruelly at the slightest offense. Because of this the children were, one after another, removed from the school by their parents, until there were only four or five remaining. About that time the School Board called upon him and demanded his resignation. He laughed in their faces and told them to read his contract, reminding them that he, himself, had drawn the contract and they had signed it, and he defied them to undertake to force him to resign from the school. He assured them that they would find that they had made a mistake.

He then proceeded to order his four or five remaining pupils to busy themselves with bringing in the wood and piling it up around the stove in the school house. He used the wood to heat the room while he studied law for the remainder of the winter.[19]

Moulton's whole article seems to deal with Jim Matteson, a final reckoning for the 78-year-old editor who would retire the following year, and yet, not naming him. He added:

Another incident, which may be of interest, was related to the writer by Mr. Elias Morris. It was reported that shortly after the murder, a letter was received by the Sheriff of Van Buren County, from the landlord of a hotel in Washington or some far western state. It contained the information that a man answering to the description given in the newspapers of the supposed murderer was there sick in the hotel. Acting at once upon this suggestion, the Sheriff left immediately for that point. He discovered upon his arrival that he had seen this same man about Van Buren County in the days before the murder. So he took a room in the hotel to wait for the man to recover sufficiently in order that he might return him to Van Buren County; however, instead of recovering, the man evidently recognized him, apparently grew worse instead of better. So, after waiting a few days and finding the man still too ill to travel, learned, to his consternation, that his prisoner had eluded him in the night and made good his escape from the hotel.[19]

The final nugget of information which Moulton left to his readers, again avoiding names, clearly refers to James Matteson´s son Ralph. A graduate of Northwestern, he then went on to pursue a law degree at the University of Michigan.

Ralph DeLeo Matteson

Upon graduation in 1903, leaving Ann Arbor to return to Chicago, Ralph felt the need to make a stop at Elias Morris´s home. Moulton wrote:

„Another circumstance which might be interesting to add to this article is a story given the writer by Mr. Elias Morris, and uncle (sic, brother) *of the murdered man, some years after the murder occurred. A young man called at his home one day to inquire if this were Mr. Morris. He stated that he came to ask for the story of that occurrence in detail; that he was ashamed and sorry to say that he was the son of the man supposed to be guilty and declared that his father was the wickedest man he ever knew. He said that his father had contrived to have*

himself appointed administrator of his father-in-law's estate (the maternal grandfather of the young man). This man was very wealthy. In the end he appropriated the estate's money for his own use, deserted his family, and was never again heard by them until the murder occurred. (Mr. Morris was glad that the young man had told him his father was dead at the time of his call upon Mr. Morris.) The young man had, by the way, just been graduated from the University of Michigan, and stopped off upon returning from college to his home in the West, for the purpose of obtaining the correct version of the Morris Murder.[49]

Merritt James Matteson is the ultimate loose end of this story. The trail of money and death ends here, as no record of where and when he died has been found to date. The Chicago City Directory of 1887 listed Annie as the widow of M.J.: "Matteson Anne. Wid. M.J. h. 528 W. Lake"[20], possibly the case, as when Alamanson Matteson made out his first will in 1894, only one son was mentioned, and the codicil in 1897 then mentioned grandson Ralph.

Where did James Matteson disappear to after the events of 1879? Probably not New York where he had escaped the insane asylum at Dewittville, and probably not Travis County, Texas where he had jumped bail, and probably not Iowa where he was wanted on charges of attempted murder. The idea that Jim's flight turned to the West is not all that hard to imagine. If not Washington, as Moulton's article in *The Decatur Republican* suggests, perhaps the mountains of Colorado where many outlaws fled, and extradition was not a given. Although he had been away for long intervals, with a penchant for creating trouble, it was James whose name appeared on the earliest mortgages in Decatur. He had testified in the Amos Morris mortgage cases, the family had entrusted him with $10,000 to conduct business in Texas, and there were witnesses who had allegedly seen James in Chicago and in Van Buren County at various times in 1879. Had the business ventures the brothers shared in the early 70's really ended, as Milo maintained, or might future detectives uncover clues as to James' fate elsewhere? For these sleuths, while Milo rests in Graceland Cemetery among Chicago's giants, the lid on James Matteson's coffin remains wide open.

APPENDIX

THE WIDOWS

EMMA HATHAWAY PRITCHARD COPLEY VINCENT

Even before Marshall Pritchard's death, his wife broke the mold placed on most Victorian housewives. Growing up on the "prize farm of Cass County", she had enjoyed an education, and in Cherry Valley, Illinois, taught school directly across from the Pritchard home. After Marshall's murder, she spent time with her family back in Michigan, but on returning to Cherry Valley, she was appointed postmaster.

Perhaps her mother Naomi's death, who had instructed Indian chiefs that "White bread costs money" or two of her sisters' deaths in 1890 drew Emma back yet again to Little Prairie Ronde:

Naomi Olney
Hathaway
1802–1889

Phebe Hathaway
Grimes
1835–1890

Jane Hathaway
Copley
1827–1890

Emma's sister Jane had been married to Alexander Bennett Copley, who came to Little Prairie Ronde only a few years after Dolphin Morris, and the Copley home was situated directly across the road from the Morris homestead. Because the Morris wealth was primarily tied up in land, Alexander Copley, his son, and his grandson, all presidents of the First National Bank of Decatur, were the successors to Milo Matteson's money loaning activities. Two years after her sister's death, Emma Pritchard married her brother-in-law Alexander, enjoying a summer house in Bay View, Michigan, and wintering in Jacksonville, Florida, until a trip to Havana in 1899 when Copley fell out of a carriage and did not regain consciousness.[2]

Emma returned to Cherry Valley and was later briefly wed to Gilbert Vincent, an old acquaintance from Little Prairie Ronde, divorcing him in 1908 on grounds of desertion.[3] According to Emma's obituary in 1917, she "was a woman of culture, being a contributor to magazines during the later years of her life."[1]

ANNIE ROBERTSON MATTESON BENGOUGH

Annie Robertson was originally Canadian, born just east of Toronto in Whitby in 1852. Her half-brother, William Ross was a physician and emigrated with his wife and two children to the United States after the Civil War. By 1870, Annie Robertson was living with William's family in Decatur.[4] She married school teacher Merritt James Matteson in Decatur on August 29, 1872,[5] and three years later, at the young age of 36, her half-brother, Dr. Med. William Ross died, another untimely death.[6] It may have been his estate which, according to his son, James had attempted to appropriate, for shortly after, records show he had left Decatur for Travis County, Texas.[7]

Annie gave birth to Ralph in September 1877, and by January 1878, James was in Cedar Falls, Iowa, once again on a collision course with his pupils' parents. After her divorce was granted, Annie maintained contact with the Matteson family in Gunnison, Kenosha, and Chicago. She was an educated woman as well, setting up a private school in Gunnison in 1882.[8]

It was after Ralph graduated from law school and then headed for Colorado in 1905 that Annie took time to revisit her roots in Ontario. There she met an old friend with whom she had gone to school in Whitby, John Wilson Bengough, a Toronto alderman as well as cartoonist, editor, and publisher of the political and satirical *Grip* magazine. Bengough was a progressive as Annie was also interested in social reform, and the two were married in 1908.[9]

It seems that Annie Matteson's second husband was the exact opposite of her first. Rather than brandishing an oversized revolver, Bengough armed himself with wit, was a proponent of women's suffrage, and had his wife accompany him to such far places as Hawaii and Australia.

John Wilson Bengough

Annie was a strong proponent of women's suffrage herself, and in 1913, as one of the vice presidents of the National Equal Suffrage League of Canada, she was among the 5,000 women who participated in the Women's March in Washington, D.C., overshadowing the Inauguration of Woodrow Wilson a day later.[10]

The Toronto World, March 16, 1913

Sadly, Annie Robertson Matteson Bengough did not live to see Canadian women acquire full suffrage in 1918. She passed away on November 22, 1917 in New York City and her final resting place is next to her husband John Wilson Bengough in Toronto, Canada.[11]

Author's note: an odd memorial stands in the Oshawa Union Cemetery, which borders on Whitby, Ontario, where Annie and John Wilson Bengough had gone to school together. It is a memorial to Annie's half-brother and reads "In memory of Wm Ross M.D. of Decatur, Mich. Died Apr. 28, 1875." As Ross's family became Chicagoans after his death, this memorial was probably placed in Oshawa by Annie herself.

LAURA SHILLING MATTESON

It remains a mystery whether Laura Matteson ever knew that she was not the first Mrs. Milo D. Matteson. In March 1867 *The Jamestown Journal* announced the marriage of Mr. M. DeHart Matteson of Cherry Creek and Estella Aldredge (sic Aldrich) of Rutledge, New York.[12] But then, only three months later, *The Daily Inter Ocean* gave an unusually detailed account of their divorce:

Milo De Hart Matteson vs. Estella Matteson. Bill for divorce. The bill states that the parties were married at Rutledge, in Cattaraugus county, New York, on the 17th day of April last; that the complainant has conducted himself as becomes a dutiful husband, but that the defendant has committed adultery with one George Sager, and has forgotten her marriage vows in numerous other cases with persons to the complainant unknown.[13]

It would be another twelve years before Laura Shilling became Laura Matteson and less than two years to leave the turmoil in Michigan for the mountains of Colorado. She seems to have fit the refined Victorian mold better than Emma Pritchard and Annie Matteson, dedicated to entertaining and music rather than to the family's dry good business, which expanded beyond Gunnison to Cripple Creek, Victor, and Aspen.

Shilling's Dry Goods, Cripple Creek   Denver Public Library Special Collections

Her contact with her father and brothers seems to have been sporadic. Besides the break-up of Matteson & Shilling after Milo emptied his father-in-law's till, Laura is left unmentioned in both her stepmother's and father's obituaries

In 1903:   *DEATH OF MRS. SHILLING.*

Word was received in the city yesterday to the effect that on the night before Mrs. I. W. Shilling died at her home in Colorado Springs. Mr. and Mrs. I. W. Shilling came to Aspen in 1884 and remained here for nearly ten years. They conducted one of the big dry goods and clothing establishments in the city. Afterwards they moved to Cripple Creek where they conducted a store on similar lines. There were two sons, step sons of the wife of I. W. Shilling named A. B. and C. H. Shilling. Old Mrs. Shilling was well known in the city and was a very prominent worker in the Presbyterian church. Her many friends and former acquaintances will recall her and sorrow over her decease.[14]

And in 1908:   *DEATH OF MR. I. W. SHILLING:*

Word was received in the city yesterday of the sudden death Monday of the Hon. I. W. Shilling, from a stroke of paralysis, at the home of his son, H. A. Shilling, at Victor, Colo.

Mr. Shilling was the father of A. B. Shilling of Grand Junction and H. A. Shilling of Victor, and would have been 86 years of age next month. He was on his way to California and had been in Victor a couple of days when death overtook him. He will be buried in Colorado Springs on Friday by the side of his wife, who died several years ago.

All old residents of Aspen will remember Mr. Shilling who, with his sons, conducted a large dry goods store here a number of years ago under the firm name of Shilling & Co.[15]

Back in Chicago, Laura could fully lead the life of refinement she had pursued in Gunnison, first in the residence on Dunning which was passed on to Milo's nephew, then at 1843 W. Wellington (later 515 W. Wellington after street renumbering), an imposing greystone which could accommodate 400 guests. The Chicago *Daily News* reported one such occasion in 1903:

An orchestra stationed in the hall gives a programme of music. Mrs. Matteson is gowned in white French bouton with point de venise and opalescent lace, and Mrs. Matilda Randall wears black lace over red. Mrs. Tabor Randall is in tan voile with trimmings of Irish point lace. The house decorations are elaborate. White hyacinths bloom in the drawing room. This evening the hostesses will entertain two distinct companies, the one at cards and the other with dancing, the dance being the last of a series of ten similar affairs. The ballroom will be decorated in Japanese effects.[16]

As the 1911 Chicago City Directory lists the Mattesons at 2618 Lakeview Avenue, Milo apparently lived long enough to look out over Lincoln Park from his new, luxurious highrise. After his death in 1912, Laura remained here, sharing the building with both of her sons. Without Milo at her side, Laura's grand receptions for 400 seem to have been relegated to the past. But she became a distinguished matron socialite listed in the *Chicago Blue Book*, a member of the Amateur Music Club, the Chicago Woman's Club, a Life Member of the Chicago Art Institute, and in 1917, a new director of the Women's Musical Society.

However, the transparency which the society pages brought to a wealthy widow could be harmful, as the Chicago *Examiner* reported in May 1915:

Evening Dress Robber Escapes; Gets $500 Gems

Mrs. Milo Matteson and Son Interrupt Lake View Avenue Flat Bandit

Chicago's gentleman burglar, clad to the minute in every detail of correct evening garb, appeared last night at the apartment of Mrs. Milo Matteson, 2616 Lake View avenue.

Mrs. Matteson must have had a premonition that all was not right in the apartment. She had been dining with her son, De Forrest Matteson, who occupies the apartment on the first floor at the same address. When dinner was concluded, she asked another son, Randolph, to accompany her upstairs.

"I'm afraid," she said.

FIND ARMED MAN.

Her sons laughed, but Randolph went ahead to open the door. The first thing that met his eyes was a young man in evening dress, who appeared very busy examining articles in the dresser drawer.

The busy stranger turned about. He drew a silk handkerchief from his pocket, wiped his hands and then replied to the query: "What are you doing here?" by whipping out a revolver.

"I'm sorry," the immaculate *young man said, "but I'm afraid I shall be compelled to ask you to remain silent. It might be well for you to place your back against the wall."*

OTHER SON HEARS CRIES:

He stepped out of the apartment, as Mrs. Matteson was about to enter. She screamed as she saw the revolver.

Her cries were heard by De Forrest Matteson, who armed himself and ran from his apartment. But the gentleman burglar had escaped. Matteson fired five times at the man in full dress, without result.

A search of the apartment showed jewelry valued at $500 was missing.[17]

And in December of the same year:

Burglars got $700 silverware, home Mrs. Milo Matteson 2616 Lake View.[18]

When the Chicago Civic Opera moved to its new home in 1929, the inaugural performance of "Aida" drew the creme de la creme of Chicago, and throngs of spectators gathered to see the prominent ticket holders. The Chicago *Daily News* reported:

Passage into the theater was difficult, for those who were not attending the performance inside the house were assembled, in ample time and record-breaking numbers, to watch the show outside. Probably not half a dozen of the persons who passed the gantlet of curious spectators thronging the spacious outdoors corridor on the east front of the building had ever so keenly felt what it was to be a personage, spied upon in the more ceremonial moments of life. Yet everybody, who by hook or crook, had procured a ticket to the opening performance had by that very fact become somebody of importance and it was well that the world should be there to look on.[19]

Reporting on the event, June Provines described "a beautifully gowned elderly woman, who was present at the opening of opera at the Auditorium and who came from California to attend this opening: name, Mrs. Milo D. Matteson."[19]

Fifty years had passed since the infamous Morris murders. No scars seem to have remained from the turmoil in Decatur. Laura must have relished her Chicago socialite role, and while she never attained the social station of a Bertha Palmer who could spend several hundred thousand dollars a season at her soirees in London and Paris, she navigated herself through the Great Depression in the luxury of the Marlborough overlooking Lakeview Avenue.

Laura Ann Shilling Matteson passed away on July 17, 1941.[20] She had weathered the rumors and inuendo during her pregnancy in Decatur and had travelled across the dusty plains with an infant son to a country where the native population was still struggling against the white man´s invasion. Even in frontier Gunnison, she pursued the culture she valued, and once back in Chicago, where she had married Milo one week after Marshall Pritchard´s assassination, she found a broad spectrum of cultural opportunities and reveled in them. Laura Matteson was laid to rest in the family plot in prestigious Graceland Cemetery, just a stone's throw from the Potter and Bertha Palmer mausoleum. Although a trail of murder had dogged the family, none could ever be proven. With Laura's death, the trail of money and prominence had come to an end.

Mrs. Milo D. Matteson

Courtesy of Chicago History Museum

The Pinkerton Investigation

Pinkerton National Detective Agency

Chicago, Oct. 9 / 1879

Elias Morris Esq. Decatur Mich.

Sir

A telegram having been received at this office to send a man to Decatur, Mich. for the purpose of investigating a murder, I detailed my son W.A.Pinkerton to proceed to Decatur, where he arrived at noon.

Tuesday, Sept 30 79

After dinner, in accordance with a telegram he received on the train from my Supt. Mr Warner; he called upon M.S.Brownbridge, a livery stable keeper at Decatur; who told him that the murdered parties lived upon a farm 5 miles from Decatur; the circumstances of the murder being about as follows:

On Sunday Sept. 28th Mr Henry Morris and wife, had been visiting one Mr John Gould, and returned home about 7 p.m. after doing the chores about the house, with the servant girl, who had also been about during the day, they all retired; the servant girl did not hear the least disturbance during the night, but upon getting up the next morning, she found the dead body of Mr Henry Morris, outside the door, with two bullet holes in it, and the body of Mrs Morris lying in the little closet off the ante-room, with four bullet holes through her.

The Morris´ were eminently respectable people, nor had so far as known any enemies, with the exception of Milo D Hart Matteson, who has been lawing the family for some time, claiming to hold mortgages for certain property, which the Morris´ claim were forgeries and never issued to, one of which for $11,000 issued in 1873 with the interest, now amounted to about $22,000 purporting to be executed by Henry Morris to Milo De Hart Matteson, and by the latter transferred to his father A.M.Matteson, now a resident of Chicago.

Hart Matteson follows the business of a usurer, loaning money at exorbitant rates of interest to farmers then taking mortgages on everything they had; in other words he was a dealer in cut-throat mortgages, and of course was universally despised throughout the whole country; this man Hart Matteson claimed to hold a mortgage against a brother of the deceased Henry Morris, which was contested, and proved to be a forgery; the case was carried to the Supreme Court, but the judge resigning before an application could be granted, Matteson got out of it in this way, the case was finally compromised by Amos Morris, paying $900 to Hart Matteson, the amount which he had actually borrowed from him.

In the case of Henry Morris vs. Matteson; Morris acknowledged that he had borrowed $600 or $700 at various times from Matteson, and Mrs Henry Morris´ signature was not on any mortgage held by Matteson, and it was expected by every one, when the case came up for trial, that the mortgages held by Matteson would be proven to be forgeries.

Henry Morris and wife were known to live happily together, and to have enjoyed the respect of every one; Matteson was known as a bad character, a man who would do any thing to make money, he had a brother James, who was a worse character than himself, who formerly lived in Texas, and was known as a horse trainer, had also been a school teacher.

„The idea is,“ – said Mr Brownbridge – „from the knowledge which the murderer evinced, about the premises of Henry Morris, that James Matteson was the man who committed the murder.“

Mr Brownbridge drove W.A.P. to the scene of the murder, and all the indications are that Henry Morris and his wife had just retired for the night, which must have been about half past eight o´clock, after being in bed for some time Mr. Morris was called by some one to the side door of the house, carrying his pants in his hand; immediately on opening the door, a shot was fired, the bullet entering his right breast, as he fell another shot was fired, entering his neck midway of the collar bone, either shot being sufficient to cause death; it is evident Mrs

Morris hearing the shooting, endeavored to come to her husband's assistance, but encountering the assassin at the door, where the first shot was fired at her; she retreated, followed by the murderer, who must have stepped over the murdered man, as she ran through the bed room another shot was fired, which passed through the fleshy part of her arm, and struck a bureau near by, knocking off one of the locks; she retreated still further to the closet adjoining the bed room, where she fell and two more shots were fired at her, piercing the body, and entering the floor; the bullets were of calibre 44, and evidently came from the largest size Colts or Remington army pistol, used principally in Texas and on the frontier. The slugs are in possession of Dr. G.L.Rose.

The assassin after doing his murderous work, evidently went to the barn, picked out the best horse in the stable, walking past several others to get it; the horse he took being a dark brown, or black horse, with a bald face and watch eye, making him a peculiarly marked horse.

The pants which Mr Morris had brought to the door with him, were found curled up in the corner of the barn, showing that the object had not been robbery, as Mr Morris carried no money on his person; the bureau drawer mentioned as having the lock shot off, contained $120, two gold watches, and some other jewelry, these were not touched, nor were any papers or valuables in the house known to have been disturbed.

The servant girl slept immediately above the doorway where Henry Morris was shot, strange to say never hearing any thing of the shooting.

In taking the horse the assassin did not take any saddle or bridle, so it is evident he brought these with him; on Monday morning the horse was found in a vacant lot in South Bend, 40 miles distant, several people met the horse and man, from 9 to 9:30 p.m. on the Sunday of the murder.

The further investigations of W.A.P. developed statements of various parties, which will be found below.

The first man examined was J.W.Phelps who lives at Marcellus 6 miles distant, and is the man who went to South Bend to identify the horse, he knew nothing but what will be narrated better from another source.

The next man examined was H.M.Sherod who lives at Porter Van Buren Co. On the night of the murder as he was driving with his family to Decatur to attend church; about sunset he met a man on foot, of whom he could give no definite description, he met the man close to the town line of Decatur, at the dug out; he said the man veered clear out of the road, as if he did not wish to be seen, and was walking toward the Henry Morris farm; at 9 p.m. as he was returning from the church, he again met a man riding very fast towards Decatur, this was on the Decatur road before it branches off to the South Bend road, he says this man was riding Henry Morris´bald faced horse, and had a saddle, he remarked to his wife that the man must be going for a doctor, he was riding so fast, about 15 minutes after he had met this man on horseback, a man named Kern, who saw nothing of the man, so he must have turned off on the road going to South Bend.

Charles Rosewarn

lives near neighbor to Henry Morris, on the the night of the murder, he was at a concert at West Valley school house, 2 ½ miles from Henry Morris´ farm, on the road to Lawton; at 8:50 p.m. he left there, and raced horses with Emanuel Wiley for a mile, when Wiley reached his home; he came on to the Decatur road and when about 40 rods from the Morris farm, he heard a horse coming very rapidly, when about 5 rods off, he recognized it as Henry Morris´ horse, by the bald face, the man riding it was leaning forward, and it appeared to Rosewarne that his face was covered; the man wore a large black slouch hat, and looked straight ahead, not giving an inch of the road, so that young Rosewarn had to pull out, although he was in a buggy, and the man on horseback, the man made no remark as he passed, he should judge this man was tall and slim; when young Rosewarn reached home, he was so much scared that he did not properly put away his horse and buggy, the clock in his home struck ten shortly after he arrived, which would make it about 9:30 p.m. when he saw the man.

Abner Hathaway

who lives ¼ miles south had also been to the concert, and when near the Warner School House, 4 miles south east, he met a man riding the Morris horse, he thought it was some one who had been sparking his girl, he was walking on right hand side of Hathaway as he passed, thought he wore a stiff hat, and butter-nut coat, his attention was particularly attracted to the man by his large eyes, and he had a ghastly white face; could give no other description.

Will Wright and Ed Gard sitting with a couple of ladies at a farm house beyond, said, the horse passed them on a rapid run; Hathaway did not recognize the horse at once, he could not explain the discrepancy between his and Rosewarne's description, thinks he would know the man if he looked just the same, it was about 9:30 p.m. when the man passed him.

Simon Sherwood

who lives at Gravel Lake, Porter Township, says on night of murder, in company of his wife and three sons, he was on his way to Decatur; between 6 and 7 p.m. they met a man going towards the Morris farm, from Decatur, he was of medium height and walking close to the fence, they would not know the man again; as they were returning home they met a man down in the hollow, on a bald faced horse, the horse nearly stopped, when the man either whipped or spurred him into a rapid gallop.

Lendell Sherwood

with his father Sherwood, he says they were all at meeting in the big wagon, as near as he can recall he was a small man, whom they saw coming through the dug way on foot, when they first saw the man on the way back, his mother remarked that the man was riding very fast, and wondered who it was; when the horse was abreast of them it slackened its speed, but was made to go very fast.

F.L.Kern

is a teacher by profession, lives one mile east of Henry Morris´farm, his brother-in-law John Heise, who lives south two miles, and who was coming there to work, told him that Henry Morris and his wife had been murdered, this was at 6 a.m. Monday morning, Kern at once came to the scene of the murder, accompanied by his brother, and found the bodies as described; when he arrived Elias Morris and his wife were there; Elias looking to see what was stolen; Mrs E. Morris showed him the corpse in the closet, with the head near the door, her night clothing had been partially burned by the explosion of the pistol.

Mr Kern appeared to be a very intelligent gentleman, whose theory was that Mr Morris had been called to the door, (after he had retired) and thinking it was John Klinger, the hired man who wanted him; was shot in the breast, the ball passing through his body and lodging in the door; the second shot was fired very close, since the face and neck were black with powder, the ball entering the neck, close to the clavical bone, lodging in the skin (after cutting the main artery) on the opposite side of the neck.

Mr Kern supposed that Mrs Morris was running to the rescue of her husband, was met in the sitting room and retreated to the bed room, pulling off the bed clothes in her search for the pistol, she retreated still further and as she passed the bureau, the shot was fired which passed through her arm, she then reached the closet, where two more shots ended the life of the already expiring woman.

Mr Kern said his brother-in-law was told of the murder by John Klinger.

Elias Morris

is a brother to the murdered man, and lives one mile south east. Mr Rosewarn his neighbor notified him of the murder, having been told by the hired man John Klinger.

The mortgage about which the trouble occurred was dated 1872, registered in Paw Paw in 1873.

Elias´ brother denied ever having given it to Hart Matteson or any body else; the proceedings were commenced by his brother Henry, to set aside the mortgage, that Milo DeHart Matteson was arrested by Amos Morris for the forgery of a mortgage of $10,000 on his place; Matteson was tried and convicted, at a new trial he was acquitted, having taken a change of venue, he foreclosed the mortgage and beat Amos, who appealed to the Supreme Court, where the mortgage was declared a forgery, Amos paid the costs, the case being compromised and dismissed; Henry Morris´ testimony would stand off Matteson´s and Morris´ wife´s name was not on either mortgage; this was the cause of getting rid of both; unless an adjournment the case was to have been tried at the next term of the U.S. Court. The judge has been favorable to Matteson. Henry Morris´ wife had no children, but she had a right of dower, and exclusive right to 40 acres; Matteson bribed Circuit Court Commissioner to go before judge. Matteson said, altogether the case had cost him $17,000. Since the difficulty Elias Morris had never spoken to Matteson. When the case was being tried Elias Morris sat and looked at Matteson, who with his hand on a revolver, demanded to know of Elias, why he was looking at him. Elias only laughed at him. Jim Matteson a brother of Hart Matteson is a horse trainer, and has a wife in Milwaukee running a millinery store.

The theory has always been that De Hart Matteson got the mortgages, and Jim who is an expert penman did the signing. Matteson had also a lot of notes, purporting to have been given him by Henry for money loaned to him from time to time, and he claimed that these mortgages were security for the notes, and that they were witnessed by Harry Church, office mate to Matteson who now lives in Crown Point, Ind. One instance related by Elias was that some years ago, Matteson came to Henry Morris, and said he had $3000 that he did not wish certain parties to know he had, he would give Henry $500 if he would take the money, and deposit it in the bank in his (H.Mo.) name; Henry did this and shortly afterwards Matteson drove to the farm, and persuaded Henry, who was very busy, to go to town, and draw the money, and a few days afterwards Matteson got the balance with the exception of the $5.00 which was offered. Aside from these two real estate mortgages, there is a paid off one of $1360. There is $180 in bank left there by Amos to pay the amount compromised upon for the $11,000.

Mr Elias Morris says that nothing whatever had been disturbed in the drawer, where the lock was shot off, although there were money and valuables there to a considerable amount; Henry might have a wallet with a small amount in it, but this could not be found.

Concerning the story about Riley Huntley, a farm lad who had worked for Henry Morris; Elias said; Huntley was in the habit of getting on sprees, and had done so once during the pressure of farm work, and finally Henry discharged him, but Riley and the whole family parted on the best of terms.

Samuel Morris

investigated if Jim Matteson had been living at South Bend; but found nothing; Samuel said that if he ever received any money from Hart Matteson, it was in gambling debts, and therefore illegal.

It appears from what Elias Morris says that Milo De Hart Matteson had a billiard table in his office, where he frequently got Henry in to gamble, there they passed sums of money backwards and forwards across the table.

Henry frequently said, if ever he signed his name to any note or paper, it was when he was drunk, and did not know it.

The next statement in order is that of

Jennie M. Bull

who said she had lived on and off with the family for 2 years.

On the day of the murder she arrived home from John Goulds (ed: Charleston) about 6:30 p.m. at that time Mr nor Mrs Morris had not arrived from home but they came shortly afterwards, after doing some chores about the house they went to attend the cows; she retired at 8 p.m. and shortly afterwards heard Mr & Mrs Morris come in with the milk; she said she was very tired and sleepy having walked a great deal that day, and was completely exhausted; she thinks she heard a jar or noise of some kind during the night, but it only aroused her momentarily, and she dropped off to sleep again; she awoke in the morning to find the sun streamng in on her face, and the day well advanced, she knew that it was late and wondered why she had not been called, she felt very drowsy, as if she had slept too much. After dressing she came down stairs, and found the dead body of Henry Morris, she had a presentiment that Mrs Morris was also killed, but she was too frightened to see; she ran as hard as she could to her mother´s about 80 rods distant, and then to the neighbors crying that Henry Morris was killed; she said when Henry Morris came home that night, he changed his clothes for a working suit.

In regard to Riley Huntly, she said that the trouble between him and Mr Morris had never amounted to anything, that Riley left there in the kindliest of spirits with every one on the place, they all came to the door to see him off, and laughed and joked on the best of terms.

In regard to Kelsie Loomis, she said, he was an intimate friend of the whole family, as much so with Mr Morris as with Mrs Morris, and when there the last time was on the best of terms with every one.

She also said when Henry Morris and wife came home that night, he noticed there was a buggy track in the lane, which she had also noticed, and asked her if any one had brought her home, she said „no" and there the matter dropped.

Sam Morris

said he saw a man pass his house at 3 p.m. with a horse and open box buggy.

Dr Curry

also saw the same man, and says he had a flat saddle in his buggy box, he was going in the direction of Henry Morris´. As near as he can recollect the man was 35 years old, dark complexion, light beard about 4 inches long, the buggy looked as if it had been driven hard; he had on a black hat, dark coat, and was a stranger in that vicinity, would probably know him if he saw him again, his upper lip was shaven.

John Klinger

Henry Morris´ hired man; on the night of the murder he was stopping at his mother-in-laws´s (Mrs Heise) house, and coming to the farm on the following morning, he found the body of Henry Morris lying in the door way; very much frightened he ran to Rosewarn's and the other neighbors giving the alarm. Klinger did not have the least idea who could have committed the murder, as Henry Morris was universally liked and respected.

W.A.P. having finished the statements at the farm, returned to town, and took the statement of

Charles Cole

aged 18 years; Hugh Roosvelt, Frank Thomas, and Lou Hendrick who were playing in a big field in Delaware St. Last Wednesday night (that is the Wednesday prior to the murder). They knew it was Wednesday night because it was prayer meeting night, they saw Hart Matteson in his phaeton driving backwards and forwards several times, as if looking for some one; a man whom they saw under the trees near by, answered to Hart Matteson, by whistling to his (Hart's) whistle, then came and got in the carriage with Hart Matteson, when they drove off, this appears to have occurred about dusk, the boys said they would not know the man were they to see him again.

W.A.P. next went to the hotel where he saw Hart Matteson sitting, saying he would like to have a few words with him, he handed him his card, at which he seemed very much agitated, and shook as with the ague. He explained to him he had been taking statements in regard to the Morris murder, and hearing of his financial difficulties with the Morris family, he thought it no more than right that he should hear his statement in regard to them.

Hart Matteson

said he had no objections to talking, the fact was Henry Morris was a splendid young fellow, and they were the best of friends, there never was any trouble between Henry Morris and himself; Henry Morris admitted to him, he owed him this money, and that Henry Morris would never have taken the stand he did, and swear that he did not owe this money, if it had not been for Elias Morris, that the money was given to Henry Morris for a legitimate purpose, which purpose will come up on trial; he said the whole trouble came from the interference of Elias Morris, that he was more the cause of H. Morris´ death than any body else, that there was nothing Elias Morris was not bad enough to do.

(In all his talk Matteson was very nervous and excited).

He said he did not hold the mortgage now, that it had been turned over to his father, whose name was A.M.Matteson, and lived at 22 Seminary Avenue, Chicago.

In regard to his brother Jim he said, he and his father had had a great deal of trouble with him, that Jim had been a wild boy, they had furnished him with $10,000 with which to go into business in Texas but he had never been successful, they did not know what had become of the money, he had been in business in Austin, Texas, but he had never been able to learn what had become of the money.

W.A.P. also learned that Milo De Hart Matteson, accompanied by his wife had attended the village church, and remained there until the meeting was over. Matteson so seldom attends the church that it was noticed particularly. After the meeting was over, accompanied by his wife, he went to the room of the landlady of the Duncombe House, and remained there until 11 o´clock chatting and talking.

My operative J.A.P. leaving Chicago Tuesday Sept 30th arrived in South Bend, in the early morning of

Wednesday Oct. 1/79

Early this morning J.A.P. proceeded to Sheriff Dougherty´s residence, and after making his business known to him, requested his assistance in the soliciting information relative to the Morris murder. The first party seen was

Lyons

whom he found a very confidential friend of Morris´. Mr Lyons said that early on Monday morning (Sept 29) there was a horse found in the 4th ward by a party named Charles Neddo, that it bore the appearance of having been ridden a great distance, and was thought to have been stolen, shortly afterwards they received a telegram from Decatur or vicinity informing them of the murder of Morris and his wife, that he went up to the stable where the horse was being cared for, and identified the animal as the property of Mr Morris, they then set to work to endeavor to ascertain, who had ridden the horse into town, but were unable to get any clue. Mr Lyons said he did not think either Hart or Jim Matteson were known in S. Bend, I don´t believe any one would know them here except myself and some of my partners on the press; he said Hart had an office in South Bend some 4 or 5 years ago, and transacted business there, but he (L.) gave him a terrible raking over in the press; Hart had not been seen in South Bend lately, as for Jim he was supposed to be in Texas, but it was d---d hard to say where he was; Jim is an expert horse trainer, and was very likely to be the party who committed the murder; Lyons said, the horse when found, had neither bridle nor saddle on, but there were marks on the horse, as if caused by the pads of the saddle.

P. next went to the M.C.R.R. depot, made himself known to the agent, whose name is

Geiddings

he said, in reply to a question concerning any stranger boarding the outgoing trains on Monday morning, that he did not know himself, but would introduce P. to his employees at the depot, who would be apt to know, he then took P. to the night ticket agent, but he did not know or notice any suspicious character going away that morning or purchasing a ticket at the office, he then went to the baggage master, and questioned him in relation to the matter, but he didn´t know any thing, they next went to the depot night policeman, but he saw no suspicious characters hanging around the depot.

P. next went to see the Sheriff but he could not give any thing reliable. P. was next introduced to the constable – Keller – as also to the City Marshall, they were both willing to assist, but at present knew nothing.

P. next had a deputy sheriff accompany him to the west section of the town, where they made a thorough search around for the saddle and bridle, but were unable to get any trace of them.

P. next saw

Wm Neddo

who said he was rather late in rising that morning, but on getting up he saw a horse in the rear part of his house, and informed his brother about it, and remarked how fatigued it looked, they agreed it must have been stolen, they went out to look it over, and found it looked as if it had been ridden hard, as its hair was as stiff as bristles, that there was what appeared to be saddle marks upon it, as also marks of a bridle, but it was minus both at that time, I had my brother Charles go up town, and report the thing immediately, subsequently the horse was taken to Mr Gesh´s stable, where it was identified.

P. next went to the M.C.R.R. depot, about a half block from where the horse was found, where he saw

Mr Elliot

the depot agent, who said no suspicious character, he felt positive, had purchased tickets at his depot, and none were seen to go out on the train, or hang around the yard.

P. next went to the Port Huron and Grand Trunk depot, but could learn nothing there.

At the telegraph office P. found a telegram of which the following is a copy,

Chicago Oct. 1/79

„J.A.P. South Bend, Ind.“

„See George Stickney 4 miles from South Bend, on Edwardsburg Road, get description of man he saw riding Morris´ horse, night of murder, ascertain if Jim Matteson, brother of Hart Matteson, money loaner at Decatur, has been about South Bend lately, examine depots for suspicious characters on Monday. F. Warner“

In accordance with the above telegram P. hired a buggy and horse at Mr Gesh´s stables, and got an old resident named Shank to drive him; they left South Bend at 10:30 a.m. on the Edwardsburg Road; Shank could name every party on the way, but he did not know any one named Stickney; they called at every house on the road, and made inquiries from parties in passing teams and wagons, but no one knew Stickney, either as farmer or hired help; the only information they could get in the vicinity of South Bend, was at a farmer's named Bucher, who resides about 4 or 5 miles from the Bend, the parties there informed P. that they heard the horseman go past their place, riding very fast, they thought it would be about ½ past one o´clock, they didn´t see him, they felt positive they could not be mistaken as their house is close to the road; they continued the inquiries all along the road, but failed to find any further trace, until they arrived at Edwardsburg, where they found a young fellow, who had been out visiting his friends at a late hour, the horseman passed him, he took no special notice of him however.

After dinner, they still continued their inquiries along the road, but learned nothing new, they finally reached Decatur at 9:15 p.m. where he met Mr Brownbridge, and related to him what had been done.

As there was some doubt existing in the public mind regarding any connection which Kelsie Loomis might have had with this murder; at Mr Brownbridge´s request P. decided to go to Niles and run the matter to an end; this action would satisfy public curiosity.

Thursday Oct.2/79

P. arrived at Niles about 7 a.m. and soon after called on Mr Tuttle, and presented his letter of introduction from Mr Brownbridge.

After some preliminary conversation Mr Tuttle said he was well acquainted with Loomis, and laughed at the idea of any thing of the kind, as Loomis having any connection with the murder being possible, but he would make inquiries at Loomis´ place of business, and let P. know what he learned.

Soon after Mr Tuttle told P. that Loomis worked up to quitting time on Saturday night, and was on hand promptly on Monday morning.

P. next called on the proprietor of the Pike House, where Loomis boards, and was informed that Loomis was at the hotel up to noon on

Sunday Sept 28th, when he changed boarding places and went to Mrs Words to board, his reason for such action, was that he hadn´t been making full time of late, and couldn´t afford to pay so much board; P. called and was Mrs Words, who told him Loomis had been there on Sunday night, this settled that matter finally.

At 3 p.m. P. took the train for Chicago, it was in charge of Conductor Colwell, who had brought the train to Chicago Monday morning, he recollected of no suspicious characters joining his train, either at South Bend or any other station.

This morning operative E.J.K. had arrived at Niles from Chicago, in regard to this same man Loomis, and to make some other inquiries; he did not see his men at the depot until 3:30 p.m. when he interviewed Conductior Wood, Messenger Smith, Mail Carrier Cooper, Station baggage man Walters, and young Smith , the driver of the Express wagon, but none of them saw any suspicious character or Loomis get on or off the train to or from South Bend.

During the evening K. was introduced to Loomis by Mr Pike, and spoke as follows:

Loomis

He said he had been informed by a man named Huntley, that there was some suspicion against him because he did not attend the funeral of Morris; he explained that Huntley used to work for Morris not long ago, that Huntley got drunk and was impudent to Morris, so Morris discharged him, but there was no ill feeling between Huntley and Morris in consequence.

Loomis said, he had years ago kept company with Mrs Morris, (before she married Mr Morris) and it was supposed and reported that they were engaged to be married, but all such reports were without foundation and untrue, as they never had been engaged to each other; both Mr and Mrs Morris were particular friends of his, he visited them quite often, he had never heard Mr Morris speak of any trouble between him and any one about mortgages, but had never asked M Morris about the matter, simply because Morris would tell him any

215

thing he asked, for that reason, and as he did not consider it any of his business, he had never inquired into the matter, he had visited the Morris' on the 28th of August last and remained with them until Sept. 1st, had never seen them since; it was not his fault, he was not at the funeral, he thought it was to take place last Wednesday, and was surely going to it, did not know it had taken place until he received the „Chicago Times" with the notice, the train the paper came, was the same he ought to have taken to go to the funeral; he expressed deep sorrow for the murder, was shocked to hear of it, and felt very bad to think he should be suspected of participating in such a foul crime.

In Chicago operatives J.C.H. and G.E.W. were detailed to shadow in the vicinity of the house of A..M.Matteson, 22 Seminary Avenue; Arriving at the house about 11 a.m. they took up positions.

At 12:30 p.m. a mail carrier called and delivered some letters.

At 3 p.m. H. passed the house and saw several women in the basement.

At 4 p.m. an elderly man and 3 women came out of the basement and went to Lincoln Avenue cars, the women got on the cars, and the man returned to the house, he again came out at 6 p.m. got a white horse from a vacant lot, and took him to the barn; soon after the women returned, and at the supper table, the one man and 3 women were the only occupants.

The parties in this house act very suspicious, all of them occasionally coming to the front gate, will stand there for some time looking up and down the street.

This morning in Chicago operative M.W.P. went to the L.S. & M.C.R.R. depot, and learned the names of the crew, who brought in the train to Chicago from South Bend on Monday morning Sept 29th.

The conductor was F.H.Palmer, the brakeman Fred Loveman and Wm Hull. The operative found Palmer at the Sherman House, he stated he took on about 10 or 12 passengers at South Bend, one half of which were females, all had tickets, most of them came to Chicago; the only man who acted suspicious, was a man about 5 feet 8 or 9 inches high, thick set, black clothes, black stiff hat, clean shaved face, dark hair; he got on at South Bend, sat down and pulled his hat over his eyes, he had a ticket in his hat, he went to Laporte, was in a hurry to get off the train, in fact jumped off before the train came to a stop, and made away from the depot.

Friday Oct 3/79

Very early this morning operative K. left Niles, and arriving in Decatur in due time, went to bed.

After breakfast K. accompanied Dr Rose, called on Mr Charles, cousin of the murdered folks who knows what Mrs Morris had said about Loomis; she had said that she liked Loomis better than she liked Morris (this was before her marriage), but her people wanted her to marry Morris on account of his wealth, she did not know what to do, and asked Mrs Charles´ advice in the matter, who advised her to marry the man she liked best.

It has been pretty well ventilated that Loomis could have nothing to do with the murder.

Yours respectfully

Allan Pinkerton

Chicago, Oct. 9, 1879

Elias Morris Esq. Decatur, Michigan

Dear Sir:

Enclosed I send you reports up to the 3rd. Last nicht I stopped the shadowing and the inquiries from the vicitinity of A.M.Matteson, being satisfied that we will not be able to get anything further than what we have, and we have made arrangements to get hold of any correspondence. I am not certain that Jim has been there, although some of the neighbors who know him are very positive he was there. We have found his wife, and she declares that she was divorced from him in Milwaukee a year ago, and has not seen him since. His mother and father both tell very contradictory stories. The mother at one time, said she had not seen him for a year, and another time she said he had not seen him for three months. She talks as if she thought Jim might have done it; but only to spite them – the old folks. The old man says he has written to Hart to remain where he is, for if he leaves he will surely be arrested. I will have the rest of the reports written up and forwarded to you.

I think Coe has struck a lead at South Bend of which he has probably informed you, as it was before he went to Decatur. It is amongst the Neddo and Bennoit crowd, and I will have that point looked up, in case it should finally transpire that Jim was not there. I am satisfied now that the man who rode your brother's bald face horse that night had on a mask, and this with the large eyes that were in it is why the boys were scared. This is one reason that made me think it was Jim who put the mask on to cover his beard. You say that we had better arrest Jim at sight; that could easily be done, but we could not hold him 24 hours without more evidence than we now have. And evidence is what we are looking for. If you could get circumstances to show that he was in your neighborhood at the time it would be conclusive, or if any of the Neddos or Bennoits were there. Unless Coe is known at Decatur he possibly might do the shadowing of Hart, but I think it would be an utter impossibility to do it; and a horse would have to be kept saddled and in readiness to follow at any time. A thorough inquiry should be made at every house within 6 or 8 miles of your brothers, to see if anyone was seen around within two or three days of the murder, as it seems utterly impossible to me for anyone to have done that deed at that time of the day without being seen by somebody. You mention about that buggy being seen that resembled Hart's. You will recollect that he took particular pains to prove a complete alibi; and an inquiry might show that his horse and buggy were in the barn. I don't think he would have let his own go out. I should have mentioned before that I received your two letters this morning of the 4th and 8th.

Yours Truly

F. Warner Supt.

Chicago, Oct. 1879

Elias Morris Esq. Decatur, Michigan

The following is a continuation of your report.

Friday, Oct. 3, 1879

This date in Chicago, operative H. and W. were shadowing 22 Seminary Ave., the residence of A.M. Matteson. At 11:15 a.m. two men came out, and entered a buggy which was standing front of the door. One of these was a man 24 years of age, wearing dark grey clothes; the other was a man about 36 years of age, full dark brown beard, rather long, and keen dark grey eyes, wore a suit of dark clothes, and low crown stiff hat, and carried a dark satchel which he put into the buggy; this man was supposed to be John De Hart Matteson. They drove away rapidly, and the operative was unable to follow them. At 4 p.m. the old gentleman, A.M.Matteson returned with the horse and buggy. The women were also away during the day until 6:30 p.m. Operative W. accosted during the day by a man named A.W.Harris who knows James Matteson; he said last Wednesday night about half past 11 as he was sitting on his door step he saw a horse and buggy drive up and turn the corner at a furious gait; the man in the buggy he said was Jim Matteson and he had a lady with him. Harris said he had not seen anything of him since.

Saturday, Oct. 4, 1879

This date in Chicago, operative W. again saw the man Harris who lives in the vicinity of A.M.Matteson, and who thinks he saw Jim Matteson last Wednesday night. Harris said he knew through his brother William Harris that Jim Matteson had to get out of Texas for some trouble with a mortgage. Harris further said that A.M.Matteson had been in the habit of selling milk to the neighbors, but this morning he told the children who came after it, that he would not sell any more milk; this would indicate that he wished to keep people out and away from his house. The operative learned today from the neighbors of A.M.Matteson, that the morning after the murder he had gone around telling them that there had been two murders committed near where his boys lived, and it was thought the hired man did it, as he had had a quarrel with the murdered parties that same day. He also told them that he had a mortgage on the farm of the murdered man for $11,000; and that his son Hartman D. Matteson had written him that he did not dare to leave his place, the people were so excited about the murder, and thought that he knew something about it. Hart D. Matteson´s wife also told one of the neighbors wives that her husband was liable to be shot at any time for taking cut throat mortgages; the neighbors also say that when the Matteson boys come to their father´s , they generally come and go in the night. Last night old man Matteson seeing the operatives around the house, and suspicioning what they were there for, got very drunk. Today the old man left with his horse and buggy about 11:30 a.m. and returned at 6 p.m.

This same date operative C. on his way to South Bend could get no trace of the man seen on conductor Palmer´s train at LaPorte, but a man answering that description had been seen at intervals last month, though (no) one knew his name or business. The ticket agent could not remember seeing any such man at any time last Monday or this week. Monday morning he sold a large number of tickets to Peru and Indianapolis and return. Arriving at South Bend, the first person that saw the horse, the operative learned was a Mrs. Redifer the wife of a horse trader. She was awakened just at daylight by a horse walking on the sidewalk, and looking out the window thought it was a mare belonging to her husband. She woke him, and he said the horse was a strange one. Mrs. Redifer said the horse had a saddle and bridle on. She was not sure about the saddle, it might have been a coat strapped on. The husbands story was the same; except he was positive that the horse did not have either saddle or bridle on.

Sunday, Oct. 5, 1879

This morning in South Bend operative C. drove out to see the Stuckeys and George Zeigler. He wanted to find some one nearer town than operative Powers had seen, who either heard or saw the horse and rider Monday morning. Just outside of town on the hill he found a man named William Dewey. C. noticed the road was hard and he told Dewey what he wanted to know; he said he did hear a horse galloping furiously by his house before daylight Monday morning. His house is so situated that a horse running by will cause the sound to appear to go both ways being in a slight hollow. He thought one of his own horses was loose so got up to see, and by the time he got out he heard the horse running down the road towards town. He judged it was about 3 o´clock in the morning. C. then told Dewey if anyone offered to sell him a saddle to buy it, and he would pay him liberally for it. This took at once, and he began to think and finally said some young fellow offered to sell him a saddle Wednesday morning last and he saw the saddle at the time on a gray horse which the fellow was riding. He called it a Spanish saddle. The young fellow told Dewey that he had bought it the day before. A great many French and others come to get small lots of hay and truck from Dewey and he could not remember who it was that had the saddle. C. asked him to try and think , and rode on. He found Kern Stuckey and asked him if he had heard the horse; he said he had not, and thought Oliver Stuckey also had not heard it, as he too lived off the road. C. asked him if he knew anyone by the name of Stickney; he though awhile and finally said he believed there some Sticksneys who lived somewhere near Edwardsburg, but he knew nothing of them. C. then went on and found George Zeigler, who said at once he did not hear the horse; and this is not surprising as the road along there is very soft loam and sand. He never heard of anyone named Stickney. C. then came back by the way of Bookers and saw Miss Booker whom operative P. saw. She said that he heard the horse distinctly being run at a furious gate as it turned the corner of her fathers house. The road is hard here and turns a corner. She thought it must have been about 1:30 or 2 o´clock. This statement as to time would bear out the statement of Dewey in regard to the time when the horse passed his house, as it is nearly four miles between the two places. C. inquired of everyone on the way back, but found no one else who had seen or heard the horse; nor could he find anyone named Stickney. There is no one named George Stuckey, and the other two Stuckeys, Oliver and Kern, did not hear the horse. On the way back when they got pretty near town, C. searched every hole and corner, behind stumps and along the hedges, in weeds by the side of the road and in every place where a saddle could be concealed. When C. reached Dewey´s again he saw him sitting on the fence; he said he believed he had seen the saddle offered him Wednesday at the house of a man named Williams when he was there on Friday, and he believed it was Joe Williams who wanted to sell the saddle. Joe is a bad one and runs with the Neddo and Bennoit crowd. The man Shank who was driving C. owns the house where Williams lives and will try and find the saddle if it is there, and he thinks he can easily do so. C. does not attach much importance to this saddle story of Dewey´s who he thinks made it up mainly to please him, but it is worth looking into. His story about hearing the horse was far differently told, and is undoubtedly true. C. looked from his place into the outskirts of the town for the saddles, though there is no place only in houses and barns to conceal it, as there is a large common along the road. C. saw where Bennoit and Neddo live, and Tom Cottrell´s wife who is also a Bennoit. Tom Cottrell is a notorious desperado having been sent up twice and is now in Berrien jail, and will probably get ten years at his trial next week. C. finds that these Neddos, Bennoits and Tom and Sam Cottrell are really desperate characters, and Tom´s wife is a perfect little French devil, having nearly killed an officer in Kansas when she was trying to get Tom away. Tom has killed one man and is continually in trouble. Arriving in town again C. saw Mr. Redifer again. He still says the horse when he saw him had no saddle or bridle on. He said his wife seemed to think differently, but he was sure of it. C. spoke of a possibility of the saddle being thrown in the river and that it might be found in that case, and asked him if there was any shallows down the river from here. He said „Yes.“ C. then asked him about the saddle being over in Lowell, where he lives. He said very likely it was, and then C. asked him if he could get it. He didn´t wait for C. to finish, but said „I don´t have a thing to do with the d—n scoundrels.“ C. said, „Certainly not Mr. Redifer, but I thought maybe you could tell me of someone who could work in with that crowd, and get the saddle.“ He thought a while and finally said Lou Kerns, a constable could do it as he was intimate with the Bennoit´s and Neddo´s, especially the women. He said he would give C. an introduction to Kerns in the morning. Redifer seems perfectly sincere in his desire to catch the murderer; at the same time he is unreliable and tricky, and C. feels positive that that saddle is in Lowell and if he doesn´t know anything about it, Neddo or Bennoit does.

This same date in Chicago, the operative in the vicinity of A.M.Matterson´s was approached by A.M.Matteson and asked if he was not looking for his son James, as he had noticed they had been watching the house for some time past. He said that it was a year since James had been around the neighborhood. He then began giving the operative a sketch of Jim´s life. He said James disappeared once for a long time, and at last he received a letter telling him that his son was confined in the Insane Asylum at Dewittville, N.Y., and after he had been there about six weeks he made his escape. He said that once when James was going along the road some place in Iowa, he met a man, and taking from him his gun, gave in his choice either to be drowned or shot. The man preferred to be drowned, and so James threw him into the river, and he would have drowned had not assistance come. The old man said that James had been deranged a long time, and that it had caused much trouble to him and his family, so much so that he had advised James´ wife to get a divorce. He said James knew all about the mortgage on the Morris farm. The operative then saw a Mr Southwick who lives one door south of A.M.Matteson, who said that he had seen James around withing three months. The operative also learned that A.M. Matteson had told some of the neighbors that if James did commit the murder he must have been insane; and that since James was thrown from his horse three years ago he had never been right in his head. He has also said that James was in Australia, to others he was in Texas, and to others he was in Iowa teaching school.

Monday, Oct. 6, 1879

This morning in South Bend, operative C. saw the constable Lou Keller not Kerns, and told him about the saddle and asked him if he did not think it probable that it was over in Lowell. He said he did think so, but whoever had it, would keep quiet now. C. questioned him for some time and he finally said that he was in with a certain woman that could get into the secrets of the Neddo gang if she had not been sick lately, and he told C. that he thought Ben Neddo would be in town pretty soon, when he would point him out to C. Neddo came in presently, riding a black mare, and C. inquired of him if he would tell him about the horse and how he looked when it was found. He said his brother Charlie´s boy „Pitchy" first saw the horse, and brought him up to the shed, where his brother looked at it. He said the horse was wet with sweat and blown, and had been ridden with a pad saddle. Previous to this Neddo had said there was no bridle or saddle on the horse when it was found. He said the saddle must have been a very large one as the impression from it extended from the shoulder to the middle of the back. He then marked on his mare how the saddle mark looked; he drew a crescent from the shoulder of the horse to the middle of his back, like this (crescent) indicating the lower line of the saddle; he said there were two girth marks and showed C. on his horse where those marks were. He said that both girth marks were pretty close together, and the ring of the girth showed also. He then described the bridle marks pretty accurately, and went on to say that he was glad he hadn´t taken the horse up for he had a kind of a bad name on account of going with Tom Cottrell, and that it would not have been very safe for him to have had that horse after what had happened. Neddo appeared very curious about the case, and finally asked C. if they suspected anyone in town. C. assured him that nobody around there was suspected in the least. Neddo promised to give C. any information that he got, and then they parted. C. now decided to go to Edwardsburg, and for that purpose engaged Shanks to drive him there. Arriving there C. inquired for the four young fellows who heard the horse going through the town. He found Fred Griffin who heard the horse go by the house where he was sitting up with his girl. The horse was running and it was about 1 o´clock. Charles Curtis who was also sitting up with his girl in a house near where Fred Griffin was, also heard the horse galloping rapidly by about the same time. Will Zeller also heard the horse; he lives on the Cass road near town and a little north. He had just got home from seeing his girl and heard the horse running by; his mother also heard it, thinks it was about 1 o´clock. C. was unable to see Frank Jerome, the other party who is said to have heard the horse. C. then tried to find out what road the horse and rider had taken from town as Shanks said that when he and the other operative were out, they lost track after leaving Edwardsburg. After a great deal of inquiry, C. found a lady living where the road leaves town some ways out, who first heard the galloping horse go by; she thought between one and two. C. found a man down the road where it turns on the main road, who remembered hearing a horse go by on a run some night about a week ago, but he was not sure that it was Sunday night. Before leaving Edwardsburg C. inquired for Stickney, but no one knew him. Dyer Cunning said he heard that John Adams could tell who the young fellow was who recognized the horse when it was going back to Decatur as the same one he had met early Monday morning. C. found John Adams after a long drive for they had been misdirected. He said he heard that this fellow who recognized the horse was one of the Stuckeys and said so in Edwardsburg, so as C. had already seen the Stuckeys this story fell through. C. then saw a Mrs Hadden further on who had not heard the horse, but had seen a very villainous looking man last Monday afternoon coming towards Edwardsburg; when she met him on the road he was dripping with sweat and walking rapidly, and she noticed particularly his savage looking eyes. She described him as 5 ft. 8, slim smooth face, black eyes and medium build, carried his coat on his arm; the same man she thought had been to her sister´s Mrs. Powell. C. went there, and found that Mrs. Powell had gone to Albany, N.Y. but her son told about the tramp; described him the same, and said he came there late in the afternoon and asked for some bread and butter; while his mother was getting it, Mr. Powers from Edwardsburg drove in the gate, and the supposed tramp seeing him, ran out of the yard and away as fast as he could. C. saw Mrs Masten who was returning from a neighbors about 7 in the evening the same night. A man got up from the fence almost under her feet and ran across the road into Wesley´s woods where she heard him go crashing through the bushes. She could not give a description as it was too dark to see plainly. She sent her boy to warn Wesley, but no one saw anything more of him. C. has now traced the horse and rider within a few miles of Bookers where Powers located him, and the trail is now pretty plain, and the time agrees with the distance. C. reached South Bend after dark and learned that L.S. Marsh the foreman of the machinery department of the Singer Company says that he heard his dog barking about three o´clock last Monday morning, he got up and went out in the yard with his revolver, and saw a man running swiftly, but making little noise towards Jefferson St.

Bridge. Marsh lives over the river and the man was going towards town.

This same date in Chicago an operative visited C. Charles whose name he had heard in making the inquiries about A.M. Matteson´s house, but Charles appeared a great friend of the Mattesons and would nave nothing to say against them. Mrs. Matteson also approached the operative today, and said she knew he was there after her son Jim. She said she was sure she had not seen Jim for a year; she also told about James being insane, and that at times they had to leave the house for fear he would kill them. His mother tells a different story from the father with regard to the cause of James becoming deranged, as she said it was caused by his being tripped up on the ice by another boy when he was 14 years of age, and struck his head. A neighbor who passed the house on last Thursday night says he saw Jim there with his father, but the father and mother both deny this. They both also say that they think James is dead, and have felt so for the last four months.

Tuesday, Oct. 7, 1879

C. left for Decatur this morning and was detained an hour in Niles; while there he visited Mr. Pike of the Pike House, and made investigation in regard to Kelsie Loomis, but developed the same facts as developed by operative K.; ny – that Loomis was at the hotel that Sunday afternoon and night. Arriving in Decatur C. called upon Dr. Rose who assured him that his horse and buggy was at his service. After dinner Dr. Rose and C. drove out in the country and went to Mr. Motts. They found no one at home, but on inquiry found that Frank Mott, the one C. wanted to see, had gone to a sorghum mill, and would not be back until night. After supper, in your company, C. saw the young man Hathaway, and it seems that his statement which was reported by W.A.P. that the man who rode the horse certainly wore a mask. C. also called at the house of Mr. Warner from whom C. had learned that De Hart Matteson had borrowed his county atlas some three or four weeks before the murder, instead of consulting, as is customary the one at the bank in town. Mr. Warner was not at home, but Mrs. Warner knew the circumstances well. She said about the last of August, Matteson came to the house and said he wanted to borrow

Mr. Warner's county atlas, and said in explanation that he wanted to locate some land at Glenwood which he thought of trading the Ball farm for; he added that he had tried several places to borrow one, but could not find any until he heard Mr. W. had one. Mrs. Warner seemed a little reluctant about letting him have it, and he insisted on depositing $5 for its safe return, he then left taking the atlas with him, and returned it to Mr. Warner in Decatur about a week afterwards. Mr. W. thought it strange that Matteson should come to his place to borrow an atlas when there were several in town. It would seem that Matteson borrowed the atlas to outline a road from Decatur to South Bend or rather from the Morris farm. C. could not find any pencil points on the atlas where Matteson might have traced out the route. Mrs. Warner said that when Matteson borrowed the map, he came from the direction of Decatur, and returned that way saying it was very hot and he wouldn't drive to the Ball farm, as he first intended doing. Mrs Warner said she and her sister had company, and that about ten o'clock they heard the horse galloping some ways off, then slow up and in a moment start up into a gallop passing the house on the run. Her sister went to the window and saw a man on horseback, but all she could tell was that he seemed rather a large man, and rode leaning forward in the saddle, and had on dark clothes. This is about the same time that young Hathaway saw the horse and rider.

This same date in Chicago, operative W. on duty in the vicinity of A.M.Matteson's was told by Mrs. Matteson, that when James left them he was very angry at both her and his father, and that he had done this horrible deed to ruin their business, but if james did do it, nobody could make her believe that Hart Matteson had anything to do with it; and they were afraid that James would come back and kill them both; and that James always carried the latest patented firearms. Mrs. Matteson also said that Mr. Morris was a worthless drunken wretch, and that he stole $400 from his father; and that he would buy his wife a box of kid gloves at a time, and she would wear one pair until they were a little soiled, and then give them away, and that she was a very vain woman, also that she had always carried a pistol with which to shoot Hart Matteson.

Wednesday, Oct. 8, 1879

This morning you and C. drove out to find young Mott. Mott said he did meet a man about four or six miles from South Bend when he was returning with the horse, and his description very much resembled Stuckey whom C. saw on Sunday. Mott said the man recognized the horse without any prompting but when Mott asked him about the man he could give a very good description of him, but he said he met the same horse with a large man or heavy built man on it running towards South Bend, very early Monday morning. Mott inquired his name and he understood him Stricknor or Strickley or some name like that, and he jerked his head backwards and said he lived about three miles back, which would make it near Edwardsburg, but as already reported C. could find no one there with a name nearer to Stickney than Stuckey or Shittler. C. next interviewed young Rosewarn and the Sherwoods but elicited nothing further than that show by the report of W.A.P. C. next saw a young lady named Miss Hubbard, who in company with another young lady and two young men from Marcellus were out riding. About nine o´clock in the evening they passed by the farm on the road from which a lane leads up to the Morris house about half a mile; somewhere along the road she and the others noticed a low open buggy and horse hitched to the fence. No one was in the buggy and no one near there; the horse was a large dark one. She thought the buggy was a low piano box, and the horse was hitched a little east of the gate. C. went to the spot indicated, and found near the gate a freshly gnawed place on the fence rail, and also the ends of two or three rails gnawed which was evidently done by the horse when hitched. C. also saw two faint wheel marks in the gravel leading to the fence.. This was not on the road which runs in front of the house, but on the side road leading through the woods back of the house. After dinner you drove C. into town, and on the way met your brother Samuel who had been to see Sterns a Jew who had a saddle stolen about three weeks before the murder. The same saddle Matteson had tried to buy of Sterns, but the price was too high; a few days after the saddle was stolen. Arriving in Decatur C. left for South Bend, and was laid over for an hour at Niles, and went to see Mr. Bacon the attorney who said he omitted to state that the package the old man had he sat on partially, and may have contained a saddle, as it was large enough, and irregularly shaped, and the old man seemed desirous of concealing the bundle. Also the rough looking man he spoke to he was certain had false whiskers; they seemed so unnaturally red and bushy, and didn´t seem to suit his face or complexion.

This same date in Chicago the operative met A.M.Matteson who was very reticent, and refused to have anything to say about the affair. The operative learned that Mr. Charles, a friend of the family had advised him to keep his mouth shut. The operative then found a Mr. Shilling whose daughter married Hart Matteson. Mr. Shilling said his son had been to Decatur to see about this affair, and had taked with a great many of the business men who did not think Hart Matteson had anything to do it. Mr. Shilling had not seen James Matteson for a year, and that when he was home he had threatened to do his father and mother all the mischief he could. The operative next found James Matteson´s divorced wife; she said she had not seen James Matteson within a year, and they were almost as strangers, and to the best of her knowledge none of his folks had seen him within that time. She was aware of the bitter feeling existing between your family and Hart Matteson, but did not think James had anything to do with it. She had heard that Mrs. Morris was always armed, and threatened to shoot Hart Matteson.

Mr. Shilling´s son said that it was rumored in Decatur that a man answering the description of James Mathews was seen to get in a buggy along with Hart Matteson and drive out of the town together. This he said was not so, as Hart Matteson said he did not ride out at all on that Sunday; that the only time he was out of the house was when he went to church with his wife, and then went to see the man whom Hart said had started the report, and that the man´s name was Miller, who did not know James at all. James Matteson´s wife says she obtained her divorce because James was insane and she could not see any reason for his committing this murder as he was not mixed up in the quarrel.

Today a letter was received at this office, of which the following is a copy.

„Austin, Texas, Oct. 6, 1879

„Dear friend William:

„I received yours of the 3rd inst making inquiries in regard to one James Matteson. My information up to the present writing is as follows: M.J.Matteson was indicted by Grand Jury of this (Travis) county in the spring term of '77 in two or three cases for perjury and swindling; he gave bond, which he at once „jumped", and has not been seen here since. He speculated in notes, and was a money lender and pawnbroker on small scale, was a good horseman and pretended to be somewhat of a horse trainer and driver. I am also informed that he taught negro school in this state; had a wife with him here, was embroiled in two or three law suits on account of his money lending proclivities. Was not a drinking man or a gambler while here, but exhibited a great desire to make money with little regard for the fairness of his transactions. When he jumped his bond here he was supposed to have some money probably four or five thousand dollars. In his money transactions he showed a desire to lend his money in „burnt proof" style, so that no one might be able to collect anything from him by garnishment or attachment, and would operate through a third party or loan in another name than his own, pretending to be simply an agent for some unknown party. His bond was forfeited here, but through some flaw or other the forfeiture was set aside by the court and bondsmen relieved. It is supposed that Matteson has money here now in the hands of a party that is operating for him. I have not been able to ascertain Matteson's present whereabouts up to writing, but have just learned that information may be had here that will locate him, which I will endeavor to get at once and notify you. I suppose that M.J.Matteson is the one you want beyond all question as he was the only person ever known here by the name of Matteson. There was a J.B.Matteson who lived here some four years ago, went from here to Rockdale, William Co. Texas, set fire to his saddlery shop and burnt it up for the insurance, for which he is now under indictment in William Co.; he is still in this state and can be found, but I am satisfied M.J.Matteson is the man you want, and I will take great pleasure in attempting to locate him which I think will be done in two or three days at the farthest and will notify you at once."

Signed, James Lucy

Yours Respectfully,

Allan Pinkerton

Chicago, Oct. 23, 1879

Elias Morris Esq. Decatur, Michigan

Sir:

The following is a continuation of your report.

Thursday, Oct. 9, 1879

Last night after supper C. was introduced (to) Mr. Marsh, foreman in the Singer manufactory, by Louis Hull, bookkeeper for A. Coquillard & Co. Mr. Marsh said he was awakened by his dog Monday morning; he got up and took his revolver and went out doors in his shirt tail, as he reached the gate he saw a man on the opposite side of the street running towards the river very swiftly but making no noise. The moon was shining brightly, and as he caught glimpse of him through the shade trees, he could see that he was heavy built and wore dark clothes, and thinks he wore a soft hat, but is not certain. The man went out of sight on Washington St. and probably headed for the bridge over the river leading to South Bend. This was a little after three o'clock.

After breakfast this morning C. called upon Cor. Haggerty, ticket agent of the L.S. and M.S. and asked him if he remembered selling any tickets to LaPorte that Monday morning. He said that a person buying a ticket that way would not be so likely to be noticed as the agent would think they belonged in town. C. heard in Niles yesterday that a man named Messenger, a paralyzed peanut merchant at South Bend had heard of a hired girl seeing the horse early in the morning with a bridle and saddle on. C. found Messenger who said that after the horse was found Monday morning some men were talking about it near his peanut stand. He heard one man whom he knew by sight say that somebody´s hired girl over in Lowell saw the horse with a saddle and bridle on standing near the house when she came down to work. He said he would try and find this man, and let C. know tomorrow. C. then went over to the jail to see Sheriff Dougherty and get a look at „Tough" Bennoit who was eating his dinner when C. got there. He is about 19 or 20 years old, and has a villainous looking face.

C. next saw Russwurm the harness-maker where the bridle was brought to be repaired, which was referred to in a previous report. Russwurm is an honest old Dutchman, but hesitated about saying anything as he was very much afraid of the Neddo and Bennoit gang. Finally he and Ben Neddo brought the bridle to him to be fixed a week ago Wednesday two days after the murder. Neddo first wanted to buy a bridle, then said he had one at home he would get fixed. He soon came back with the bridle. It was a driving bridle and belonged to a double harness and the blinders had been cut off; the rein was new. Neddo took away the rein and bits so that nothing was left but the crown piece, cheek pieces, and throat latch. Mr Russwurm then said very impressively, „there is a mate to that bridle somewhere, for it was taken from a double harness." The bit was an ordinary one. Russwurm begged not to be given away, and C. assured him he would get into no trouble.

Friday, Oct. 10, 1879

C. heard that a suspicious looking man had been seen hanging around two houses which don´t bear a good reputation on the Monday after the murder, that this man lived in South Bend and had been in the vicinity of Decatur the week prior to the murder. C. thought he had better investigate this matter, so he took a walk, about a mile out of town to these places. He first went to the house of Geo. Williams who is a hard case, and his wife is a prostitute. Mrs. Williams opened the door in answer to C´s knock, and said, „My husband is at home, come up tonight won´t you." C. hastened to assure her that he came on different business, and told her what he wanted. She said her husband knew more about the fellow than anyone and C. had better see him. C. found him at the barn, and he said Mrs. Washburn knew more than he did. C. saw Mrs. Washburn, who attempted to tell C. that she did not remember any fellow calling that day, and didn´t know anything. C. saw that she could be scared, and went at her accordingly. She then admitted that the fellow had been to her house once or twice, but she didn´t like him for he was a dead beat. She described him as five feet, eight inches high, dark eyes and hair and black moustache. He always had plenty of money, and he had said at one time, it wasn´t anybody´s business how he made it. She said he went off at times and came back again, and just before this murder occurred he went up into Michigan, near Decatur. She still refused to tell the man´s name, but promised to find out by Sunday. C. then went to see Williams again; he tried to play off innocent of knowing anything for some time but finally said „Well, you ask Chum Neddo who sold him that little bay mare or ask Harry Hans about it, and he´ll tell you.“ C. then came back to South Bend and after dinner saw Messenger the peanut man, who said that a Mr. Price made the remark near his peanut stand, that a hired girl saw the horse early Monday morning with a saddle on. C. saw Mr. Price who said that it was not he that made the remark about the hired girl, but just heard it surmised, and had forgotten, who said it as there were several standing around. C. heard that a fellow called „Sport“ was seen going up the street towards an auction store with a saddle on his shoulder last night; a watchman named Logan heard of it and went up to the auction room, but he hadn´t been there. Logan came and told C. of it, and said all he knew of the fellow was, that he was called Sport, and that he had no horse, so it seemed strange he should have had a saddle. C. inquired a great deal for Sport, but could not find anyone who knew him. Later in the evening he saw Mr. Hull who said he thought the fellow was named Long, and he would find out for certain and let C. know. C. so far can get no trace of Stickney.

Saturday, Oct. 11, 1879

C. spent a great deal of the time about the streets today, as a great many people from the country were in. He found the name of the man who met Mott taking the horse back to Decatur to be Nick Rine instead of „George Stickney.“ There is no doubt but what he is the man referred to. He was not in town, and lives seven miles out in the country. C.

found the man alluded to as „Sport", but his going up the street with a saddle on his shoulder is a false report, and C. can find no one that started the report. „Sport´s" name is DeLong, and he is quite an expert pool player and hunter from which amusements he derives his nickname. C. also ascertained the name of the man who was up to Williams´ and Mrs. Washburn´s the day after the murder, to be John Barrett; he is a jocky and horse trainer, and there is nothing in the idea that he was connected with the affair. C. also saw Mrs. Dr. Reeves and learned from her regarding the two men who called on her husband the Sunday afternoon of the day of the murder. From what Mrs. Reeves said C. concluded the men wished to avoid much observation as one of the men wanted the doctors services to cure his daughter of „dropsy". Dr. Reeves is known as a specialist and abortionist, and the fact of the two men acting as they did, and seeming to avoid being noticed is thus explained.

C. spent most of the afternoon along both banks of the river for a mile down and examined closely the banks and all dark and weedy places, but found nothing in the shape of a saddle. Later in the day C. saw Ben Neddo who spoke very politely, and took special pains to speak to C. and seemed to expect to be questioned. C. saw Ex-Sheriff Turnock today, and unlike Neddo he describes the saddle marks as a small pad saddle, and he thinks only one girth. Mr. Shanks tells the same story, and said he greased the two places on the horses back that were puffed up by the pads, on each side of his foreshoulder. C. has made cautious inquiries hereabouts of anyone who has missed a bridle from a double harness, but can find no one who has lost anything of the kind. C. examined Ben Neddo´s bridle while he was talking with him, and noticed it had been newly fixed and that the blinders had been cut off as Russwurm had said.

Sunday, Oct. 12, 1879

C. started after breakfast this morning with Shanks to go out to see Nick Rine. The weather was excessively hot and the horses suffered very much. After a drive of seven miles they came to the farm where Nick Rine lives, and met him just as he was starting off on horseback. C. told him at once what he wanted, and then asked him if he met Mott or a young man riding the horse towards Decatur Tuesday morning. He said he did, and described the man and horse. C. then asked him if he saw the horse early Monday morning. He said he had, and went on to tell how he met the horse and the rider. He said he left South Bend about 1:30 Monday morning, and when he got near Stovers school house, which is near where Miss Booker lives whom C. interviewed, he heard a horse running towards him. He saw as the horse came up that it had three white feet and a bald face, and he kept trying to recognize the man by the horse thinking it someone he knew. As the man approached him, Rine said „good evening" but received no answer, the horse rushing by on the run, and giving half the road. His first thought was, that somebody was going for the doctor, next that it was a horse thief. He did not notice the man closely, as he had so little time, but thinks he had a beard and that he was a large man with a dark suit, and black hat on, and that he rode on a saddle and leaning well forward. C. then came back to Mr. Chaffen whom he heard had also heard the horse go by his house early Monday morning. C. examined a long row of osage orange trees on each side of the road, and also the woods and underbrush coming into town. C. found that Mr. Chaffen was away from home but would be back in a day or two. His son said he did not know whether his father heard it or not as he never said much anyway. At dinner at the hotel in South Bend today C. learned that a German farmer living in Olive township and not far from Olive swamp met an old man and a young man, both strangers to him coming out of South Bend early Tuesday morning after the murder. The old man he remembered had on a long jean „warmers" or jacket and had a fringe of gray whiskers under his chin. The young man he described very vaguely, as he didn´t notice him particularly. He could only say that he was a heavy set large man with a black hat. In the back of the wagon was a small Spanish saddle with a quilted black seat, a kind of saddle used in Texas, and would make such marks on a horse as were described by Mr. Turnock and Mr. Shanks.

Monday, Oct. 13, 1879

C. today heard a rumor that someone saw a fellow they call „crazy Neddo" on the horse early Monday morning. This „crazy Neddo" is a singular carse, and it is possible that he may have been riding the horse around as he is up all times of the night. C. could not ascertain who saw him however, and it is more than likely that it is one of the rumors that grow out of nothing. C. wrote to Dr. Rose today asking for an accurate description of the saddle stolen at Decatur.

Tuesday, Oct. 14, 1879

C. went out to Mr. Chaffen´s place today, but he was still away. If he heard the horse go by it will show that the man left the Edwardsburg road about half a mile out, and came in by a soft sandy road, and if he did perhaps C. can find out someone living on that road who knows something about his coming into town as a number of the people are teamsters and get up very early. C. learned today that Charles Neddoo says there were no saddle marks whatever on the horse when he was taken to the stable. This is a direct lie, as there are a number who saw the marks and Ben Neddo himself told C. about them, although he lied also in regard to the size. C. was up in a suburb of South Bend today known as Irishtown. Eveybody was willing enough to give information if they knew anything, but C. could not find anyone who heard the horse. Mr. Hull, already referred to, is keeping a lookout on one of the Bennoit crowd who works at the Coquillard works and will let C. know of any suspicious moments on his part, as he has seemed very anxious to get information about the murder and has been quite inquisitive of late.

Wednesday, Oct. 15, 1879

C. spent today in making inquiries about Lowell, and in houses along the various roads by which the horse could have come in after leaving the Edwardsburg road. He would have gone over to see Mr. Chaffen but learned down town that he was not at home yet, being off to the fair somewhere. C. is inclined to think that William Dewy was correct about hearing the horse on the Edwardsburg road, and he is pretty sure of the road by which he left, though parties living on the corner did not hear him, but this is easily accounted for as the road is very soft and sandy and a horse tread would make no noise. The main road leading into town is very hard, and is down hill, and a horse running or even trotting down this road would make sufficient noise to wake anyone. The other road by which C. thinks the horse left leads directly by Chas. Neddo´s house where it turns and comes toward the river. It is very deep sand, and a horse going through it would not make a particle of noise. From there to where Roedifer (Rodefor) saw it is not very far, though on another street.

Thursday, Oct. 16, 1879

C. met Lou Keller tonight, and was told by him, that he had been approached by Neddo who proposed to „fix" up a saddle which they were to find, and get a reward from Coe. It was finally decided that Keller should appear to fall in with Neddo´s proposition, that they might find out if anything should come from it. If Neddo attempts to get up a saddle, he will be apt to catch himself in a lie, as he described it as a large pad saddle, and C. has two men who will swear that the marks were those of a small pad saddle. C. has got a pretty fair description of the saddle bargained for by Matteson at Decatur, and stolen sometime afterwards. One important fact is that it has no horn, but is a flat saddle. It is very probable that this was the one used as it is light and rides easy. C. drove out to Chaffen´s place today, and discovered that he had never heard the horse at all, but remarked to someone that he had heard of someone else hearing it, and from this the whole story sprang.

Friday, Oct. 17, 1879

C. tramped about Lowell today inquiring of people along the roads leading into town if they heard anything of the horse the Monday morning after the murder. He found one man who lives near Charles Neddo´s who heard a horse or something walking by sometime in the morning. C. is pretty certain now of the route the horse took coming into town, but it is lost in the sand about Neddo´s place; at least that is his supposition as no one could hear a horse walking or even running after coming down the hill there as the sand is fully six inches deep. C. went out in the country today to see a man named Buckley who worked on a farm, and was reported as having seen the horse and rider about two miles from town. Upon finding Buckley, C. learned it was all a mistake, as it was late last Sunday night when he saw a horse and rider, and it was a gray horse.

Saturday, Oct. 18, 1879

Ben Neddo has disappeared somewhere, and C. cannot get any idea from anyone where he has gone. C. saw him yesterday, as also did Lou Hull and some others. Very likely he has gone after a saddle somewhere, though Lou Keller said that he had not seen him to speak to him about the matter.

Sunday, Oct. 19, 1879

Today being Sunday C. was unable to do much. Towards evening he was introduced to a Mr. Andrews who said that a man named John Alexander knew a woman who saw the man riding into town on the horse Monday morning. It was arranged that C. should meet Alexander at Andrew´s store in the morning.

Monday, Oct. 20, 1879

This morning C. saw the man Alexander, from whom he ascertained that the woman he referred to was Tom Cottrell´s wife. C. soon shook Alexander and went to see Mrs. Cottrell. She said that she heard her dog barking early Monday morning, and also heard a horse running down hill near her house. She got up and looking out the window saw the horse wet with sweat and panting, an recognized the man that was riding it. She said she did not notice whether there was a saddle on the horse, but she knew there was some deviltry on foot when she saw him coming in that matter. She said she would tell who the man was for money, and that he lived right in town. C. succeeded in getting an admission from her that it was a relative; she would not set any price upon her information until she could see her husband.

Tuesday, Oct. 21, 1879

C. received orders from Supt Warner to return home. He left South Bend at 4:50 pm and arrived in Chicago at 7 pm. Before leaving he saw Mrs. Cottrell, who had ascertained that the man to whom she referred was then in town.

Yours Respectfully,

Allan Pinkerton

Chicago, Oct. 28, 1879

Elias Morris Esq. Decatur, Michigan

Sir:

The following is a report of operative E.J.K. who was sent to Decatur in response to your telegram of the 13th inst.

Monday, Oct. 13, 1879

K. left Chicago at 4 pm and arrived in Decatur at 9 pm and met Dr. Rose on the street, and together they found Dr. Broderick. He informed K. that suspicion had been aroused against a man name Floyd Smith who is a tool of Hart Matteson's, and who lives upon 40 acres of Matteson's land about five miles in the country. On the night of the murder, some young people going home from a party or dance about 9.30 or 10 o'clock met a man driving a white and bay horse hitched to a light buggy furiously through the deep sandy road. He was coming from the direction of Henry Morris's house and was going towards Decatur, and as Matteson has a gray horse at Smith's, and on account of his frequent visits to Smith's within the last ten weeks, and the circumstance of his (M's) going out to Smith's last Sunday and bringing in this white or gray horse, has aroused their suspicions, that Smith was the man who was in that buggy on the night of the murder, and that he is the man who drove the murderer to Henry Morris' house, and as he at one tme did work for Henry Morris, and knew the premises well, he told the murderer about the horse in Morris' stable, and then drove away as above described; and on account of the relative time between when this team and buggy was met at some distance from Henry's house, and the time of the murder.

Tuesday, Oct. 14, 1879

K. met you at Dr. Broderick´s house this morning, and heard about the same statement as above related; also that a man living in Decatur named Botsford, and who used sometimes to do dirty work for Hart Matteson had called at your house the other day, and said he had changed his mind in regard to Matteson and now thought that hart Matteson was concerned in the murder, and in speaking about the team that was met upon the road the night of the murder, he (Botsford) said that he believed that Floyd Smith was the man who drove that team, and that Smith took the murderer over to Henry´s house, and leaving him in the vicinity drove back home again, and it was decided that K. should see Botsford and get his statement, as you thought he could be trusted although he used to work for Hart Matteson. It was also decided that K. should see Ed Arnold, a merchant who has been working hard on the case, and who you thought had some important information to give. Dr. Broderick brought in Mr. Arnold and the following is his statement.

Statement of Mr. Arnold.

On the 8th inst I went to Breedsville to fix the postmaster in regard to any letters that Hart Matteson might leave there or any that might come for him. The postmaster informed me that on the week previous a couple of letters were put in the night box of his office, and he is quite certain that the man who put those letters in the box drove a small black horse, but could give no further description of him, and could not remember to whom the letters were addressed, but the envelopes were a little larger than the ordinary size and of a reddish color. I arranged with the postmaster so that I will know of any letters that Matteson mails, or any that come for him. I went from Breedsville to Grand Junction and fixed the postmaster there also; and in conversation with John Wright, owner of a saw mill he related to me the following circumstance which happened at his house on the 6th inst.: Wright and his wife were away from home and left a servant in charge of the house. While they were about a stranger came to the house and inquired for Mr. Wright; the girl informed him that Mr. and Mrs. W. were not at home, but that Mr. W. would be in shortly, and invited him to a seat in one of the rooms. The stranger took a seat, and the girl went about her work; her duties were such as to cause her to pass the room door in which the stranger was seated. Once she looked into the room and could see nothing of him, she stepped inside, and as she did so the stranger got out from behind a safe that is in the room, where he had been crouched down as though hiding from someone; she wanted to know what he was doing there, and he replied „Oh! Nothing"; some other remarks passed between the two, and she went about her work again; and in passing the room again discovered, in company with another girl, that he was not there. She found him in the sitting room examining some books and papers that lay on the table. The second girl asked him if he wanted to see Mr. Wright. He said he did, and she advised him to go down to the mill where he might be, but the man said he would as leave wait where he was, and after remaining a while longer he went out and towards the town. When Mr. Wright returned the girl told him of the peculiar actions of the stranger, and gave him a description of the man. Mr. Wright went immediately down the street, and meeting the stranger, asked him what he meant by skulking about his house. The stranger put his hand to his hip-pocket as though to draw a pistol (and Mr. W. saw a pistol in his pocket) and stated that he was a physician and had called at Wright's house to see if he did not want some medicine. Wright informed him that he did not want any medicine and did not believe he was a doctor. The fellow then drew from his inside coat pocket a bundle of doctor's prescription blanks, and wanted to know how he would come by those things if he was not a physician. Wright allowed that anyone could get those blanks from any drug store. They bandied words for a while, and the stranger finally made out a prescription for Mr. Wright of which the following is a copy:

Fluid extracts of Dandelion -- zi

Golden Seal -- aa

Princess Pine -- aa

Buchen -- aa

Wahoo -- ff ½

Port Wine – ½ pt.

M. Leg. 1 tablespoonful 3 times per day ½ hour before meals.

The heading of the original prescription blank was M.M.Dale, druggist and apothecary, South Haven, Mich., and at the bottom the stranger wrote his name as Dr. G.M.Bates. Drs. Rose and Broderick assert that the prescription is not made out proper, and that no regular physician would have made it out as it is. K. has therefore written to M.M.Dale enclosing the prescription and asking for information regarding Dr. H.M.Bates. Mr. Wright stated to Mr. Arnold that while talking with this stranger he noticed something about his eyes that seemed familiar, and gave his description as being about 5 ft. 10 inches high, rather slim build, but broad shouldered, kind of hollow chested, had dark or sandy short burnside whiskers, and heavy mustache, and the points of the mustache extended across the face to the side whiskers. At this point in Mr. Wright´s description, Mr. Arnold asked him if he ever knew Jim Matteson. Mr. Wright started suddenly, and bringing his hand down hard upon the box on which they were sitting, exclaimed, „By George, that was the man!" and said the man had dark eyes, and he knew Jim Matteson and was quite positive that this stranger was he, who said also, that he would visit a couple of small towns first and finally bring up in Kalamazoo. It is said that Jim Matteson is a very eccentric individual and the actions of this man at Mr. Wright´s corresponded exactly with some of his former capers.

H.W.Botsford´s statement.

One week ago last Sunday he was down to Floyd Smith´s house in company with his neighbor, Mr. E.L.Hanks, for the purpose of pumping him about the murder. He spoke to Smith about the talk about Hart Matteson being concerned in the murder. Smith said he had been to Paw Paw, and the same opinion prevailed strongly there. Botsford told Smith that he had the bullets that killed Morris and his wife, but Smith manifested no desire to see them, on the contrary, when Mr. B. took them from his pocket and held them out for Smith´s inspection, Smith cast his eyes upon the ground, and would not look at them, and Mr. B. could not catch his eye. Mr. B. remarked that they were large bullets, and Smith said perhaps they had been fired from a rifle. Mr. B. held the bullets towards Smith thinking he, like everyone else would be curious to examine them and would not raise his eyes from the ground. George Testil, a neighbor of Smith´s told Mr. B. that Hart Matteson had been to Smith´s house seven times in two weeks, and Mr. B. knows that Matteson took his wife to Smith´s house last Sunday, and remained to dinner. Mr. Wilkins, a brother-in-law of Smith´s says that he is a very bad man, and that when Smith swore in the interest of Hart Matteson that he saw Amos Morris going down the valley road, he swore to a lie, for he (Wilkens) knew that Smith was not at home on that day. This evening as K. was riding out to see a Mr. Hall, they met Hart Matteson who was coming from the direction of Smith´s. K. saw Mr. Hall who said that about 10 pm on the night of the murder he was standing near the road in front of his house, which leads by Smith´s house, and that someone passed along on horseback, riding like the devil; it was a bright moonlight night and he could see that the horse had a white stripe down his face, but he could not give any further description of the horse or man, as he did not pay any particular attention to them, but they went at a break neck pace down the road in the direction of Smith´s.

Wednesday, Oct. 15, 1879

K. was informed by Dr. Broderick this morning, that Norwood would be up from the country this afternoon after him. K. learned that Hart Matteson intended to leave for Chicago on the 3 pm train, and telegraphed Mr. Warner to that effect. In the afternoon K. learned that Norwood had declined to take him to board so that he could work upon Smith because he was afraid he would become mixed up in the matter. But Botsford knew another man named Sutfin who might take K. and who lived near Smith. Botsford drove K. out there in the evening but Sutfin had gone to stay all night at his fathers and his house was closed up, so as Dr. Rose intended to see Norwood and endeavor to persuade him to take K. they returned to town without seeing Sutfin. It turned out that Hart Matteson instead of going to Chicago by train drove to St. Joe, and thence to Chicago by boat.

Thursday, Oct. 16, 1879

While at Dr. Broderick's this morning, Botsford came and informed K. that Floyd Smith and his wife had gone to Dowagiac to the county fair, and Botsford was afraid that Smith had left for good. Smith told his neighbors that he was going to Dowagiac, and remain at the fair one day, and then visit some of his relatives near Niles and return home next Sunday. It is probable that visit of Smith's was made at the instigation of Matteson, who did not want him where he would be subject to questioning, while he himself was not around to look after him. Dr. Rose arranged with Norwood today for K's boarding with him for a time, and he is to go on Saturday. Tonight Dr. Rose and K. drove to Smith's house, and K. searched it thoroughly, thinking that he might possibly obtain some evidence, showing him to be a participant in the murder; but more to ascertain whether his intention was to pack up and move away. K. found nothing about the house that would give any further clue, and everything indicated that no attempt had been made to move.

This same date in Chicago operative W. left the agency at 4 pm and shadowed the house of A.M.Matteson until dark, but did not see anyone except the wife of A.M.Matteson. The operative then went by Mr. Shilling's and saw two ladies and one gentleman in there. The latter he took to be Milo D. Matteson. At 7:30 pm one of the ladies put on her wraps, and was seen to the door by a lady whom the operative took to be Mrs. M.D.Matteson. Presently Milo D. Matteson came out, and went to his father's house and went into the barn; he remained there for a few minutes, and then returned to his father-in-law's house.

Friday, Oct. 17, 1879

K. met you and your brother Samuel this morning, and received instructions to come to your house tomorrow afternoon, and interview some parties who were supposed to know something about the saddle in question.

The operative in Chicago today saw the mother of Hart Matteson at 2 pm take a street car going south into the city. During the remainder of the afternoon A.M.Matteson was seen about the house doing odd chores. At 6:20 pm Milo D. Matteson and his wife drove up to Mr. Shilling´s, and after Mrs. Matteson had alighted, Hart drove the team to his father´s, and remained at the house a few minutes and then returned to Mr. Shilling´s. The operative learned from a neighbor that Hart Matteson and his wife had spent the day at the exposition.

Saturday, Oct. 18, 1879

K. remained very quiet about the hotel today, until about 4 pm, when according to agreement he met Dr. Rose a little ways out of town. They drove first to the vacated premises of Henry Morris, and then to your house where they remained to tea. Upon arriving again in Decatur, it was found that it was too late to go to Norwoods tonight, and as Smith would not be home until tomorrow it was concluded to wait until Monday to make the move.

This same date in Chicago operative W. obtained a letter from a Mr. King, 540 Montana St. of which the following is a copy:

„I noticed your remarks about the Mattesons, and I am surprised to learn that his folks live in your neighborhood. I had been informed that he or his folks lived in Chicago, and have had some track of him since the occurrence at Cedar Falls. He undertook to kill a man in New York state last summer, at or near where the Champlin boys used to live. Who gave you your information, and what prospects are there that the detectives will get him? I do not know as I want him, but we don´t want to forfeit his bail bond. I recollect of reading about the murder you speak of in Michigan, and if Matteson had the law suits and indictments against him you speak of, there can be no doubt but what he is the right man. Some of them pretend to say that he is crazy; that he is a terrible desperado there is no question, and I am only afraid he will come to my back sometime. He tried not to have me prosecute the indictment against him, and caused a letter to be written to me. This was in the summer of 1878. I do not want to meet him again, and hope he will soon be locked up as he is a dangerous man.“

Signed, T.L.French, of Adams and French, Sandwich, Ill.

Sunday, Oct. 19, 1879

K. paid his hotel bill early this morning, and then walked out of town a little ways and met Dr. Rose, who was accompanied by Ed. Arnold. The latter gentleman had been to Grand Junction since K. last saw him, but had learned nothing new. Upon arriving at Norwoods, K. was introduced to Mr. And Mrs. W. and Mrs. Doty, Mrs. N.´s mother. Smith returned home about 4 pm and began to chop wood, and prepare for supper. The window of K.´s room look out upon Smith´s house, and he has a good opportunity to see when anybody visits him. K. remained up until midnight but did not see anyone come there.

Monday, Oct. 20, 1879

After breakfast this morning K. took his gun and went out shooting. He circled around Smith´s farm all the forenoon, and made himself thoroughly acquainted with the locality. He got no chance to approach Smith who was drawing in his buckwheat and thrashing it near the barn. In the afternoon Norwood and K. took the guns, and arranged it so they would pass by where Smith was working, and K. was introduced as Doty, Mr. N.´s cousin. They passed a few pleasant words with Smith, and joked about the amount of game they would shoot, and finally left him. In the evening K. watched Smith´s house again, but saw no one come there.

Tuesday, Oct. 21, 1879

K. was up early this morning, and taking his gun loafed around Smith´s buckwheat field, hoping to get a chance at him, but he was thrashing near the barn, and a neighbor was with him most of the time. He went over to Smith´s house about 5 pm and found him carrying corn to his hogs. K. talked with him upon different subjects for a time, and then gave him a drink of whiskey. Smith related all about a „girl scrape" that a young man named Sutfin had got into in the neighborhood some time ago, and gave his opinion, that Sutfin was innocent of the charge the girl preferred against him. K. gave his views of the matter, and continued the conversation long enough to make himself pretty well acquainted with Smith, so that he can now approach him any time, and when a favorable opportunity offers, broach the subject of the murder.

He invited K. to come over and see him, and K. promised to go and help him fan out his buckwheat tomorrow.

Wednesday, Oct. 22, 1879

Immediately after breakfast, K. went over to Smith´s, and helped him finish fanning out his buckwheat. The noise and clatter of the fanning mill made conversation almost impossible, but they managed to yell a joke at each other occasionally, and the whiskey K. furnished for him made Smith very sociable and talkative. Circumstances seemed against K. however, for when they landed the fanning mill upon the stone boat and started to draw it back to the owner, they met this person, a negro, and he and Smith had a few moments conversation about crops, and then they started on, and K. was about to begin the murder subject when they met the negro´s son, with whom Smith also talked a few moments, and when they finally started again Smith began telling K. about those negroes, their fortunes, and K. could not broach the subject without interrupting him, and perhaps arousing his suspicions. Coming back they rode upon the stone boat, and here again conversation was out of the question, as it took all their time to keep from falling off. When they reached Smith´s house, K. helped unhitch, and put the horses in the barn. Smith was in a big hurry to get through so as to attend a husking bee, about half a mile north. He wanted K. to go along, but he declined, saying he had no invitation, as he knew it would not avail him anything. Smith did not get back from the bee until evening, and though K. visited his stable and yard twice afterwards he did not catch him out of the house.

Thursday, Oct. 23, 1879

It stormed so hard all day that it was almost impossible to go out of the house. K. started several times to go to Smith´s house, but was driven back by the storm. After dinner K. saw Smith hitch up, and drive to Decatur, and as he did not get back by dark, K. had no chance to talk with him during the afternoon. In the evening K. was over to Smith´s house. In the presence of Smith´s wife, K. broached the subject thinking he might get from her an opinion of Matteson, but they did not seem inclined to talk about the matter.

Friday, Oct. 24, 1879

Mr. Norwood was getting ready to kill a hog this morning, and K. was going to assist him, but as they were preparing for it, Smith came into the yard, and having his axe upon his shoulder said he was going over into Coles woods to get some base-wood bark for bindings. K. got the gun and accompanied him. They stopped at Mr. Coles´ house, and K. was introduced to Frank Coles who treated them to some cider, and they talked upon different subjects for about an hour, and then Smith and K. went into the woods. K. gave Smith a good pull at the whiskey bottle, and then said he would look about for a while, and try and shoot some game (he wanted to give the liquor time to take effect.) K. walked through the timber, and back to where he was stripping a bass-wood tree, that he had cut down, and K. carefully broached the subject of the murder, and Matteson´s connection with it. Smith talked freely about it. He had talked with Matteson regarding the suspicions that were aroused against him, and Matteson had said he didn´t know anything about the affair: that he knew everybody suspected him of having a hand in the crime, but that if people would consider a moment they would see that since the suit between him and Henry Morris had been carried to the Supreme Court, that no witnesses would be required and that the suspicion that Mr. Morris and his wife were put out of the way because they were witnesses, was simply absurd, and that these suspicions against him, would hurt him a great deal more in court than if Mr. And Mrs. Morris were alive. Smith told K. about Henry Morris borrowing money from Hart Matteson, and said he (Smith) used to work for Henry Morris who used often to go into town, when he knew of his borrowing money from Matteson, as he would also borrow from him (Smith) and that this was how Matteson got the mortgages upon the farm. He explained, at K.´s suggestion, about Matteson being arrested for forgery and convicted, and that Matteson then took the case to St. Joe County and was acquitted. Smith said Matteson had a great many enemies in this county simply because he had loaned money to them, and had taken mortgages for security, and that when Matteson saw there was no chance to get his pay he would foreclose, and for this would be considered a mean man and a sharper, and it was these that were so open in their assertions that he had caused the death of Mr. and Mrs. Morris.. Smith said he had bought his place from Matteson, and that Matteson held a mortgage upon it. In reply to K.'s remark that Matteson would eventually foreclose on him, Smith said that he was a bit afraid of that, and that Matteson, as far as he knew, never harried anybody. He had had several deals with Matteson in horses, etc and had always been used well. He did not think that Matteson had anything to do with the death of Mr. and Mrs. M., but then of course he could not say positive, but if Matteson was concerned he did not know anything about it, and did not think Matteson was that kind of a man.

The assertion that Matteson might have been concerned in the murder, Smith repeated twice, but added each time that he did not believe Matteson to be that kind of a man. K. questioned him closely for over an hour, but he did not contradict himself, or seem in the least embarassed. Smith on their way home remarked that he liked fun and spent as much money as anybody, still he got along as well as those that never took a drink, and always remained at home.

Yours respectfully,

Allan Pinkerton

(At this point in the investigation report an itemized bill to Elias Morris from Pinkerton's National Detective Agency for $560.82)

Chicago, Nov. 4, 1879

Elias Morris, Esq.   Decatur, Michigan

Dear Sir:

Enclosed please find reports up to Nov. 1st in relating to investigation that has been made hunting for your brother's murderer. We have received a number of letters from different parties, making suggestions on the matter. Among others was one received today from Mr. Bacon of Niles, in which he mentions a man named Ottinger whom he says is a great friend of Hart Matteson´s, and very skillful with the pistol; says he lives in the city, but don´t know where. We have no definite information in relation to the whereabouts of James Matteson, but we have points guarded so that I think that if his friends are in communication with him we shall be able to learn it. The copy of the letter I sent you from the warden of the penitentiary at Jackson, Michigan, I have not heard from you whether the parties he mentions live at Lawton or Paw Paw, or whether there is anything in it. We have written the warden asking to give further particulars if he can.

Also enclosed please find bill for services and expenses, amounting to $560.82. You can send the amount of the bill here either by express or check. Any points you get please let me know. We have nobody now specially working upon the matter.

Yours Truly,

F. Warner Supt.

Chicago, Nov. 4, 1879

Elias Morris, Esq. Decatur, Michigan

Sir:

The following is a continuation of your report.

Saturday, Oct.25, 1879

This morning K. went over and saw Smith who said he was going to Lawrence, and asked K. to go along with him. Smith was busy fixing his corn-crib, and K. took a stroll through the timber. About 2 pm Smith and K. started for Lawrence, and Smith said on the way there that he had bought the farm he now lives on, from Matteson for $1000, and that Matteson held a mortgage upon it for about $700, and that the papers had all been made out to that effect, and were in the county clerk´s hands. He intended to stay on the place until he had paid for it and if Matteson tried to foreclose the mortgage he would endeavor to get someone to advance him the money, and take the mortgage out of Matteson´s hands. They arrived in Lawrence at 2:30 pm and after hitching the team went into the hotel and had something to drink. Smith went off to do some errands about town, but presently came running back very much frightened, and said he believed he had lost a ten dollar bill, and explained that before he left home he remembered of his wife laying the bill upon the table, and he could not remember whether he got it or not, and if he did he must have pulled it out of his pocket with his tobacco box on the road and lost it. He finally decided that he could get the goods for his wife on credit, as he was acquainted in the store, but he felt worried over his loss. They had another drink, and as Smith did not have any money K. had to do all the treating. Smith searched the buggy, but failed to find the money, and K. attempted to console him by saying that he surely must have forgotten to take it from home. They remained around town until 5 pm and Smith met several friends of his, Dan Simmons a horse jockey among the number, and they had several drinks together. Smith likes whiskey wonderfully well, and K. expended $2.00 in treating and buying a bottle-full to carry home with them. On the road home he was quite jolly and communicative and, K. opened the murder subject at once. Smith told K. that he knew nothing about the murder, only what he had heard, and that on the night of the murder he was home, and that the day previous the negro Hamilton had helped him to sow some wheat, and that on the Monday after he had finished it alone, and in the afternoon of the same day had hitched up and drove to Lawrence on some business, to get some wheat ground or something of that sort, and while at the butcher shop in Lawrence someone came in and told about one of the Morris´ being killed, and that was the first time he had heard of the murder, and when he heard it he did not know at the time which one of the Morris´ had been murdered, but when he got back home all his neighbors knew about it, and then for the first time he learned that Henry Morris and his wife were the ones that were assasinated. Smith then went on to tell how he had worked for „Hank" Morris, and what a good fellow he had been to him, and that he felt very bad over his death. Smith told K. that Henry Morris used to gamble with „Dan" Stevenson and „Bill" --- (he could not remember his surname) in Decatur. Smith had never seen Henry gamble, but he had seen him around with these gamblers. He had often asked Henry for money when they would be in town together, and sometimes Henry would say he did not have any, but knew where he could get it, and then he would go to Matteson and borrow money, and Smith said he had been present when Matteson had given Henry money. Smith said he owed Henry money at one time, and had afterwards worked for him and paid it back in that manner. Smith said he thought more of Henry Morris than any man in the county, and if he knew that Hart Matteson had anything to do with the murder, he would get out of his clutches as soon as he could, and would tell then what he knew, even if he lost all he had, and if he knew of anyone who assisted in the murder he would be the first man to help hang them, and he would help hang Hart Matteson, if he was positive he had been the cause of this murder, but he did not think that Matteson knew anything about it. He knew Matteson was a sharper, and had a great many enemies, but he could not bring himself to believe that Matteson had any hand in the crime. Of course he could not say whether Matteson did have a hand in the murder or not, because he only knew what he had heard, and he had heard twenty different stories, when he was at the Paw Paw fair of the suspicions against Matteson. He had spoken to Matteson about this talk that was going around, and Matteson had denied it and told him that such talk made him sick at heart, and he did not know why people would think him guilty of such a crime. Smith did not deny that he had been very intimate with Matteson, but it was because he had a great deal of work for him, such as pasturing horses, threshing etc, and that Matteson always paid him for it; that Matteson had come to his house quite often, and more so lately because they were settling about the property, but that Matteson never spoke a word about the murder during these visits. When Matteson left the gray horse at his barn the Friday following the murder, he was at the Paw Paw fair. Upon his return at night he was unable to recognize the horse, and went over to Norwoods to see about it. Abe Norwood came back with him, bringing a lantern, and when Smith saw the horse by light he recognized it as Matteson´s. He thought nothing strange of Matteson´s leaving the horse because he often brought horses to him, that he had taken upon the mortgage to pasture. Matteson´s wife was with him on this night, and they were leading a black horse, but hitched the black in the wagon after turning the gray horse into the barn. In regard to Smith being a witness in the suit against Amos Morris, he explained that it came about in this way: His brother-in-law „Kit" Parsons wanted to raise some money, and asked him about getting it, and he took Parsons to Matteson whom they found on the street in Decatur talking to Amos Morris, and when Smith informed Matteson what Parsons wanted, Matteson told them to come to his office. There Amos Morris and Matteson figured for sometime, and then Matteson informed Smith and Parsons that he could not let them have any money just then, as he had just let Amos have all the ready money he had, but that he could let Parsons have the money in three or four days. Smith thinks Parsons gave Matteson a mortgage upon a team for security. This was his evidence in the Amos Morris mortgage case. K. questioned and cross questioned Smith very rigidly, but he did not contradict himself at all, denying emphatically any knowledge of the murder, and repeatedly asserting that he would assist all in his power to bring the murderers to justice, and also stated that he was at home on the night of the murder. About Matteson and his wife being to his home one Sunday to dinner, he explained that Matteson came that day to make the final settlement about the farm, and that was all that was talked about that day. Smith did not hesitate to talk freely about the murder, but said he could tell nothing only what he had heard.

Arriving at Norwood´s K. questioned Mr. „Lant" Norwood as to whether Smith was home on the night of the murder. Mr. Norwood said on that Sunday, Smith´s brother-in-law, a Mr. Emery who lives at Paw Paw was visiting Smith. Mr. Norwood went to Keeler in the afternoon, and when he returned about 6 pm he saw Smith husking corn for his hogs, and Emery had gone home. Mr. Norwood did not know whether Smith went anywheres that night or not.

Sunday, Oct. 26, 1879

This morning K. questioned the Norwoods in regard to Smith´s whereabouts on the night of the murder. Abe could not remember of seeing Smith that day, as he did not pay any attention to it, but Raime and Lant remembered having seen Smith about his place late in the evening. K. had another talk with Smith today, and he again and again denied any knowledge of the murder, and all he knows about it is what he has heard. He did not act at all frightened or suspicious, but said he felt very sorry than anyone would suspect him, and if he had any proof that Hart Matteson was concerned he would ( ) him away at once. This afternoon Dr. Rose drove K. to Hartford to see a Mr. Waterman, proprietor of the Olds House, who had some information to impart; Mr. Waterman´s story is as follows: Sometime early last spring, Hart Matteson drove into Hartford, put his horse into Mr. W´s stable, and also took dinner with him. He told Mr. W. that he had a chattel mortgage upon some property in Hoppertown and he was going up there to see about it as he was afraid the parties would, or intended to clear out. On his return from Hoppertown that same Matteson stopped all night with Mr. W. The next morning Matteson in paying his bill, which was $2.50, only had two dollars in change besides a hundred dollar bill, and promising to send the other 50 cents to Mr. W. he drove toward Decatur. Now on the day of the murder one J.W. Ackley who lives in Hoppertown drove into Hartford, and put up with Mr. W., and leaving his horse in the stable told the stable man that he was going up the street to get a team, and was then going to Decatur. He left the stable about 4 pm and the stableman did not see him again until about 11 pm the same night, wehn he saw Ackley board the 11.15 pm train for Hoppertown. The next day Ackley put in appearance again at Hartford, and informed Mr. Waterman that he had a long drive the day before (Sunday) and said he had been to Decatur; and took his horse from Mr. W.´s stable and drove off. News of the murder had reached Hartford by this time, and Mr. Waterman thinking this man´s actions rather suspicious, and besides remembering that Matteson had told him that the name of the man he had those mortgages against at Hoppertown was Ackley, Mr. W. took the pains to inquire at the livery stables, whether Ackley had hired a team on that Sunday, but learned that he had not. After hearing this statement Dr. Rose remembered that Ed. Arnold owned a saw mill in Hoppertown, and that this Ackley either worked for Arnolld or owned a share in the mill. He would therefore learn if Ackley had been to see Arnold that night, or if he had been to see his brother who lives in Decatur.

Monday, Oct. 27, 1879

Immediately after breakfast K. went to Hamilton´s (the negroes) house and pumped him in regard to Smith´s whereabouts on the day and night of the murder, and his statement was about the same as „Lant" Norwood´s. He said he had seen Smith around home all day, and that Emery was there upon a visit, until about the middle of the afternoon when he went towards home. He remembered having seen Smith husking corn quite late in the evening, and was quite sure that he was home all night, because he knew that Smith was up early and finished planting some wheat. K. then went over onto Smith´s farm where he and old Jim Hall were digging potatoes, and talked with them until dinner time. K. then watched until Smith had had his dinner, and then went to his house and got into conversation with his wife about the murder. She said that her husband had been at home all that night, and that since the murder when he was to be away all night, she always got Miss Norwood to come over and stay over night with them. She had heard that Matteson was suspected of being concerned in the crime, but she did not hardly believe he was such a wicked man. She said that Matteson used to come down to see Floyd often on business, but she could not remember of ever hearing him speak of the murder. She was sure that Smith was home on the night of the murder, and was positive that he did not know anthing about it. About 6:30 pm Dr. Rose came, and after settling his board bill, K. returned to Decatur.

Tuesday, Oct. 28, 1879

K. met you this morning, and after a consultation with regard to Matteson´s suspicious actions about his barn it was decided that my Superintendent Mr. Warner or my son W.A.Pinkerton should come to Decatur to consult with regard to the operation. K. received $15 from you, and took the 11:35 am train for Battle Creek where he arrived at 1 pm. He met Mr. Crosby who drove him to Johnson´s house; there they found that Johnson was at work in Nicols, Sheppard and Co´s painting. Mr. Crosby went there, and made an appointment at 7 pm with Johnson to meet K. The appointment was kept, and Johnson made a statement as to how he came by the saddle. He said he was employed by the „Homestead View Company" to sell their photographs, and had some views of James Stanton´s farm house, three miles straight west from Rolling Prairie. He exhibited the views to the Stanton folks, and they could not agree upon the price, and Johnson had almost given up hopes of selling them any, when he and young Stanton were in the barn talking, and Johnson noticing the saddle hanging up on a peg offered to trade $6 worth of views for the saddle and bridle. This Stanton refused, but said he would swap the saddle alone for the views, and they finally made the trade and Johnson shipped the saddle to Battle Creek. Johnson wanted a saddle and that is why he traded, and before he started out, it was understood between him and the manager of the View Co. that should he get a chance to trade for the saddle to do so. Johnson saw nothing about the saddle, or the actions of the Stantons, that would lead him to think that they were either anxious to get rid of, or reluctant to part with the saddle, and he said it was an old looking one, and appeared as though it had not been used in a long time. Johnson thinks that young Stanton told him that they had owned the saddle foor a good while. There was another saddle in the barn, but much older and rougher looking than the one he traded for. The Stanton folks seemed to be very respectable people, and were well acquainted in that neighborhood, and Johnson did not think there was anything of importance in the matter.

Wednesday, Oct. 29, 1879

K. arrived in Decatur this morning at 3 o´clock. At 10 am he met you, and shortly afterwards met Supt. Warner who had arrived on the morning train. It was decided that K. should go to Rolling Prairie and investigate the saddle matter there.

Thursday, Oct. 30th, 1879

K. left Decatur this morning at 5 o´clock, ate breakfast at Niles, and then took train for South Bend, Indiana. Arriving there he found that the 8 am accomodation train had left, and he could not get another train until 4 pm, a local freight. He therefore made arrangements that the hotel-keeper´s son should drive him to Stanton´s in the morning, and then on to Laporte in time for the 5 pm train for Chicago.

Friday, Oct. 31st, 1879

The landlady´s son drove K. out to Stanton´s immediately after dinner, and K. questioned Mr. Stanton closely in regard to the saddle he had let Johnson have, in exchange for views of his homestead. Mr. Stanton informed K. that this saddle had been in his possession for 8 or 9 years, and that his son bought it that length of time ago in Laporte, Indiana. They had not used the saddle much lately, but his son used it occasionally. It always hung in the barn, and he could not remember when it was last used. His son used to ride it upon a bay horse, and sometimes upon a black one. They had loaned it a few times to their neighbors, but not in a great while, and not time inside of two months, and he was sure that the saddle hung in the barn at the time of the murder. K. satisfied himself after questioning them closely that there was nothing of consequence in the matter, and the fact of the saddle having been shipped about the time of the murder, was merely a coincidence. K. was then driven on to Laporte where he took the train for Chicago arriving there at 10.20 pm.

Respectfully yours

Allan Pinkerton

AFTERWORD

In more than 140 years, despite countless attempts to solve the Morris and Pritchard murders, no solid evidence has ever come to light. While Milo Matteson had made himself clearly visible at church and in the lobby of the Duncombe House the day of the Morris murders, the whereabouts of James Matteson then or thereafter has never been established.

But the trail of money and death did not go cold in 1879, leaving more than enough circumstantial evidence for the reader to ponder.

Tom Parsons´ detailed version of the murder scene published in *The Chicago Herald* in 1891 seems eerily plausible, but did it have its basis in reality or was it just part of a battle he was waging against his brother Kit? Or alternatively, was it perhaps not Kit but rather his brother-in-law Floyd Smith who had been the accessory after all and had confided the details of the crime scene to Kit, who then later related them to Tom? But Floyd Smith had been let down from that tree in 1879 and remained silent, dying in 1884.

The summer of 1884, particularly July, was unlucky for so many more. Besides Smith, Milo´s young nephew Arthur Thomas, a witness to the Amos Morris mortgage, experienced an untimely death at 26. Alan Pinkerton had died in Chicago. Kit Parsons had survived an assault with intent to do bodily harm, but oddly, resisted having his assailants´ names published. And Jerome Coleman, the disbarred attorney and questionable witness in the Matteson forgery case, did not survive that month of July.

One other incident from 1884 presents such a strange coincidence, it should not remain unmentioned. According to the Pinkerton Investigation, John Wright described a visit paid him by James Matteson posing as a doctor prior to the Morris murders. To prove he was a physician, the man wrote out a prescription on a blank piece of paper with the heading "M.M. Dale, Druggist and Apothecarist, South Haven, Michigan".[1] The druggist in South Haven, however, was Edgerton E. Dale, who at only 39, was the victim of an untimely death himself in July 1884. The "M.M. Dale" was his wife, Marietta M.

Hawks Dale, originally from Cherry Valley, Illinois, home of Marshall Pritchard. Her father had operated a hotel in Cherry Valley, and in the 1870 Census, Edgerton is listed at Hawks' hotel as "house painter".[2] In a town of only 1400 inhabitants, it is very likely that Dale knew Marshall Pritchard's father, who was listed in the same census as "carpenter & joiner."[3]

The only inference which may be drawn from this anecdote is that the murders of Charles and Esther Morris and Marshall Pritchard should not be stamped as unsolvable mysteries, too long gone to reveal new clues or insights. This trail of money and death is not cold. With modern search engines and online resources, more and more interdependencies surface. But for now, at least, the trail might find its end with *The South Bend Tribune's* October 1 report of the Morris funeral:

The funeral of the victims of this, the most cold blooded and brutal tragedy known in the state, occurred yesterday afternoon at 2 o'clock, at the residence. Long before that time teams from all around the country and from the neighboring villages brought sympathizing friends and curious lookers-on, until the number swelled to at least two thousand. Carriages, and all manner of vehicles lined the fence along either side of the lane leading to the main road, and the spacious yards about the premises were crowded full. It was a peculiarly sad and solemn occasion, so out of harmony with all the surroundings. The day was charming. A soft breeze from the west played among the branches of the grand old forest trees about the place, whose leaves dressed in their gayest autumn hues glistened in the sunlight and formed a most beautiful picture to the eye. All nature was smiling, although the hearts of the thousands gathered there were bowed with great sorrow.[4]

Three Decatur ministers spoke at the outdoor services. In his brief remarks, Reverend J.W.H. Carlisle issued a call to action for all yet to come:

We should not let this matter rest until the perpetrator of this awful deed is apprehended and brought to justice. Let every living thing, every flower that blossoms on the hillside, every leaf of the forest, every ray of light, every inch of soil, if need be, upon this great globe, turn detectives and reveal the true murderer of these innocent people.[4]

Morris Grave, Anderson Cemetery / Photo by author

ILLUSTRATIONS

Note: historical photographs prior to January 1923 are considered in the public domain (PD) and not subject to copyright.

Marshall S. Pritchard Grave / Photo by Author

Photo of Jennie Bull Phillips / Public Domain

Alleged Photo of Newton Foster / Public Domain

Anne Madison Bradley, Arthur Brown, Isabel Cameron Brown / Public Domain

Decatur Township, Van Buren County, Michigan 1873

Excerpt of 1870 U.S. Census, Van Buren County, Michigan

Excerpts of Bloomingdale Township Plat Map 1873 and 1912

Steamship *Chautauqua* / Public Domain

Excerpt of 1870 U.S. Census, Van Buren County, Michigan

Chautauqua Lake / Historical Atlas of Chautauqua County, NY, 1867

Ralph DeLeo Matteson / Public Domain

Emma Hathaway Pritchard Copley Vincent / Public Domain

Naomi Hathaway, Phebe Grimes, Jane Copley / Public Domain

John Wilson Bengough / Public Domain

Canadian Suffragettes March in Washington, D.C. / Public Domain

William Ross's Grave, Whitby, Ontario / Public Domain

Shilling's Dry Goods, Cripple Creek, Colorado / Denver Public Library

Mrs. Milo D. Matteson / Chicago History Museum

Morris Grave, Anderson Cemetery / Photo by author

SOURCES

Foreword

1. *Van Buren County Republican*, (Decatur, Michigan, October 8, 1879), 3

Chapter 1 Little Prairie Ronde

1. Frederick Webb Hodge, *Handbook of American Indians North of Mexico, Vol 3 N–S*, (Washington Government Printing Office, 1912), 530
2. Catherine Howland, *A Scrapbook History of Early Decatur, Michigan and Vicinity*, (Decatur Bicentennial Committee, 1976), 899–900
3. Catherine Howland, *A Scrapbook History of Early Decatur, Michigan and Vicinity*, (Decatur Bicentennial Committee, 1976), 355
4. Catherine Howland, *A Scrapbook History of Early Decatur, Michigan and Vicinity*, (Decatur Bicentennial Committee, 1976), 8
5. Catherine Howland, *A Scrapbook History of Early Decatur, Michigan and Vicinity*, (Decatur Bicentennial Committee, 1976), 346
6. Ellis, Franklin, *History of Berrien and Van Buren counties, Michigan. With ... biographical sketches of its prominent men and pioneers.* (Philadelphia: D. W. Ensign & Co., 1880), 448
7. Catherine Howland, *A Scrapbook History of Early Decatur, Michigan and Vicinity*, (Decatur Bicentennial Committee, 1976), 8
8. Ellis, Franklin, *History of Berrien and Van Buren counties, Michigan. With ... biographical sketches of its prominent men and pioneers.* (Philadelphia: D. W. Ensign & Co., 1880), 447
9. "Michigan Deaths and Burials, 1800–1995." Index. FamilySearch, Salt Lake City, Utah, 2009, 2010.

Chapter 2 The Morris Murders

1. Catherine Howland, *A Scrapbook History of Early Decatur, Michigan and Vicinity*, (Decatur Bicentennial Committee, 1976), 736

2. *The National Democrat*, (Cassopolis, Michigan, October 2, 1879), 1

Chapter 3 Alleged Forgeries and a Jury Verdict

1. Decatur (Mich.) Murder Investigation Records, 1879, Pinkerton's National Detective Agency, Clarke Historical Library, Central Michigan University

2. New York State Census, 1865

3. Catherine Howland, *A Scrapbook History of Early Decatur, Michigan and Vicinity*, (Decatur Bicentennial Committee, 1976), 254

4. Decatur (Mich.) Murder Investigation Records, 1879, Pinkerton's National Detective Agency, Clarke Historical Library, Central Michigan University

5. *The True Northerner*, (Paw Paw, Michigan, May 12, 1871), 7

6. *The True Northerner*, (Paw Paw, Michigan, January 26, 1872), 1

7. Illinois, U.S. Marriage Index, 1860–1920

8. *The True Northerner*, (Paw Paw, Michigan, February 24, 1871), 4

9. *The True Northerner*, (Paw Paw, Michigan, January 2, 1874), 1

10. *The True Northerner*, (Paw Paw, Michigan, December 12, 1873), 1

11. *The True Northerner*, (Paw Paw, Michigan, December 19, 1873), 1

12. *The True Northerner*, (Paw Paw, Michigan, December 19, 1873), 4

13. *The True Northerner*, (Paw Paw, Michigan, January 2, 1874), 4

14. Decatur (Mich.) Murder Investigation Records, 1879, Pinkerton's National Detective Agency, Clarke Historical Library, Central Michigan University

Chapter 4 A Decade of Litigation

1. *The True Northerner*, (Paw Paw, Michigan, March 27, 1874), 5

2. *The True Northerner*, (Paw Paw, Michigan, May 15, 1874), 5

3. *The True Northerner*, (Paw Paw, Michigan, April 11, 1873), 5
4. *The True Northerner*, (Paw Paw, Michigan, March 27, 1874), 5
5. *The True Northerner*, (Paw Paw, Michigan, June 26, 1874), 5
6. *The True Northerner*, (Paw Paw, Michigan, August 7, 1874), 5
7. *The True Northerner*, (Paw Paw, Michigan, July 10, 1874), 5
8. *The True Northerner*, (Paw Paw, Michigan, August 21, 1874), 5
9. *The True Northerner*, (Paw Paw, Michigan, September 18, 1874), 5
10. *The True Northerner*, (Paw Paw, Michigan, January 24, 1879), 4
11. Death Records. Michigan Department of Community Health, Division for Vital Records and Health Statistics, Lansing, Michigan.
12. Decatur (Mich.) Murder Investigation Records, 1879, Pinkerton's National Detective Agency, Clarke Historical Library, Central Michigan University
13. *The True Northerner*, (Paw Paw, Michigan, December 10, 1880), 1

Chapter 5   String Him Up

1. "Michigan Deaths and Burials, 1800–1995." Index. FamilySearch, Salt Lake City, Utah, 2009, 2010. Index entries derived from digital copies of original and compiled records.
2. Decatur (Mich.) Murder Investigation Records, 1879, Pinkerton's National Detective Agency, Clarke Historical Library, Central Michigan University
3. Catherine Howland, *A Scrapbook History of Early Decatur, Michigan and Vicinity*, (Decatur Bicentennial Committee, 1976), 738
4. *The True Northerner*, (Paw Paw, Michigan, December 26, 1879), 5
5. *The True Northerner*, (Paw Paw, Michigan, December 26, 1879), 5
6. Catherine Howland, *A Scrapbook History of Early Decatur, Michigan and Vicinity*, (Decatur Bicentennial Committee, 1976), 714
7. *The Chicago Herald*, (Chicago, Illinois, December 3, 1891), 3
8. *The True Northerner*, (Paw Paw, Michigan, March 12, 1880), 5

9. *The True Northerner*, (Paw Paw, Michigan, April 16, 1880), 5
10. *The True Northerner*, (Paw Paw, Michigan, December 3, 1880), 4
11. *The True Northerner*, (Paw Paw, Michigan, April 15, 1881), 5

Chapter 6 Counterfeiting and Dry Goods

1. *The True Northerner*, (Paw Paw, Michigan, December 3, 1880), 4
2. 1860 U.S. Census, population schedule (Washington, D.C.: National Archives and Records Administration)
3. Ohio, U.S. County Marriage Records, (Miami, 1860–1868), 342
4. 1870 U.S. Census, population schedule (Washington, D.C.: National Archives and Records Administration)
5. *The Paxton Record*, (Paxton, Illinois, June 17, 1875), 4
6. *History of the Regulators of Northern Indiana*, (Indianapolis, Indiana, Indianapolis Journal Company, 1859), 51
7. *The Hillsdale Standard*, (Hillsdale, Michigan, January 19, 1858), 3
8. *The Wheeling (West) Virginia Daily Intelligencer*, (Wheeling, Virginia, July 13, 1858), 4
9. *The Hillsdale Standard*, (Hillsdale, Michigan, July 20, 1858), 3
10. *The White Cloud Kansas Chief* (White Cloud, Kansas, March 22, 1860), 2
11. *The National Republican* (Washington, D.C., December 7, 1868), 1
12. *The Wheeling (West) Virginia Daily Register*, (Wheeling, Virginia, December 9, 1868), 4
13. *The National Republican* (Washington, D.C., February 6, 1869), 1
14. *The Evening Telegraph* (Philadelphia, Pennsylvania, October 26, 1870), 1
15. *The Chicago Daily Tribune* (Chicago, Illinois, August 13, 1876), 2
16. *The True Northerner*, (Paw Paw, Michigan, February 6, 1880), 7
17. 1880 U.S. Census, population schedule (Washington, D.C.: National Archives and Records Administration)

18. *The Gunnison Daily News-Democrat*, (Gunnison, Colorado, October 29, 1881), 5

Chapter 7   A New Beginning

1. *Famous Scouts, Including Trappers, Pioneers, and Soldiers of the Frontier*, Charles Haven Ladd Johnston, (L.C. Page, 1910)
2. *Kit Carson's Life and Adventures, from Facts Narrated by Himself*, Peters, Dewitt C. (Dustin, Gilman, Hartford, Connecticut, 1873)
3. Annual Report of the Commissioner of Indian Affairs, (Washington, D.C., 1866)
4. Speech to the Cherokee, President James Monroe, 1817
5. *The Colorado Daily Chieftain*, (Pueblo, Colorado, May 17, 1880), 1
6. *The Colorado Magazine*, (The State Historical Society of Colorado, Denver, Colorado, July 1931), 127
7. *The Pueblo Daily Chieftain*, (Pueblo, Colorado, May 17, 1882), 3
8. *The Colorado Magazine*, (The State Historical Society of Colorado, Denver, Colorado, November 1932), 205

Chapter 8   Business and Pleasure

1. *The Free Press*, (Gunnison, Colorado, December 7,1881), 3
2. *The Gunnison Daily Review*, (Gunnison, Colorado, December 16, 1881), 3
3. *The Gunnison Daily News-Democrat*, (Gunnison, Colorado, December 22, 1881), 6
4. Decatur (Mich.) Murder Investigation Records, 1879, Pinkerton's National Detective Agency, Clarke Historical Library, Central Michigan University
5. *The True Northerner*, (Paw Paw, Michigan, May 14, 1880), 2
6. *The True Northerner*, (Paw Paw, Michigan, October 29, 1880), 2
7. *The Gunnison Daily News-Democrat*, (Gunnison, Colorado, December 22, 1881), 6
8. *The Gunnison Daily News-Democrat*, (Gunnison, Colorado, December 23, 1881), 6
9. *The Gunnison Daily News-Democrat*, (Gunnison, Colorado, February 11, 1882), 4

10. *The Gunnison Daily News-Democrat*, (Gunnison, Colorado, February 21, 1882), 4
11. *The Gunnison Daily News-Democrat*, (Gunnison, Colorado, February 22, 1882), 4
12. *The Free Press*, (Gunnison, Colorado, February 22, 1882), 3
13. *The Free Press*, (Gunnison, Colorado, March 15, 1882), 4
14. *The Free Press*, (Gunnison, Colorado, March 25, 1882), 3

Chapter 9   Breaking with the In-Laws

1. *The Gunnison Daily News-Democrat*, (Gunnison, Colorado, June 4, 1882), 4
2. *The Free Press*, (Gunnison, Colorado, June 14, 1882), 3
3. *The Free Press*, (Gunnison, Colorado, June 21, 1882), 3
4. *The Gunnison Daily News-Democrat*, (Gunnison, Colorado, July 1, 1882), 3
5. *The Free Press*, (Gunnison, Colorado, July 5, 1882), 3
6. *The Free Press*, (Gunnison, Colorado, July 26, 1882), 4
7. *The Free Press*, (Gunnison, Colorado, July 26, 1882), 3
8. *The Free Press*, (Gunnison, Colorado, July 29, 1882), 4
9. *The Gunnison Daily News-Democrat*, (Gunnison, Colorado, May 13, 1882), 8
10. *The Gunnison Daily News-Democrat*, (Gunnison, Colorado, May 14, 1882), 4
11. *The Gunnison Daily News-Democrat*, (Gunnison, Colorado, June 6, 1882), 4
12. *The Free Press*, (Gunnison, Colorado, June 7, 1882), 2
13. *The Gunnison Daily News-Democrat*, (Gunnison, Colorado, July 7, 1882), 1
14. *The Gunnison Daily News-Democrat*, (Gunnison, Colorado, February 24, 1882), 1
15. *The Gunnison Daily News-Democrat*, (Gunnison, Colorado, May 19, 1882), 3
16. *The Free Press*, (Gunnison, Colorado, June 7, 1882), 2
17. *The Colorado Magazine*, (The State Historical Society of Colorado, Denver, Colorado, November 1932), 207
18. *Rocky Mountain News*, (Denver, Colorado, August 14, 1882), 2

Chapter 10   Rise and Fall of Gunnison

1. *Gunnison Review-Press*, (Gunnison, Colorado, April 28, 1883), 2
2. *Gunnison Review-Press*, (Gunnison, Colorado, March 29, 1883), 1
3. *Gunnison Review-Press*, (Gunnison, Colorado, March 31, 1883), 3
4. *The Gunnison Daily News-Democrat*, (Gunnison, Colorado, May 28, 1882), 4
5. *Gunnison Review-Press*, (Gunnison, Colorado, June 33, 1883), 1
6. *Gunnison Review-Press*, (Gunnison, Colorado, July 28, 1883), 6
7. *Gunnison Review-Press*, (Gunnison, Colorado, August 3, 1883), 3
8. *Gunnison Review-Press*, (Gunnison, Colorado, November 9, 1883), 1
9. *Silver World*, (Lake City, Hinsdale County, Colorado, November 17, 1883), 3
10. *The Colorado Daily Chieftain*, (Pueblo, Colorado, September 3, 1884), 5
11. *The Sun*, (Gunnison, Colorado, February 2, 1884), 4
12. *Gunnison Review-Press*, (Gunnison, Colorado, March 22, 1884), 7
13. *Gunnison Review-Press*, (Gunnison, Colorado, April 12, 1884), 8
14. *Gunnison Review-Press*, (Gunnison, Colorado, July 8, 1886), 4
15. *Gunnison Review-Press*, (Gunnison, Colorado, July 17, 1886), 8
16. *The Solid Muldoon*, (Ouray, Colorado, July 23, 1886), 3
17. *The Colorado Daily Chieftain*, (Pueblo, Colorado, September 12, 1888), 1
18. White Pine Cone, (White Pine, Colorado, January 20, 1888), 1

Chapter 11   Back East Again

1. *Daily Inter Ocean*, (Chicago, Illinois, February 13, 1887), 6
2. *Daily Inter Ocean*, (Chicago, Illinois, January 29, 1888), 6
3. *Daily Inter Ocean*, (Chicago, Illinois, April 29, 1888), 23
4. *Daily Inter Ocean*, (Chicago, Illinois, September 2, 1888), 10
5. *Daily Inter Ocean*, (Chicago, Illinois, December 2, 1888), 22
6. *Daily Inter Ocean*, (Chicago, Illinois, June 15, 1890), 18

7. *Daily Inter Ocean*, (Chicago, Illinois, July 27, 1890), 24
8. *Daily Inter Ocean*, (Chicago, Illinois, January 4, 1891), 27

12   Gilded Chicago

1. *The Congregationalist*, (Boston, Massachusetts, July 4, 1895)
2. *Gunnison Review-Press*, (Gunnison, Colorado, November 29, 1884), 8
3. *Daily Inter Ocean*, (Chicago, Illinois, December 24, 1891), 27
4. *Daily Inter Ocean*, (Chicago, Illinois, May 5, 1893), 6
5. *Chicago Herald*, (Chicago, Illinois, December 3, 1891), 3
6. *Chicago Herald*, (Chicago, Illinois, December 4, 1891), 3
7. *Daily Inter Ocean*, (Chicago, Illinois, November 28, 1886), 10
8. *Record of Wills, 1879-1928* (Illinois, Probate Court, Cook County)
9. *Altgeld of Illinois: A Record of His Life and Labor*, (New York, B.W. Huebsch, 1924), 287
10. *Rockford Republic*, (Rockford, Illinois, April 30, 1897), 4
11. *St. Paul Globe*, (St. Paul, Minnesota, April 14, 1897), 6
12. *Chicago Record*, (Chicago, Illinois, April 14, 1897), 2
13. *Topeka State Journal*, (Topeka, Kansas, July 23, 1898), 3
14. *Boston Journal*, (Boston, Massachusetts, July 24, 1898), 1
15. *Kimball Graphic*, (Kimball, South Dakota, June 4, 1898), 3

Chapter 13   More Tales of Fraud and Forgery

1. *Chicago Daily News*, (Chicago, Illinois, November 3, 1902), 2
2. *Record of Wills*, 1897-1898 (Illinois, Probate Court, Cook County)
3. *Daily Inter Ocean*, (Chicago, Illinois, June 7, 1878), 3
4. *Chicago Daily News*, (Chicago, Illinois, March 12, 1903), 4
5. *Evening Bulletin*, (Providence, Rhode Island, August 20, 1903), 8
6. *Chicago Eagle*, (Chicago, Illinois, December 11, 1897), 6
7. *Chicago Daily News*, (Chicago, Illinois, August 20, 1903), 2
8. *Chicago Daily News*, (Chicago, Illinois, August 21, 1903), 2
9. *Chicago Daily News*, (Chicago, Illinois, November 12, 1903), 4
10. Daily Illinois State Register, (Springfield, Illinois, November 28, 1905), 4

Chapter 14   Colliding with the 20ᵗʰ Century

1. Decatur (Mich.) Murder Investigation Records, 1879, Pinkerton's National Detective Agency, Clarke Historical Library, Central Michigan University
2. *Chicago Daily News*, (Chicago, Illinois, September 4, 1903), 19
3. *Chicago Tribune*, (Chicago, Illinois, March 16, 1903), 9
4. *Chicago Record*, (Chicago, Illinois, March 19, 1901), 6
5. *New York Times*, (New York, New York, May 5, 1902), 9
6. *Chicago Tribune*, (Chicago, Illinois, January 10, 1909), 1
7. *Chicago Daily News*, (Chicago, Illinois, June 18, 1910), 15
8. *Annual Report of the Commissioner of Patents*, (Washington, D.C., 1912), 351

Chapter 15   An End for Three Mattesons

1. *Buffalo Sunday Morning News* (Buffalo, New York, February 4, 1912), 31
2. *Buffalo News*, (Buffalo, New York, September 30, 1912), 3
3. *Historical and Biographical Sketch of Cherry Creek, Chautauqua County, New York*, (Cherry Creek, New York, 1900), 152
4. *Historical and Biographical Sketch of Cherry Creek, Chautauqua County, New York*, (Cherry Creek, New York, 1900), 64
5. *Chicago Examiner*, (Chicago, Illinois, April 1, 1912), 7
6. *Chicago Tribune*, (Chicago, Illinois, April 1, 1912), 17
7. *The True Northerner*, (Paw Paw, Michigan, April 5, 1912), 1
8. *The True Northerner*, (Paw Paw, Michigan, April 12, 1912), 1
9. *Elias Morris Papers,* Clarke Historical Library, Central Michigan University

Chapter 16   Assassinated

1. *The Chicago Daily Tribune*, (Chicago, Illinois, January 27, 1879), 3
2. *The Marshall Statesman*, (Marshall, Michigan March 27, 1896), 3
3. *The True Northerner,* (Paw Paw, Michigan, December 26, 1879), 5
4. *The Rockford Journal,* (Rockford, Illinois, November 20, 1880), 5

5. *The Rockford Journal,* (Rockford, Illinois, February 10, 1877), 6
6. *The Daily Register,* (Rockford, Illinois, July 12, 1878), 3
7. *The Daily Register,* (Rockford, Illinois, April 24, 1884), 3
8. *The Daily Register,* (Rockford, Illinois, March 4, 1879), 1
9. *The Daily Gazette,* (Rockford, Illinois, April 28, 1884), 4
10. *The Daily Register,* (Rockford, Illinois, January 21, 1885), 3
11. *The Daily Gazette,* (Rockford, Illinois, July 18, 1885), 4
12. *The Daily Register,* (Rockford, Illinois, November 18, 1885), 3
13. *The Daily Globe,* (Saint Paul, Minnesota, March 7, 1886), 2

Chapter 17   Milo's Factotum

1. Decatur (Mich.) Murder Investigation Records, 1879, Pinkerton's National Detective Agency, Clarke Historical Library, Central Michigan University
2. Catherine Howland, *A Scrapbook History of Early Decatur, Michigan and Vicinity,* (Decatur Bicentennial Committee, 1976), 714
3. *The Saginaw Herald,* (Saginaw, Michigan, December 25, 1879), 7
4. *The True Northerner,* (Paw Paw, Michigan, December 26, 1879), 6
5. *The Kalamazoo Gazette,* (Kalamazoo, Michigan, January 9, 1880), 4
6. *The True Northerner,* (Paw Paw, Michigan, January 5, 1883), 6
7. *The True Northerner,* (Paw Paw, Michigan, November 1, 1883), 6
8. *The True Northerner,* (Paw Paw, Michigan, October 30, 1884), 1

Chapter 18   Jennie's Account

1. Catherine Howland, *A Scrapbook History of Early Decatur, Michigan and Vicinity,* (Decatur Bicentennial Committee, 1976), 97–98

Chapter 19   The Attorneys

1. *The True Northerner,* (Paw Paw, Michigan, January 30, 1874), 5
2. *The True Northerner,* (Paw Paw, Michigan, December 12, 1873), 4

3. *The True Northerner,* (Paw Paw, Michigan, March 27, 1874), 5
4. *The True Northerner,* (Paw Paw, Michigan, August 17, 1877), 5
5. *The True Northerner,* (Paw Paw, Michigan, October 12, 1877), 5
6. *The True Northerner,* (Paw Paw, Michigan, December 12, 1873), 4
7. *The True Northerner,* (Paw Paw, Michigan, September 18, 1874), 5
8. *The Kalamazoo Gazette,* (Kalamazoo, Michigan, July 8, 1879), 4
9. *The True Northerner,* (Paw Paw, Michigan, July 18, 1879), 4
10. *The Grand Rapids Evening Leader,* (Grand Rapids, Michigan, March 20, 1880), 4
11. *The True Northerner,* (Paw Paw, Michigan, July 31, 1884), 5
12. *The True Northerner,* (Paw Paw, Michigan, May 1, 1874), 5
13. *The True Northerner,* (Paw Paw, Michigan, July 24, 1874), 5
14. *The True Northerner,* (Paw Paw, Michigan, December 11, 1874), 4
15. *Michigan, U.S. Marriage Records,* (Kalamazoo County, 1872), 415
16. "The Gentile Polygamist" by Linda Thatcher, (*Utah Historical Quarterly,* Vol. 52, Nr. 3, 1984)
17. *Utah, U.S. Wills and Probate Records,* (Salt Lake City, Utah, 1904–1906), 862
18. *Elias Morris Papers,* Clarke Historical Library, Central Michigan University
19. *Death Records, Michigan Department of Community Health* (Lansing, Michigan)

Chapter 20   Stabbed in the Back

1. Catherine Howland, *A Scrapbook History of Early Decatur, Michigan and Vicinity,* (Decatur Bicentennial Committee, 1976), 714
2. *The True Northerner,* (Paw Paw, Michigan, November 6, 1884), 1
3. *The True Northerner,* (Paw Paw, Michigan, April 24, 1889), 1
4. *The True Northerner,* (Paw Paw, Michigan, July 24, 1884), 5
5. *The True Northerner,* (Paw Paw, Michigan, July 9, 1890), 5
6. *The True Northerner,* (Paw Paw, Michigan, August 27, 1890), 5

7. Marriage Records, *Michigan Department of Community Health* (Lansing, Michigan)
8. *The True Northerner*, (Paw Paw, Michigan, August 5, 1891), 1
9. *The True Northerner*, (Paw Paw, Michigan, September 2, 1891), 5
10. *The True Northerner*, (Paw Paw, Michigan, October 21, 1891), 1
11. *The True Northerner*, (Paw Paw, Michigan, December 2, 1891), 1
12. *The Chicago Herald*, (Chicago, Illinois, December 2, 1891), 1
13. *The Muskegon Chronicle*, (Muskegon, Michigan, January 29, 1892), 2
14. *The True Northerner*, (Paw Paw, Michigan, February 3, 1892), 1
15. *The Jackson Citizen Patriot*, (Jackson, Michigan, October 22, 1892), 3
16. *The True Northerner*, (Paw Paw, Michigan, January 11, 1893), 8
17. *The True Northerner*, (Paw Paw, Michigan, October 25, 1895), 8
18. *The True Northerner*, (Paw Paw, Michigan, June 3, 1896), 5
19. *The True Northerner*, (Paw Paw, Michigan, August 12, 1896), 5
20. Marriage Records, *Michigan Department of Community Health* (Lansing, Michigan)
21. Catherine Howland, *A Scrapbook History of Early Decatur, Michigan and Vicinity*, (Decatur Bicentennial Committee, 1976), 1186

Chapter 21 The Wickedest Man

1. *The True Northerner*, (Paw Paw, Michigan, April 12, 1912), 1
2. 1860 U.S. Census, population schedule, Cherry Creek, Chautauqua, New York, (Washington, D.C.: National Archives and Records Administration), 158
3. 1870 U.S. Census, population schedule, Decatur, Michigan, (Washington, D.C.: National Archives and Records Administration), 330a
4. Marriage Records, *Michigan Department of Community Health* (Lansing, Michigan), 406
5. Catherine Howland, *A Scrapbook History of Early Decatur, Michigan and Vicinity*, (Decatur Bicentennial Committee, 1976), 728

6. Decatur (Mich.) Murder Investigation Records, 1879, Pinkerton's National Detective Agency, Clarke Historical Library, Central Michigan University

7. *The Weekly Democratic Statesman*, (Austin, Texas, February 25, 1875), 4

8. Decatur (Mich.) Murder Investigation Records, 1879, Pinkerton's National Detective Agency, Clarke Historical Library, Central Michigan University

9. Illinois, Deaths and Stillbirths Index, 1916–1947 (Provo, Utah)

10. *The Cedar Falls Gazette*, (Cedar Falls, Iowa, January 4, 1878), 3

11. *The Cedar Falls Gazette*, (Cedar Falls, Iowa, February 1, 1878), 3

12. *The Buchanan County Bulletin*, (Independence, Iowa, February 8, 1878), 3

13. *The Waterloo Courier,* (Waterloo, Iowa, October 30, 1878), 5

14. *The Daily Inter Ocean,* (Chicago, Illinois, June 7, 1878), 3

15. Decatur (Mich.) Murder Investigation Records, 1879, Pinkerton's National Detective Agency, Clarke Historical Library, Central Michigan University

16. *The True Northerner,* (Paw Paw, Michigan, November 29, 1878), 7

17. Decatur (Mich.) Murder Investigation Records, 1879, Pinkerton's National Detective Agency, Clarke Historical Library, Central Michigan University

18. *The Chicago Herald,* (Chicago, Illinois, December 2, 1891), 1

19. Catherine Howland, *A Scrapbook History of Early Decatur, Michigan and Vicinity*, (Decatur Bicentennial Committee, 1976), 1186

20. *Chicago, Illinois, City Directory*, (Chicago, Illinois, 1888), 1147

The Widows

1. *The Rockford Republic*, (Rockford, Illinois, October 13, 1917), 2

2. Catherine Howland, *A Scrapbook History of Early Decatur, Michigan and Vicinity*, (Decatur Bicentennial Committee, 1976), 80

3. *The Rockford Republic*, (Rockford, Illinois, January 16, 1908), 6

4. 1870 U.S. census, population schedule, Decatur, Michigan, (Washington, D.C.: National Archives and Records Administration), 33

5. Marriage Records, *Michigan Department of Community Health* (Lansing, Michigan), 406

6. Michigan, U.S., Wills and Probate Records, (Van Buren County, Michigan, September 20, 1875)

7. *The Weekly Democratic Statesman*, (Austin, Texas, February 25, 1875), 4

8. *The Free Press*, (Gunnison, Colorado, April 19, 1882), 4

9. *The Toronto Star*, (Toronto, Ontario, Canada, March 24, 1908)

10. *The Toronto World*, (Toronto, Ontario, Canada, March 16, 1913)

11. *New York City Deaths*, 1862–1948

12. *The Jamestown Journal*, (Jamestown, New York, March 22, 1867), 2

13. *The Daily Inter Ocean*, (Chicago, Illinois, July 17, 1867), 3

14. *The Aspen Daily Times*, (Aspen, Colorado, April 26, 1903), 4

15. *The Aspen Democrat*, (Aspen, Colorado, February 5, 1908), 3

16. *The Chicago Daily News*, (Chicago, Illinois, March 12, 1903), 3

17. *The Chicago Examiner*, (Chicago, Illinois, May 21, 1915), 13

18. *The Chicago Day Book*, (Chicago, Illinois, December 10, 1915), 7

19. *The Chicago Daily News*, (Chicago, Illinois, November 5, 1929), 13

20. *The Chicago Tribune*, (Chicago, Illinois, July 19, 1941), 8

Afterword

1. Decatur (Mich.) Murder Investigation Records, 1879, Pinkerton's National Detective Agency, Clarke Historical Library, Central Michigan University

2. 1870 U.S. Census, population schedule, Cherry Valley, Illinois, (Washington, D.C.: National Archives and Records Administration), 35
3. 1870 U.S. Census, population schedule, Cherry Valley, Illinois, (Washington, D.C.: National Archives and Records Administration), 20
4. *The South Bend Tribune*, (South Bend, Indiana, October 1, 1879)

ABOUT THE AUTHOR

Having grown up near Edwardsburg, Michigan, William G. Kohler has deep roots in Decatur. Every Sunday, as a young boy, he and his sisters visited their grandmother, who lived only a few steps from the Webster Memorial Library, coincidentally built on the original site of the Matteson home. His ancestors were among the early settlers in Van Buren County, and genealogy has been a passion of his for more than fifty years, despite moving to Germany after graduating from the University of Michigan. He has dedicated the last ten years to studying the Morris murders and the Matteson family

Made in the USA
Monee, IL
19 September 2021